Ruling the Spirit

THE MIDDLE AGES SERIES

Ruth Mazo Karras, Series Editor
Edward Peters, Founding Editor

A complete list of books in the series
is available from the publisher.

RULING THE SPIRIT

Women, Liturgy, and Dominican Reform
in Late Medieval Germany

CLAIRE TAYLOR JONES

PENN

UNIVERSITY OF PENNSYLVANIA PRESS

PHILADELPHIA

Published by
University of Pennsylvania Press
Philadelphia, Pennsylvania 19104-4112
www.upenn.edu/pennpress

Printed in the United States of America on acid-free paper
10 9 8 7 6 5 4 3 2 1

Library of Congress Cataloging-in-Publication Data

Names: Jones, Claire Taylor, author.
Title: Ruling the spirit: women, liturgy, and Dominican
    reform in late medieval Germany / Claire Taylor Jones.
Other titles: Middle Ages series.
Description: 1st edition. | Philadelphia : University of
    Pennsylvania Press, [2017] | Series: The Middle Ages series
    | Includes bibliographical references and index.
Identifiers: LCCN 2017007706 | ISBN 9780812249552
    (hardcover)
Subjects: LCSH: Dominican sisters—Spiritual
    life—Germany—History—To 1500. | Dominican
    sisters—Germany—Liturgy—History—To 1500. |
    Monastic and religious life of women—Germany—
    History—Middle Ages, 600–1500. | Mysticism—Catholic
    Church—History.
Classification: LCC BX4337.Z5 G4374 2017 | DDC 271/
    .972043—dc23
LC record available at https://lccn.loc.gov/2017007706

CONTENTS

ABBREVIATIONS

BdRP   Meyer, Johannes. *Buch der Reformacio Predigerordens*. Ed. Benedict
      Maria Reichert. 2 vols. Leipzig: Harrassowitz Verlag, 1908–1909.

DLL   Achnitz, Wolfgang, ed. *Deutsches Literatur-Lexikon: Das Mittelalter.*
      Autoren und Werke nach Themenkreisen und Gattungen. 8 vols.
      Berlin: Walter de Gruyter, 2011–2015.

DS   Seuse, Heinrich. *Deutsche Schriften im Auftrag der Württembergischen*
      Kommission für Landesgeschichte. Ed. Karl Bihlmeyer. Reprint.
      Frankfurt am Main: Minerva, 1907.

MBK   *Mittelalterliche Bibliothekskataloge Deutschlands und der Schweiz.*
      Vol. III/3. München: Die bayerische Akademie der Wissenschaften
      in München, 1939.

PT   Tauler, Johannes. *Die Predigten Taulers. Aus der Engelberger und der*
      Freiburger Handschrift sowie aus Schmidts Abschriften der ehemaligen
      Straßburger Handschriften. Ed. Ferdinand Vetter. Berlin: Weidmann,
      1910.

Introduction

> Mitt wie grosser minnender begird sy geflissen wer den orden an
> allen stuken ze haltend, da von wer fil ze sagen [Of the great and
> loving desire with which she zealously observed the order in every
> detail there would be much to tell].
>
> —Töss Sisterbook, Life of Margret Fink

Toward the beginning of her *Büchlein der Gnaden Überlast* (*Book of the Burden of Grace*, c. 1345), Christina Ebner illustrates the power of the Dominican liturgy with a tale about Sister Hailrat, the Engelthal convent's first choir mistress. The event occurred in the early days of the convent, during the first Advent in which they performed the Office according to the Dominican Rite.

> In dem ersten advent da sie nach dem orden sungen . . . da sie nu
> komen zu dem virden suntag im advent, da sie sungen die metin,
> da sie nu komen hintz dem funften respons "Virgo Israel," und der
> vers "In caritate perpetua," daz sank sie teutsch und sank so un-
> menschlichen wol, daz man brufet, sie sunge mit engelischer
> stimme. . . . Diser heilig covent wart von grozer andaht sinnelos und
> vilen nider als die toten und lagen also biz sie alle wider zu in selber
> komen: do sungen sie ir metin mit grozer andaht auz.[1]

> During the first Advent that they sang according to the order . . .
> when they came to the fourth Sunday in Advent, while they were
> singing matins and had come to the fifth responsory "Virgo Israel"
> and the verse "In caritate perpetua," she sang it in German and with
> such inhuman beauty that one thought she was singing with an
> angel's voice. . . . This holy convent became senseless from great

devotion and fell down as if dead and lay thus until they had all
come to themselves. Then they sang their matins to the end with
great devotion.

While singing the solo verse of a responsory, the choir mistress had been
seized by divine insight, spontaneously translating the Latin song into her
mother tongue and performing the inspired text with inhuman beauty.
Rather than responding with the prescribed text of the chant response, the
rest of the community fell, rapt in ecstasy.

This story exemplifies some commonly accepted characteristics of late
medieval female piety: liturgical devotion, embodiment, vernacularity,
ecstatic experience, and community. In keeping with Caroline Walker
Bynum's analysis of bodiliness and embodied response as a trait of women's
spirituality, the Engelthal sisters are physically overcome by the beauty of
Hailrat's song.[2] A vernacular translation replaces the Latin of the Office,
supporting the frequent association of women with vernacularity.[3] Peter
Ochsenbein has interpreted the story as an example of mystical exceptionalism, arguing that Hailrat was so overcome by a private experience of grace
that she disturbed the performance of the Office for the entire convent.[4]
Erika Lauren Lindgren, on the other hand, asserts that the episode "emphasized the communality of monastic life," since Hailrat mediates and communicates extraordinary devotion to her sisters.[5] This account of communal
ecstasy is indeed a rich testament to fourteenth-century female piety. Yet if
one attends to the event's context in the convent's history, another aspect
emerges: praise of life under the Dominican order.

Like many of the southern German Dominican women's houses, the
Engelthal community had begun as an assembly of beguines, that is, women
living a pious life together but without having taken vows and without being
enclosed in a convent.[6] Their road to incorporation in the Dominican order
was a long one, and they adopted some of the order's practices, including
the Dominican liturgy, before being fully incorporated. As Christina Ebner
informs us, this experience of ecstatic song was granted to the community in
the first Advent sung *nach dem orden*, that is, according to the Dominican
Office. The miracle that graces their newly ordered liturgical song thus confirms the early Engelthal sisters in their decision to join the Dominican order
by demonstrating the worthiness of its practices. Standing at the beginning
of the sisterbook, the story foreshadows the importance of the order as a font

of spiritual experience throughout the sisters' lives as portrayed within the book.

Ruling the Spirit suggests a new paradigm for female liturgical piety in late medieval Germany by intervening at the nexus of two productive spiritual movements: fourteenth-century female Dominican spirituality and the fifteenth-century Observant reform. Rather than placing works *by* German Dominican women in conversation with spiritual writings by women of other orders and nationalities, I examine texts *for* German Dominican women for their statements about the Dominican order and the role of the order in fostering piety. *Ruling the Spirit* argues three related claims. First, contrary to received opinion that the Dominicans were not particularly interested in the liturgy, the friars placed the Divine Office at the center of Dominican women's spiritual lives from the order's origins through the end of the Middle Ages. Second, female Dominican liturgical piety was not a subversive expression of resistance or an attempt to wrest spiritual power away from the friars, but the fruition of the spirituality that the order's *forma vitae* was intended to entrain. Third, fourteenth-century mysticism does not represent a moment of radical ecstatic spirituality that had to be stamped out by the fifteenth-century Observant reform. Rather, these two devotional movements represent two points in a continuous devotional history of ordered liturgical piety.

I approach this literature with the understanding that no texts exist, or ever existed, that record mystical experience as such. As Werner Williams-Krapp has argued for Heinrich Seuse (Henry Suso),[7] the texts that purport to record mystical experience are always already mystagogy. Their primary purpose is not to relate a past experience but to teach others how to achieve spiritual fulfillment. Even the lives of Dominican nuns as recounted in the sisterbooks do not provide access to past performance. The experience of hearing Hailrat's song is unavailable to us. All we can know is that the author, Christina Ebner, valued the Dominican Office as a source of devotion.

Pushing this argument even further, *Ruling the Spirit* is not, in a sense, about the lives of Dominican women at all. Rather, it is about the normative ideals presented to them in a variety of texts and genres by the friars responsible for their spiritual care. This holds true even in the case of the fourteenth-century sisterbooks, on which I focus in Chapter 3. These female-authored narratives present exemplary models of piety as much as they recount the lives of historical women. Moreover, they were revived and put back into circulation in the fifteenth century by the Observant reformer Johannes Meyer, who saw their pedagogical value. The Observance witnessed another

blossoming of female chronicling, and Anne Winston-Allen and Heike Uffmann have done invaluable work bringing the first-hand accounts of
fifteenth-century German religious women to scholarly attention.[8] Whereas
their work recovered women's participation in and reactions to the late
medieval regular reforms, this book examines the rhetoric of pious observance
of the order in German Dominican normative literature produced primarily
by friars for women from the early fourteenth through the fifteenth century.
With remarkable continuity across genres and centuries, this literature
encourages strict observance of the Dominican order and devotion to its
Office as the wellspring of spiritual experience and reward.

The Southern German region, encompassed by the Dominican province
of Teutonia, lends itself to such a study for two reasons. First, the imbalanced
proportion of Dominican sisters over friars in this province made the *cura
monialium* a special concern. Second, within this region the Observant
reform movement enjoyed an unusual degree of success. In 1303, the General
Chapter of the Dominican order carved the province of Saxony out of Teutonia's northern regions, leaving the southern province with the vicariates of
Brabantia (encompassing the Rhineland up to and including Cologne),
Alsatia (which also contained Switzerland), Suevia (together with Franconia),
and Bavaria (including Austria).[9] At this time, a total of 141 communities of
women were under Dominican care. Sixty-five of these lay within the province of Teutonia alone.[10] The friars of Teutonia, possessing in 1303 only forty-
seven houses, were significantly outnumbered by the houses of sisters.[11] A
hundred years later, Teutonia would become the first province to establish a
reformed Observant friary;[12] it would bury the first Master General to support the Observance;[13] and it would see the greatest institutional success of
the movement.[14] The disproportionately large number of Dominican women
and the success of the Observant reform (to which the women contributed
no small part[15]) made Teutonia fertile ground for vernacular devotional and
didactic literature urging adherence to the order and spiritualizing performance of its Office.

I ground my study in the library collection of the Dominican convent
of St. Katherine's in Nürnberg. Every text I treat was held by the convent
library in the fifteenth century. St. Katherine's was reformed to the Observance in 1428 and grew to be one of the most significant Observant women's
houses in the province, both by virtue of its zeal in sending reforming parties
to sister houses and because of its vast library of books, both received from
outside and copied by the sisters themselves.[16] By the end of the fifteenth

century, St. Katherine's owned at least 726 manuscripts, of which 161 were Latin, primarily liturgical manuscripts. The remaining 565 contained a broad variety of German texts.[17] Most importantly, a library catalog and two table readings catalogs survive. The library catalog and the second table readings catalog were drawn up in the 1450s by Kunigunde Niklas, who served St. Katherine's as a prolific scribe before becoming librarian in 1451. Her catalogs reveal information about reception and use of the convent's holdings. For example, Kunigunde Niklas allotted Johannes Tauler's sermons, discussed in Chapter 2, for extensive reading before the community when they assembled for a meal. The surviving epistolary exchange between St. Katherine's in Nürnberg and the convent of St. Katherine's in St. Gallen, Switzerland, also contains information about the use and reception of this literature. The women of Nürnberg sent their St. Gallen sisters Johannes Meyer's *Book of Duties* and the *Book of the Reformation*, discussed in Chapter 6, in order to help them in their effort at self-reform.[18] The presentation and transmission of these texts as recommended reading supports my methodological decision to read these texts as didactic or edifying literature rather than as mystical accounts.

One further concern requires preliminary discussion. My argument deals with ideals and exhortations for Dominican women's liturgical spirituality. As a study of didactic and devotional literature, *Ruling the Spirit* does not, nor does it aim to, recover the realities of late medieval women's Latinity. Nevertheless, the extent to which Dominican sisters understood the Latin Office texts affected their ability to participate in liturgical piety, and many of the arguments I make, especially in Chapter 3, assume a basic level of Latin comprehension. Although it was long assumed that late medieval nuns of all orders were generally Latin-illiterate, a growing body of scholarship argues for reassessing the Latinity of medieval religious women, often by adding nuance to the very notion of literacy.[19] Adjusting our lens in this way allows us to move beyond reliance on women's original compositions or reception of prose literature as a means of assessing Latin comprehension to address liturgical Latin as a unique competency. Liturgical literacy and accuracy was an essential component of the order; reading theological treatises (for women) was not.

Despite evidence of flourishing vernacular literacy, the state of Latin fluency among the Dominican women of Teutonia remains an open question. While the library collections of several Southern German convents have been studied in some detail, the vast preponderance of German-language devotional material has led scholars to focus on vernacular sources within these collections.[20] Marie-Luise Ehrenschwendtner has conducted the most comprehensive study of the educational expectations and practices of Southern German Dominican women. She notes that recruits to Dominican convents were expected to be *litterata* and able to read the psalter upon entrance to the novitiate.[21] The sisterbook of St. Katherine's St. Gallen records that the Nürnberg sisters expected a novice to learn to read a little Latin from the psalter as well as singing and solmization before entering the convent.[22] Dominican novices would have developed literacy either at home or in a city school.[23] However, "literate" could mean anything from phonetic decoding to nuanced comprehension. Ehrenschwendtner assumes that the designation *litterata* did not imply understanding the Latin language but simply deciphering the signs on the page.[24] In her recent study of the Observant Dominican convent of St. Katherine's in St. Gallen, Simone Mengis largely concurs with Ehrenschwendtner.[25] Latin instruction in St. Gallen was practical and performance-oriented, so successful mastery did not necessarily entail comprehension of the Latin words, only accurate recitation.

The composition of the Latin holdings of St. Katherine's conforms to Ehrenschwendtner's and Mengis's assessments. Of the 161 Latin-language manuscripts, only 19 (12 percent) contained prayers, sermons, and treatises, while the rest were liturgical. None of these, nor any Latin text, are indicated as table readings in the catalog.[26] It is possible that the few Latin prose manuscripts were not for the nuns at all but rather for the use of their male confessors, as Marie-Luise Ehrenschwendtner has argued for Altenhohenau and Simone Mengis for St. Katherine's in St. Gallen.[27] It seems not even Latin regular documents were used; St. Katherine's owned multiple manuscripts with German translations of the Augustinian Rule and the Dominican Constitutions.[28] The broad vernacularization of the order's legislation leads Mengis to conclude that a revival of higher standards of Latin literacy among women was not part of the Observant reform program.[29] Although the Dominican women of Nürnberg avidly acquired and read vernacular literature, there is no evidence that they read Latin prose.

Eva Schlotheuber argues for a more optimistic assessment of late medieval religious women's Latin. She insists that in the Middle Ages *litteratus/litterata* always indicated facility in Latin language, not just phonetic literacy.[30] She disagrees with the assumption that Latin-language volumes must have been intended for a male chaplain, and points to Karin Schneider's identification of several scribes among the Dominican nuns who copied liturgical Latin fluidly and accurately.[31] Schlotheuber's more recent work on the northern German convent of Paradies bei Soest has borne out earlier claims, as her team has been able to demonstrate quite advanced levels of Latin literacy in the richly decorated choir books these women produced.[32] Their study of this Dominican convent joins an explosion of recent research on the Cistercian communities of northern Germany, which similarly reveal high levels of Latin fluency, especially in the wake of the fifteenth-century reforms.[33]

Despite differences in tenor and emphasis, all three scholars agree that the level of Latin literacy within a convent cannot have been uniform but varied from woman to woman.[34] This observation conforms to more systematic assessments of Latin literacy in late medieval English convents. David Bell outlines levels of literacy prior to the ability to compose an independent text in the target language. These levels of ability range from phonetic decoding, to basic comprehension of commonly encountered liturgical texts, to full comprehension of nonliturgical Latin.[35] Performance of the liturgy involved a great deal more than Latin language competency; it required a spectrum of literacies that encompassed music and musical notation in addition to grammar and letters. Katherine Zieman describes this "liturgical literacy" as also incorporating musical ability, swift decoding of script, and good memorization. Like Mengis, she emphasizes that this form of literacy did not aim for nuanced comprehension of a text, but rather that the range of abilities were subordinated to the goal of accurate performance.[36]

Building on Bell's and Zieman's work, Anne Bagnall Yardley proposes a scale of liturgical literacy that ranges from singing the basic chants of the Divine Office from memory, to familiarity with the repertoire and ability to use the choir books, to knowledge of musical theory and even ability to compose polyphony. From consideration of the English sources, she concludes that the first two levels of ability would have been common and expected, whereas anything further was exceptional.[37] Any choir nun would have been expected to be able to read not only Latin but also musical notation, in the sense that she needed to produce the sounds signified by the marks on the page. Latin literacy, like any linguistic fluency, was not an all-or-nothing game but could be acquired to varying degrees of competence. The extent to which she understood the words must have varied widely from nun to nun even within the same convent.

The paucity of Latin devotional literature in St. Katherine's in Nürnberg does not necessarily reveal any information about the sisters' ability to understand liturgical Latin. Indeed, sweeping generalizations about Latin fluency must give way to a more nuanced picture of varying competence, talent, and ability. In the absence of evidence that the women of a given convent wrote or read Latin tracts, we still cannot conclude that none of them understood the texts of the liturgy. As Bell, Zieman, and Yardley have argued, liturgical and prose Latin comprise two different levels of literacy, and it is entirely possible to understand the psalms of the Office without being able to read the Constitutions. Reception of prose literature cannot be used to draw conclusions about women's engagement with the Office.

It is worth noting, however, that in the argument over medieval women's literacy modern scholars often are picking up on the doubts of contemporaries. Fifteenth-century friars were deeply concerned by the idea that the nuns were merely parroting sounds without comprehending the words of the Office. This anxiety was motivated by an association of liturgical devotion with regular virtue. In 1454 Sister Katharina Holzschuher recorded a sermon delivered to St. Katherine's by a Friar Alanus, who asserts, "darumb ist es nütze vnd heilsam züuerstëen das man alle tag list und pet, wann die verstantnüße meret die süssen andacht, vnd wenn man verstet daz man singt, so außlaufft nit daz gemüte durch unzimlich züfell [It is useful and salutary to understand what you read and pray every day, since understanding increases sweet devotion, and when you understand what you sing, you do not lose your concentration to inappropriate thoughts]."[38] A wandering mind is almost inevitable when singing what amounts to nonsense syllables.[39] Since the choir nuns spent a hefty portion of the day singing Latin texts in the canonical hours, it was critical that this time be well spent in attentive contemplation rather than bored and mechanical rote performance, which too easily gave way to impure distraction.

I have elsewhere argued that the Observance did, in fact, witness a promotion of women's Latin literacy that has gone unrecognized as pedagogical material. Vernacular hymn translations did not replace the Latin hymns of the Office, but instead were used pedagogically for Latin language instruction that was oriented around the goals of the reform.[40] Dominican friars in Teutonia encouraged Dominican women to understand enough liturgical Latin to engage in the Divine Office intelligently and in a way that would foster spiritual devotion. Throughout the later Middle Ages, Dominican friars approached comprehension of liturgical Latin and access to prose texts as separate issues, one of which was essential for their sisters' spiritual well-being and one of which was irrelevant. Interest in boosting women's Latin fluency was motivated by this concern alone: that observance of the Office in the manner prescribed by the order serve as a source of contemplation and devotion for the Dominican women of Teutonia.

Chapter Overview

My first chapter contends that, although the Dominicans prioritized preaching and study over liturgical observance among the friars, the Office held pride of place in the lives of the sisters. The legislative and normative documents produced at the foundation of the order demonstrate the central importance of liturgical piety in the regulations for Dominican women. Reconsidering Dominican legislation with close attention to the differences between the expectations for friars and for sisters provides a solid ground from which to approach the spiritual literature and devotional treatises which provide the subject of the remaining chapters. That is, having established what legally constituted the order and the Office, I turn to the vernacular treatises that urged women to observe it.

The second chapter explores the didactic interests of the early fourteenth century in the sermons of Johannes Tauler (c. 1300–1361) and the German writings of Heinrich Seuse (1295–1366). I argue that observance of the order also serves as a foundational tenet in the spiritual programs of these friars. Although they adopt the mystical concepts of *Gelassenheit* (detachment) and the ground of the soul from the quasi-heretical Meister Eckhart, both Tauler and Seuse insist that spiritual perfection be pursued with prudence and orderliness. The practices of the Dominican order, prominently including the Divine Office, constitute a form of spiritual training that orders the ground of the soul so that it might receive divine experience. Through presenting the life and liturgy of the order as a spiritual pursuit, Tauler's sermons and Seuse's writings offer ways to find divine experience within strict adherence to the Office.

In the third chapter I examine the collections of exemplary lives known as the sisterbooks. These pseudo-hagiographical narratives were collaboratively composed by the Dominican women of Teutonia in the first half of the fourteenth century to memorialize remarkable women of their own communities. Long seen as evidence of feminine mystical hysteria, these narratives seem to celebrate unruly women, and the Observant interest in them has defied explanation. I argue that, far from celebrating rebellious behaviors, the sisterbooks promote observance of the mandates of the order, foremost among which is the Divine Office. In transmitting the sisterbooks, Observants did not co-opt and tame subversive monuments to women's independent spirituality, but rather promoted a body of edifying literature that had shared their emphases and concerns a century earlier. Finally, I show that the innovative force of the life narratives contained in the sisterbooks is expressed in a combinatorial creativity whereby not only the text but also the liturgical context of a citation is deployed in order to produce a mosaic of spiritual meaning that expands upon but grows out of the Dominican *forma vitae*.

In Chapter 4 I turn to the fifteenth century to consider the place of the Office in Observant legislation and regulatory documents. The recent explosion of scholarship on the Observance has not systematically examined the place of the liturgy in the fifteenth-century reform. Yet, as perusal of visitation letters and the acts of the General Chapters shows, the liturgy was arguably more important to Observant reformers than it had been to the founders they venerated. The Observants insisted that both friars and nuns revive a strict and zealous performance of the order's liturgy. Moreover, they developed a pedagogical program aimed at helping the Dominican sisters understand the Office they were bound to observe.

In the final two chapters I examine texts by prominent and prolific Dominican Observant reformers active in the province of Teutonia in the fifteenth century. In Chapter 5 I consider two early fifteenth-century German versions of the patristic writer John Cassian's *Conferences*, a set of spiritual dialogues with desert fathers. One version presents a direct and unabridged translation, while the other consists of a loosely inspired sermon cycle worked up into a treatise and known as *The Twenty-Four Golden Harps*. The Dominican reformer Johannes Nider (d. 1438) was either catalyst or composer of both texts, which were initially both received by the Dominican convent of St. Katherine's in Nürnberg. The direct translation remains practically unstudied, but the treatise has been taken as evidence both of Nider's misogyny and of his imposition of a monastic lifestyle on the laity. A comparison of the texts, however, reveals drastically different treatments of Cassian's statements concerning liturgical performance and visual piety. I argue that Nider held that contemplative visualization was sufficient for lay devotion, but devout recitation of the Office was the foundation on which Dominican women should build their spiritual lives.

In the final chapter I turn to Johannes Meyer (1422/23–1485), a prolific vernacular chronicler and staunch supporter of the Observance, particularly in the women's branch of the order. Meyer's *Book of Duties*, a practical description of a convent's various jobs, and the *Book of the Reformation*, a chronicle *cum* sisterbook of the Observance, both present normative visions for convent life in which the Office plays a pivotal role. Meyer presents community as the most important factor in Observant life and spirituality. For him, the liturgy is both the common task of the Observant community and the means by which this community is founded and defined. The *Book of Duties* describes a team of sisters collaborating to organize and perform the Office, as well as to prepare the younger generation to assume these duties. In the *Book of the Reformation*, Meyer shows how public processions and enclosure ceremonies involving the laity define the Observant community by ritual separation, but also underline and celebrate the convent's embeddedness in and dependence on the surrounding civil society. For Meyer, the Office was the means by which Observant Dominican women would define their communities, reform devotion, and carry the order into the future.

CHAPTER I

The Office in Dominican Legislation, 1216–1303

De florido orto ecclesie, rose quedam in Alemania prodiere [From
the flowery garden of the church, certain roses blossomed forth in
Germany].

—Hugh of St. Cher

My epigraph is taken from a letter written by Hugh of St. Cher, a Dominican
friar who served as a cardinal and papal legate to Germany. The letter, sent
to the provincial of the Dominican province of Teutonia in February 1257,
urges him to replant the sweet-smelling roses back into the blossoming garden of the Order of Preachers. These roses, he explains, are none other than
the sisters following the Rule of St. Augustine, who had been first placed
under the care of the Friars Preachers and then cut off from the order by
Innocent IV.[1] Hugh's flowery language was meant to put a good face on a
bitter controversy, namely the Dominican order's battle over the *cura monialium*. This issue would come to an initial resolution in 1259, but the forty-
year struggle was to have a lasting impact on the place of women in the
Dominican order, their interactions with their brothers Preachers, and the
expectations laid on their lives and spirituality.

The lengthy controversy over the *cura monialium* coincided with pro-
tracted debates over the Dominican liturgy. The order's administrative procedures and Constitutions were largely finalized by 1228, and even the
monumental intervention of Raymond of Peñafort in 1239–1241 entailed
more reorganization than rewriting.[2] Despite the success of this effort to

unify and centralize the international community, the friars were unable to agree upon a uniform liturgy until 1256. At the same time, the development of the Constitutions for Dominican women was hampered by the order's continual efforts to be relieved of the *cura monialium* entirely.[3] Both these controversies were finally laid to rest through the diplomacy and force of will of Humbert of Romans (1200?–1277), Master General of the order from 1254 to 1263. His involvement in finalizing the Dominican Rite influenced his formulation of the sisters' Constitutions.

The main chapters of this study focus on didactic literature intended for German Dominican nuns from the fourteenth and fifteenth centuries. In the later Middle Ages, German Dominican convent literature would explore and develop a variety of ways to experience and foster devotion to the Divine Office. Yet this spiritual advice continued to draw on the legislation and regular documents that were hammered out in the early days of the order. In this chapter, I recruit Dominican legislative and normative documents in order to demonstrate that the Divine Office was central to the role of Dominican women from the very origins of the order.

Dominican Legislation

The Augustinian Rule constituted the foundational legislation for both the male and female branches of the Dominican order. Dominic himself had been an Augustinian canon before founding his own order. Once canon 13 of the Fourth Lateran Council dictated the selection of a previously approved rule,[4] it cannot have been a difficult choice. The Benedictine Rule, which provided the major alternative, commands enclosure and delineates a comprehensive cycle of daily prayer and manual labor. Separation from the world does not accord with a preaching mission, and the full daily schedule leaves no time for the study that Dominicans understood to ground and nourish good preaching. The Augustinian Rule is far more flexible than the Benedictine in that it "outlines a disposition as much as a praxis."[5] Indeed, Humbert of Romans, the order's fifth Master General and its great systematizer, argues in his commentary on the Augustinian Rule that the Rule's great strength lies in its vagueness, which allows the Dominicans to follow its spirit while suiting daily life to their calling.[6]

The Augustinian Rule, in keeping with its apostolic inspiration, places the greatest emphasis on communal property. It lingers over the difficulty that formerly rich and poor will experience in learning to cohabit and specifies that even clothes are to be centrally held, cleaned, and distributed for use.[7] The Rule thus stipulates individual poverty and encourages but does not mandate communal ownership, thus permitting the absolute poverty that the Friars Preachers would adopt in 1220.[8] Regarding the separation of the community from the world, the Augustinian Rule merely enjoins that one should never go out alone but must always be accompanied by a fellow. This "buddy system" institutes mutual policing and reporting, which also receives lengthy exposition. Yet these stipulations are only necessary because the Augustinian Rule envisions an unenclosed community that does work in the world, an imagination that fits well with the Dominican mission to preach but is incommensurate with the strict enclosure increasingly imposed on women's communities in the high and late Middle Ages. Dominic and his successors who codified the women's legislation chose to write enclosure into the Constitutions for Dominican Sisters, rather than placing their second order under a different Rule.

The liturgical portions of the Rule are similarly vague. In comparison to the Benedictine Rule's detailed psalm cycle, the chapter on prayer is extraordinarily short, enough so that it may be cited here in full:

II.1. Orationibus instate horis et temporibus constitutis.

2. In oratorio nemo aliquid agat nisi ad quod est factum, unde et nomen accepit; ut si forte aliqui, etiam praeter horas constitutas, si eis uacat, orare uoluerint, non eis sit inpedimento, qui ibi aliquid agendum putauerit.

3. Psalmis et hymnis cum oratis deum, hoc uersetur in corde quod profertur in uoce.

4. Et nolite cantare, nisi quod legitis esse cantandum; quod autem non ita scriptum est ut cantetur, non cantetur.[9]

II.1. Be constant in prayer at the hours and times appointed.

2. No one should do anything in the oratorium other than that for which it is intended and from which it takes its name. If perchance some want to pray there even outside the appointed hours, if they are free, one who thinks to do something else there should not be an impediment to them.

3. When you pray to God in psalms and hymns, consider in your heart what you offer with your voice.

4. Do not sing anything other than what you read is to be sung; moreover, what is not written that it should be sung, should not be sung.

As is characteristic of the Augustinian Rule more generally, these directives describe a prayerful disposition more than they lay out a specific prayer practice. Rather than defining the "horas constitutas," the Rule protects the space of the oratory as a haven for prayer at any time of day. It enjoins devout and contemplative attention to the content of the prayers and denounces mere lip service.[10] Curiously, however, despite the repeated mentions of the "appointed hours" and the final command to sing only "what is written" and nothing more, the Rule dictates neither what hours are to be observed nor what specifically is to be sung. Those observing the Augustinian Rule would need a supplementary document providing instructions for the observance of the liturgy in order to be able to observe the Rule fully.

Accordingly, both the Dominican friars and sisters possessed Constitutions which further regulated life within the order. Some sort of customary must have been developed at the order's founding in 1216, but the earliest surviving set of Dominican Constitutions were ratified at the Most General Chapter in 1228.[11] The Constitutions detailed procedures for making changes and amendments, which was steadily and continuously done, especially in the early years.[12] The greatest revision of the Constitutions was completed by Master General Raymond of Peñafort, submitted to the General Chapter in 1239, and approved in 1241.[13] Although the Dominicans continued to introduce small changes, the bulk of this version of the Constitutions would survive throughout the Middle Ages.

Raymond of Peñafort's successor as Master General, John of Wildeshausen, initiated a similar revision, unification, and consolidation of the order's liturgy.[14] The General Chapter in 1245 appointed four friars, who were to assemble with all their liturgical books at the Dominican house in Angers to correlate and harmonize the Rite. Although their efforts won final approval at the General Chapter in 1248, implementation of the unified Rite proved difficult in the face of vigorous protest and dissatisfaction. A measure to make adherence to the uniform Rite part of the Constitutions was proposed in 1252 but was never passed into law.[15] Only John of Wildeshausen's successor, Humbert of Romans, would succeed both in creating a uniform liturgy codified in a master exemplar and in enforcing adherence to this Rite through an amendment to the Constitutions.[16] From this point forward,

Humbert's Rite was treated as if it were legislation, and changes to the liturgy followed the same procedure of approval as amendments to the Constitutions.[17]

Having settled the issue of the Dominican liturgy, Humbert turned to the regulation of the women associated with the order. At the time there were at least two sets of statutes in use among the communities of women under Dominican care. In Teutonia many communities followed Constitutions derived from those Dominic himself had composed for the nuns of San Sisto in Rome and which had been imposed by papal bull on the penitent communities known as the Magdalenes.[18] While serving as provincial prior of France, Humbert of Romans himself had formulated statutes based on the friars' Constitutions for the women of Montargis.[19] In the capacity of Master General, Humbert revised the Montargis statutes and, in an encyclical appended to the acts of the General Chapter of 1259, declared these Constitutions binding. Any community that refused to adopt Humbert's statutes would lose affiliation with the Friars Preachers.[20] Any grumblings over Humbert's Rite or his Constitutions for the sisters were silenced when in 1267 Clement IV issued two papal bulls which separately confirmed Humbert's legislative legacies, the Rite and the women's Constitutions, and forbade changes to them without papal approval.[21]

Both the male and female branches of the order accordingly had a number of different documents that laid out the Dominican *forma vitae*. In addition to the Augustinian Rule, each had a set of Constitutions, and the friars, ideally, also possessed a uniform liturgy. The Rule gave little opportunity for adjustment,[22] but the composition of the Rite and the different Constitutions for friars and sisters was a fraught process that lasted decades and only achieved relative stability through the firm guidance of Humbert of Romans. The very energy with which the early Dominicans disputed the form of the Divine Office signals its importance to those who shaped the order's practices, and the liturgy furthermore occupied a central place in the *forma vitae* of Dominican women.

Differences in the Constitutions for Friars and Sisters

In both the Constitutions for the Dominican friars and those of the sisters, the first chapter, simply entitled *De officio ecclesie*, lays the groundwork for liturgical practice within the order, although other chapters touch on liturgical matters, as well. This first chapter is nearly identical in the two sets of Constitutions, but slight differences have significant consequences for the status of the Office and liturgical observance in the lives of friars and sisters. Here I will consider three changes which concern the way of reciting the canonical hours and the matins of the Little Office of the Virgin, as well as the status of Humbert's Rite. The regulations concerning the Divine Office in the Constitutions for the friars reveal that, although liturgical observance was important, study and preaching took precedence over communal prayer. Dominican women, however, did not share this calling, and the Office replaced formal study in their spiritual and intellectual lives.

For the friars, the prioritization of study and preaching over liturgical practice went beyond the dispensations from singing the hours in the church to affect the very manner in which the community was to perform the Office. The Constitutions specify that "hore omnes in ecclesia breuiter et succincte taliter dicantur, ne fratres deuotionem amittant et eorum studium minime impediatur [all hours are to be said in the church briefly and succinctly so that the brothers do not lose their devotion and their study is minimally impeded]."[23] Indeed, Humbert had composed his Office with these injunctions in mind, and, although it was not as abbreviated as the Franciscan Rite, it could be performed quite expeditiously. Prior to the institutionalization of Humbert's Rite, the General Chapters had attempted to restrict ornamental singing.[24] Whether these denouncements stemmed from a fear of music's sensuality or the recognition that complex singing took longer to perform, they limit the amount of energy and attention a friar should be devoting to the Office hours.

Since Dominican women neither preached nor studied, their daily agenda resembled that of Benedictine monastics more than that of their Dominican brothers. The sisters were expected to concentrate on the Office hours and spend their remaining time on handiwork and manual tasks in the workroom.[25] The introduction of a chapter *De labore*, On Work, represents a significant divergence in the Constitutions of the sisters from those of the friars.[26] Despite this and the major changes concerning enclosure, much of the chapter on the Divine Office is identical in the friars' and sisters' Constitutions, with the broad shift of focus taking place instead via smaller changes. The passage of the women's Constitutions corresponding to the brothers' injunction cited above reads, "hore canonice omnes in ecclesia tractim et distincte taliter dicantur, ne sorores deuocionem amittant et alia que facere habent minime impediantur [All canonical hours should be said in church slowly and distinctly so that that the sisters do not lose their devotion and the other things they have to do are minimally impeded]."[27] This passage repeats the friars' Constitutions word for word, except for two very revealing substitutions. "Study" is replaced with the vaguer "other things they have to do" and, more importantly, saying the hours "briefly and succinctly" gives way to "slowly and distinctly."[28] Unlike the friars, who speed through the Office, the sisters devote more time and thought to it.

This difference affects the expectations for matins of the Little Office of the Virgin. As soon as the friars heard the first bell, they were to start singing the Little Office of the Virgin while getting up (*surgant fratres dicendo matutinas*), apparently to save time.[29] The acts of the General Chapters show that this phrasing was debated for almost three decades, revealing disagreement over the level of respect and attention that was due this Office. The wording was finally changed in 1270, when the General Chapter passed a measure clarifying that the friars had to recite the Little Office standing after having gotten out of bed (*surgant fratres et stando dicant officium de beata virgine*).[30] Matins of the Little Office still was nevertheless said in the dormitory. The sisters, on the other hand, were required to assemble in the choir even for matins of the Little Office. Their Constitutions specify that "hore uero de beata virgine prius horas canonicas dicantur in ecclesia [they should say the Little Office of the Virgin before the canonical hours in the church]."[31] Whereas the friars were permitted to say the Little Office while rising, the sisters were required to perform it with the same solemnity as the canonical hours. Late in the thirteenth century, an anonymous ordinance concerning the implementation of the women's Constitutions in Teutonia permitted the sisters to sing the Little Office matins in the dormitory, as the friars did.[32] The Constitutions of the sisters, however, were never updated, and this practice technically remained a deviation.

The difference in both the solemnity of the Little Office and the speed with which the canonical hours were sung shows that the Constitutions for the sisters demand a far greater degree of devotion and attention to the hours than do those of the friars. The friars were expected to show up and fulfill their duty, but the primary font and wellspring of their devotion was the study to which they would devote the greater portion of their day. Their Office should be suitably concise. Dominican women did not share this intellectual vocation, and although their Constitutions make some provisions for brief moments of private contemplation and reading, the Divine Office remains central to its formation of their spiritual lives. While the brothers rush through the hours in order to get to their books, the sisters must linger in the choir singing "distinctly" in order to allow time to process the words that are their spiritual food.

The different place of the liturgy in the spiritual lives of Dominican men and women may ground the most surprising difference between the chapters on the Divine Office in their Constitutions. The General Chapter in 1256 had confirmed a clause imposing Humbert's Rite on all friars. Since Humbert both organized the Dominican liturgy and wrote the Constitutions for the sisters out of a concern over disparity of practice, it seems logical that he would write his own Office into the Constitutions of the sisters, as well. Yet, in the place of this clause in the friars' Constitutions, in the sisters' we read, "aliquis autem locus statuatur, in quo ad preuidendum officium diuinum sorores conueniant, presente priorissa uel alia cui commiserit tempore oportuno [some place should be established in which the sisters convene at an appropriate time to review the Divine Office with the prioress presiding or another to whom she entrusts this]."[33] Instead of imposing his own Office on the women, Humbert simply includes a vague passage ordaining that each convent should have a committee to determine and prepare for its own liturgical practice. Not only were the sisters not bound to the same Rite as the friars, it would seem that they also did not need a unified liturgy among themselves.

Since Humbert had devoted so much energy to the revision and organization of the Dominican Rite, it is baffling that he would not impose its observance on the sisters, as well. Perhaps Humbert felt that the concise Office of the brothers would not suit the women's need for a longer, slower, and more contemplative service. I find it more likely that the concern was financial or practical: requiring the sisters to obtain all fourteen volumes of Humbert's Rite would impose an unnecessary expense. The sisters did not need all of the books, since they did not perform Mass as the ordained brothers did.[34] This situation must also be considered when interpreting the portion of the women's Constitutions that Raymond Creytens takes as proof that the Dominican women did not use Humbert's Office. The chapter on ingress and egress details the procedure for allowing a priest into the cloister to administer communion to a bedridden nun, "prout in ordinario continetur [as contained in the Ordinary]."[35] Since Humbert's Ordinary does not contain the rubrics for administering to the sick, Creytens argues that the nuns must have continued to use a pre-Humbertian Office in which these rites had not been displaced to another liturgical book.[36] However, the priest would have had his own book and, especially in the early days of the order, may well have been a secular chaplain appointed by the friars but not belonging to them and therefore not bound to their Rite.[37] This passage provides evidence for nothing further than that Humbert did not require the nuns to follow his exemplar.[38]

Nevertheless, after the decade of labor and strife that had gone into the creation of the Dominican Rite, it seems mad to expect that each individual convent should have begun the process for itself. Indeed, that this was ultimately not expected of them can be seen from surviving ordinances clarifying the implementation of Humbert's female Constitutions in Teutonia. The anonymous author invokes the injunction from the Augustinian Rule (*quod autem non ita scriptum est ut cantetur, non cantetur*) but reverses it, enjoining that "quod cantare tenentur, non legant [what they are required to sing, they should not read]." Lest this injunction remain, like the Rule and the Constitutions, too vague to be enforced, he adds, "notulas et libros chorales habeant secundum ordinem [they should have notes and choral books according to the order]."[39] The German sisters, at least, were thus expected to make an effort to conform to the same Office as that celebrated by the male branch of the order.[40] Their ability to use the Latin text of this Office as a source for contemplative devotion is a different issue, to which I will now turn.

Women's Literacy in the Constitutions

The Constitutions for Dominican Sisters prescribed a *forma vitae* in which the Latin-language Divine Office would provide the devotional centerpiece for women of the order. In order to evaluate this expectation fully, we must examine the place of Latin in the sisters' Constitutions and clarify what we mean by "Latin literacy" among female religious. In the Introduction I surveyed the recent work that has been done to recover the levels and forms of literacy attained by medieval nuns through careful scrutiny of surviving manuscripts. Many of these studies have briefly addressed the issue of normative expectations but correctly conclude that the norms can tell us little about the reality.[41] Furthermore, despite recognition of multiple levels of literacy, whether women knew Latin continues to be bound up with discussions of whether they read Latin theological treatises or whether they were capable of composing Latin documents, both of which are separate issues from the Latin of the Office.

With regard to the expectations for Dominican nuns in particular, the question is more difficult to answer, because Humbert of Romans's final version of their Constitutions contains very little on the matter. Scholars of Dominican women's literacy have taken recourse to other sources for more insight. Some have looked to the earlier stages of statutes for Dominican women which address the sisters' education more explicitly and thoroughly.[42] One may also turn to Humbert's model sermon treatise, *De eruditione praedicatorum*, where he declares women inept for higher learning but advises parents to teach their young daughters the psalter, the Office for the Dead, and the Little Hours of the Virgin in order to prepare them for a religious career.[43] It is not clear, however, that these statements affected or were even received by Dominican women.[44] Recently, Julie Ann Smith has examined the expectations for literacy as they changed over the evolution of the women's Constitutions.[45] I follow her diachronic approach here but arrive at a different conclusion. Namely, the vagueness of the final Constitutions as regards literacy and learning is legible as something closer to positive encouragement when read against the earlier San Sisto Rule for Magdalenes and the Constitutions for Montargis.

In the 1259 Constitutions, the only instructions concerning teaching or learning within the community are to be found in the chapter on novices.

> Item nouicie, et alie sorores que apte sunt, in psalmodia et officio diuino studeant diligenter, preter conuersas, quibus sufficiat ut sciant uel addiscant ea que debent pro horis dicere. Omnes uero in aliquo laborerio addiscendo uel exercendo occupentur.[46]

> Item, novices and other sisters who are fit should apply themselves diligently to psalmody and the Divine Office, except for the laysisters, for whom it is sufficient to know or learn the things they ought to say for the hours. Certainly, in some workroom all should be occupied with learning or doing exercises.

Despite the brevity of this passage it reveals greater expectations than that the sisters would merely learn to sing the Office. True, the *conversae* simply should learn (*addiscant*) what they need for the hours, which the previous

chapter of the Constitutions had specified as the *Pater noster* alone.[47] Nevertheless, the novices who were to become choir sisters should apply themselves
to (*studeant*) the psalms and the Office. The word choice is telling, as is
the injunction that apt sisters should continue to do this after profession.[48]
Interested and intelligent women are expected to engage the Latin text of the
psalms and the Office outside the times ordained for worship. The use of
exercendo is also interesting, although ambiguous. *Exercitia* could refer to
contemplative or even mortificatory spiritual exercises, but the Constitutions
exclusively use the term *disciplina* to describe this kind of activity. It would
seem, therefore, that some sort of schoolroom is foreseen where sisters may
do educational exercises in Latin grammar.

In addition to the passage above, the chapter on prayers for the dead
reveals some further information regarding what the laysisters are supposed
to say for their hours instead of the Office: yet more repetitions of the *Pater
noster*. "A festo sancti dyonisii ad aduentum pro anniuersario fratrum et sororum, litterate sorores psalterium, non litterate quingenta pater noster dicant
[On the Feast of St. Denis in Advent for the anniversary of the brothers and
sisters, literate sisters should say the psalter, illiterate sisters five hundred *pater
nosters*]."[49] These specifications regarding the prayers of the laysisters help
explain why the laysisters must be taught enough to say their prayers. They
are also expected to be praying in Latin, even if only the one prayer
repeatedly.

Performance of the liturgy and the literacy entailed are briefly at issue in
the chapters on punishments. Not paying attention during the hours, laugh-
ing in choir, being absent for a silly reason, and singing anything other than
what is intended are all considered a medium fault. Not bringing the book
with the appropriate reading to collation and, more interestingly, reading or
singing badly are considered light faults, although the Constitutions specify
that the offending sister is not to be publicly humiliated for her mistake
immediately.[50] The Constitutions reveal no further information concerning
the time of day when learning or studying liturgical texts should occur, nor
about appropriate reading or learning material aside from the Office.

In her study, Julie Ann Smith notes that the 1259 Constitutions introduce a clause not found in the earlier statutes. She interprets the passage as a
restriction on the women's reading material, stipulating that "no community
was to be given books for reading or transcribing without permission of
the Master General or provincial prior."[51] The clause she cites, however, is
the last sentence in the section on receiving new houses and therefore in the

entire Constitutions. It reads "nulli eciam libellus iste tradatur ad transcribendum uel uidendum sine licencia magistri uel prioris prouincialis [this book is to be given to no one for transcribing or viewing without permission of the Master General or the provincial prior]."[52] The clause refers to one book alone, "this book," that is, the book of the Constitutions, which is not to be circulated without the permission of male superiors. The passage therefore does not regulate the reading material of Dominican nuns, but rather attempts to restrict the affiliation of new convents.

Smith is correct in noting that only one passage regarding learning is added to the 1259 Constitutions, although the particular passage she chooses to focus upon is puzzling. The chapter on novices in the Montargis Constitutions includes the injunction that sisters should diligently study the psalter and the Office. This earlier version lacks the different regulations for laysisters and the mention of the workroom, which first appear in the 1259 Constitutions.[53] Otherwise, the final Constitutions are primarily interesting for their deletions, which Smith does not address.

Namely, both the San Sisto Rule for the Magdalenes and the Constitutions for Montargis contain regulations concerning learning in the chapter on work. In the Montargis statutes, we read that "sorores postquam officium ecclesiasticum didicerint diligenter, addiscere poterunt tantum ut quod legitur intelligant, ut maiorem habeant devotionem [after they have diligently learned the Office of the church, sisters will be able to learn enough that they understand what is read, so that they may have greater devotion]."[54] No mention is made of grammar, exercises, language learning, or theological texts, so the content of this instruction remains vague. Nevertheless, the *tantum* limits the extent as well as the purpose of this further learning.

The Rule for the Magdalenes provided more thorough stipulations, which not only dictated the content and purpose of the convent education but also restricted who qualified to benefit from it.

> Iuniores discant legere et cantare, ut divinum officium valeant exercere; grammaticalia vero et auctores discere non oportet. Sorores que viginti quatuor annos transcenderunt, si nesciunt psalterium, de novo non discant. Que viginti annos compleverunt et nichil adhuc de cantu vel musica didicerunt, etiamsi sciant psalterium, de cetero non addiscant.[55]

The young should learn to read and sing, so that they are good at practicing the Divine Office; it is not appropriate, however, to learn

grammar and the authorities. If sisters who are older than twenty-
four do not know the psalter, they should not learn it from nothing.
Those who are twenty and have learned nothing of song or music,
even if they know the psalter, should not learn anything else.

The Magdalenes were expected to know enough Latin to perform the Office
well, but further study is forbidden them. The injunction against *grammati-
calia et auctores* encompasses even more than the corresponding warning in
the friars' Constitutions. In the chapter on students, the friars' Constitutions
enjoin that no one is to study "in libris gentilium et phylosophorum [in the
books of the gentiles and philosophers]," and moreover "seculares scientias
non addiscant, nec artes quas liberales uocant [they should not learn the
secular sciences, not even those arts called liberal]."[56] Whereas the young
brothers are protected from pagan sources, the Magdalenes were forbidden
even from reading Christian authorities.

Even more striking is that women beyond a certain age are deemed
incapable of new learning, but that they nevertheless might be admitted as
novices. The Constitutions of the friars stipulated that potential novices were
to be carefully assessed for scholarly aptitude and, especially early on, the
order zealously recruited men already educated at the universities.[57] In contrast, the Rule for the Magdalenes displays no such concern for the relative
intelligence of their novices. Moreover, this passage from the chapter on work
outright forbids the education of women who entered the order at an older
age, even in areas that supported the Divine Office.

Although they recognize that a certain amount of Latin education is necessary for the purpose of singing the Office, both the San Sisto Rule for Magdalenes and the Montargis Constitutions prohibit further study. In addition,
the Magdalene Rule restricts access to education to the young entrants who can
be taught from an early age. In comparison with these earlier statutes, the
vagueness of the 1259 Constitutions becomes positive information. Ehrenschwendtner speculates that women's literacy was controversial, and stipulations
were cut out of the 1259 Constitutions in order to avoid the issue.[58] Certainly,
in the final version, Humbert did not explicitly encourage theological learning
for the Dominican sisters. He did, however, delete all the passages placing
restrictions upon them and included a provision for a schoolroom of sorts.

A set of late thirteenth-century ordinances survive which clarify the
implementation of the 1259 Constitutions in Teutonia. These instructions
expand upon the matter of the women's education, largely absent from

Humbert's final version, by drawing on the obsolete Rule for Magdalenes. Although the admonishment not to teach old sisters new tricks is not repeated, this author clarifies the qualifier "que apte sunt" with regard to sisters continuing their education beyond the novitiate. "Item si aliqua recipitur XVIII annorum vel citra, si durioris est ingenii, non occupentur ad discendum amplius quam legere et cantare, ne declinando et huiusmodi faciendo tempus perdat [If someone eighteen years old or younger is received, if she is of a harder intelligence, such should not be occupied with learning more than reading and singing, lest she waste her time declining and doing similar things]."[59] The reference to declinations suggests that some sisters were indeed doing grammar exercises as part of increasing their Latin comprehension. While this was something more commonly expected of the young (as indicated by the age), it was also difficult. Some women simply did not have the brain for it and, whatever their age, were not to waste their time and strain their devotion in a frustrating task.

Furthermore, although the 1259 Constitutions lack any reference to learning or education in the chapter on work, these Teutonic injunctions include two relevant instructions. First, despite the strict imposition of silence during work hours in the Constitutions, this document permits women to have someone read to them in the workroom, especially admonitions from order superiors and commentaries on the Rule.[60] Second, we find a number of admonitions concerning scribes, including the previously lacking restriction on material.

> Scriptrices sedeant cum aliis laborantibus in communi domo, sed hae non scribant aliis, donec conventus habeat libros necessarios. Scribentibus vero aliis taxetur pretium per librarium fratrem, sicut magister ordinavit, et in utilitatem conventus vertatur acquisitio. Quibus autem aliquid iniungitur scribendum, nullo modo supponant furtiva opuscula, immo hoc diligentibus caveatur.[61]

> Scribes should sit with the other workers in the common house, but they should not write for others until the convent has the necessary books. A price should be assessed for the other writers by the Brother Librarian, as the master ordered, and the payment should go toward the use of the convent. Those charged with writing anything should by no means include secret little works, no—this is to be avoided by the diligent.

The scribes should not be segregated in a scriptorium dedicated to this work but rather must sit together with the women doing other sorts of work, for example, the seamstresses who shortly will be admonished not to embroider designs on the friars' habits. Both this information about the seamstresses and the detail that the scribes are to be paid by the Brother Librarian reveal a close practical relationship between the two branches of the order. Furthermore, the sisters fulfilled an important ancillary role in the educational system of the friars. The men were supposed to spend all free time in study, and their Constitutions did not include manual labor. The friars therefore had no provisions for copying books on their own and evidently relied not only upon professional scribes but also on the sisters for their books.[62] The warning against *furtiva opuscula* is likely to be understood in this context. The author forbids the scribes from including extraneous material, whether edifying meditations or personal notes, in commissioned books.

Such was the state of the legislation for the Dominican nuns at the end of the thirteenth century. Both the male and the female branches of the order were subject to the Augustinian Rule, which was so vague as to provide little guidance for daily conduct. Both men and women therefore had sets of Constitutions which determined the expectations for members of the order and detailed their structures of governance. The Constitutions of the friars included procedures for enacting changes in the legislation, whereas the sisters had no such mechanism for adaptation. On the other hand, the friars were bound by Constitution and papal decree to Humbert's Rite, whereas the sisters were given free rein, at least nominally. Similarly, the friars were subject to a strict curriculum and a hierarchy of schools, degrees, and privileges, whereas the sisters had no legislation regarding their education except that they must devote themselves to liturgical study. These were the standards and expectations for literacy in the service of liturgical piety to which the early sisters presumably were held and to which the Observant reformers wished to return.

In the next chapter, I turn to Johannes Tauler and Heinrich Seuse, two fourteenth-century friars who occupy key positions in this history of Dominican female spirituality, both by virtue of their role advising women during their lifetimes and through the avid reception of their work by the Observants. Both friars promote a form of spirituality that soars to mystical heights while remaining grounded in the practices of the order. What they describe in theory is portrayed in narrative examples by the contemporary sisterbooks, the subject of Chapter 3.

CHAPTER 2

Detachment, Order, and Observance in Johannes Tauler and Heinrich Seuse

Der sang us dem grunde der gienge gar hoch [The song from the ground would rise high indeed].

—Johannes Tauler

The Dominican friars Heinrich Seuse (1295–1366) and Johannes Tauler (1300–1361) both served in the vicariate of Alsace within the province of Teutonia. Seuse's writings, especially his Latin treatise the *Horologium sapientiae*, enjoyed an extraordinarily broad circulation, both complete and in excerpts. A fairly large number of extant manuscripts (fifteen) contain Seuse's complete *Exemplar*, a compilation of four vernacular works: the *Vita*, the *Little Book of Eternal Wisdom*, the *Little Book of Truth*, and a collection of edited letters. In contrast, Tauler's thought survives exclusively in German-language sermons, possibly recorded by but certainly distributed to the women to whom he preached.[1] Taken together, their works represent some of the main genres of spiritual writing received by late medieval Dominican women, including those that will concern us throughout this book: sermons, treatises, and exemplary lives.

Both Tauler's sermons and Seuse's devotional works were widely transmitted in female communities, especially within the Observance.[2] They are both strongly attested within the convent library of St. Katherine's in Nürnberg, in part thanks to the labors of the librarian Kunigunde Niklas. Niklas had been a member of the convent prior to the 1428 Observant reform, and her activities on behalf of St. Katherine's are attested from 1436 when she first becomes visible as a scribe. Niklas copied more than thirty manuscripts before her appointment as librarian in 1455.[3] Among the works she copied for her convent was Seuse's *Exemplar*, which she entered into her own library catalog under the signature J II.[4] As librarian, Niklas was also responsible for developing the community's cycle of table readings, edifying texts that were read aloud to the assembled sisters during a meal. Although she did not herself copy the manuscript she used, Niklas incorporated all eighty or so Tauler sermons in E V (Nürnberg, Stadtbibliothek, Cod. Cent. IV, 29) into the yearly schedule.[5] Kunigunde Niklas thus single-handedly assured that Seuse's *Exemplar* was available to her sisters and that they would regularly hear Tauler's sermons.

Scholarship on the fourteenth-century vernacular writings of German Dominican friars often conceives of such literature as combatting the immediate and corporeal feminine spirituality of Dominican women by imposing a male rationality. In a statement representative of this position, Werner Williams-Krapp writes that Seuse worked to convince Dominican nuns that "wild hallucinations achieved through rigorous asceticism are not to be understood as the consummation of spiritual perfection."[6] In other words, Williams-Krapp paints a picture of rational and prudent friars working to rein in the delusional visions of women spurred by bodily excess. Although returning a measure of value to embodied female devotional practices has proven a useful corrective in certain contexts, simply turning the paradigm on its head does not correct the problem. As Ulrike Wiethaus has compellingly argued, feminist approaches that celebrate the bodiliness of female spirituality still essentialize women and their engagement with Christian tradition and practice.[7] As I show in the following chapter, the visions of the sisterbooks represent carefully constructed mosaics of spiritual meaning: literary lessons which, far from being "wild hallucinations," in fact often teach obedience and devotion to the Office. In this chapter I approach the writings of contemporary friars not as a corrective measure aimed at reining in the sisters, but as a contiguous element that lays the conceptual and practical groundwork for a broader construction of German Dominican spiritual practice and convent life, including the complex negotiation of female liturgical piety.

Treating Tauler and Seuse together reveals that, despite generic differences in their surviving works and different emphases in their patterns of thought, both friars present the Dominican *forma vitae* as a devotional and ascetic exercise that fosters spiritual life. Adapting the philosophy of the condemned Dominican teacher Meister Eckhart, Tauler and Seuse posit a "ground" of the soul in or through which the human mind accesses divine experience. Detaching oneself from the world in a state of *Gelassenheit* in order to prepare for this experience represents the ultimate goal of their spiritual programs. Nevertheless, both men reject ascetic exceptionalism and insist that spiritual perfection can only be attained through orderly practice or, better, through the practices of the order. By submitting oneself to the regulations of the Dominican order, one learns to let go of one's own will in *Gelassenheit*, such that only the prayers of the Office remain as expressions of self rising from the ground of the soul. Tauler's ideal expressions of piety prove different from Seuse's, and Seuse's again from those of the sisterbooks, yet these very differences reveal the spiritual productivity of life under the Dominican statutes.

The Ground and *Gelassenheit*

Gelassenheit and its partner concept, the ground, constitute key terms for both Tauler and Seuse, as for their Dominican predecessor Meister Eckhart, and these ideas govern their devotional and spiritual programs.[8] Since their liturgical spirituality is both founded in and aims back toward the ground of the soul, I must address these concepts first, building their devotional programs from the ground up, so to speak. These terms govern how Tauler and Seuse conceive the human relationship to the divine and the effectiveness of human activity, including the Dominican *forma vitae* and the Office. Using the concept of the ground, Tauler and Seuse outline a schematic theological anthropology that explains in philosophical terms how and why observance of the order's regulations brings one closer to God.

Indebted to Neo-Platonic notions of emanation, the ground represents the part of the human person that shares in the divine being as it pours itself out into creation.[9] Seuse famously depicts this dependence or identity visually in a full-page illustration of the cycle of emanation and return found in the earliest manuscript witness of the *Exemplar*. The divine ground, represented as a dark double circle, rests at the top left of the image. From this point a red thread traces stages in Christ's life allegorized in poetic couplets as a spiritual progression. At each stage, the thread draws through a small double disk in the center of the figure's chest, echoing the divine ground from which the thread originates.[10]

Whereas Seuse uses the term *grunt* to designate divine mystery and avoids it when describing aspects of the human self,[11] Tauler employs the term primarily with regard to the human soul.[12] In Tauler's sermons, the ground often spatially describes the location of the *gemuete*, which is only imprecisely translated as mind, since it designates the mind's natural dependence upon and desire to return to God. Paul Wyser concludes that "dieses Streben ist eben doch das Gemüt selber, nicht nur eine Kraft: es ist der Menschengeist, der Seelengrund mit seiner Neigung zu sich selbst [this striving is the *gemuete* itself and not only a faculty: it is the human spirit, the ground of the soul with its inclination towards itself]."[13] Bernard McGinn accordingly translates *gemuete* as "essential inclination" and defines the ground for Tauler as the "place" of God's reflection in the human soul.[14] Although McGinn's translation is more accurate, it becomes unwieldy with frequent use. I will translate *gemuete* as "mind," with acknowledgment of this term's shortcomings.

Whether the ground represents the divine font itself or the place within the human soul where it may be sought, both Tauler and Seuse set access to the ground as the goal of contemplative practice. One may achieve this through a process of self-divestment which they both call *Gelassenheit*. Derived from the verb *lassen*, to leave or let go, *Gelassenheit* entails letting go of the world and worldly concerns in order to access the ground. Nevertheless, perfect contemplation neither entails nor permits quietism, but rather orients a person's works to the will of God. As Amy Hollywood argues in her analysis of Eckhart's sermon 86 on Mary and Martha, "the highest contemplation is compatible with, and in fact brings about, a state of heightened activity."[15] Virtuous practice is also an important component of spiritual perfection for both Tauler and Seuse, but unlike Eckhart, who offers no concrete prescriptions, the later friars promote specific devotional programs in order to foster *Gelassenheit*.[16] As we shall see, the Dominican *forma vitae* represents a central component of their programs. However, since their understandings of the ground differ, their conceptions of *Gelassenheit* and the methods of achieving it differ, as well. Although both urge surrendering the will to God in *Gelassenheit*, Seuse prioritizes the path of suffering in imitation of Christ, whereas the Virgin Mary's obedience proves more emblematic of Tauler's approach.

Of the works included in Seuse's *Exemplar*, the *Vita* and the *Little Book of Truth* contain the most extensive discussions of *Gelassenheit*.[17] The *Vita*

constitutes the life narrative and spiritual progression of an anonymous pro-
tagonist called simply "ein diener der ewigen wisheit [a Servant of Eternal
Wisdom],"[18] who nevertheless represents Seuse, if not with precise historical
accuracy.[19] The work is divided into two books, the first of which narrates
the Servant's own spiritual journey, while the second, beginning in chapter
33, recounts the path of his spiritual daughter, Elsbeth Stagel of the Töss
convent, who is explicitly named.[20] Walter Blank has pointed out that these
two books are each further divided into two sections. The first half of book
one recounts Seuse's path as a "beginner," after which a conversion experience in chapter 19 allows him to advance to intermediate status on the path
to perfection. At the beginning of the second book, Stagel is introduced,
having already completed the path of the beginner. Seeking Seuse's mentorship marks her transition to the intermediate step. The genre shift from life
narrative to dialogical treatise in chapter 46 marks the moment of Stagel's
achievement of spiritual perfection, confirmed by Seuse in a vision after her
death.[21] In these later chapters, Seuse himself occasionally seems to taste this
perfection as he continues to grow through his relationship with Stagel.

Throughout the *Exemplar* Seuse delights in playing with the word *Gelassenheit* in its various grammatical forms and realms of meaning. Whether in
spite of or because of this, he does not represent *Gelassenheit* as something
one could discursively or intellectually grasp, but rather, as Susanne Bernhardt argues, "als praktisches Wissen, das es nachzuvollziehen gilt [as practical
knowledge that one must understand by doing]."[22] For Seuse, *Gelassenheit*
and its attendant practices link the philosophical-theological concept of the
ground of the soul to the concerns of practical theology. Seuse does not rest
at providing a theoretical description of the human soul, but further presents
a devotional program, illustrated in the three stages of the *Vita*. Each of the
three stages of spiritual progression entails particular exercises which gradually reveal new levels of meaning corresponding to new forms of *imitatio
Christi*.

The first stage involves developing the appropriate attitude toward one's
own body. The Servant practices severe self-castigation in many ways similar
to those used by Elsbeth von Oye, a sister from the convent of Oetenbach
whose life is recounted in their sisterbook. For example, he explicitly compares himself to the tortured Christ while flagellating himself with a thorny
scourge.[23] This practice, however, must be surpassed, because in choosing to
inflict such discipline on himself, Seuse still follows his own will rather than

God's.[24] Similar to many accounts in the sisterbooks, the transition to the intermediate stage entails ceasing self-castigation in order to accept suffering inflicted by "wolfish people."[25] *Gelassenheit* at this stage is understood in the sense of humility and patience or equanimity in the face of adversity, which Richard Kieckhefer has identified as one of the characteristic virtues of fourteenth-century holiness.[26] This advanced stage entails not literal imitation of Christ's acts or suffering but creative imitation of his virtue in all events and experiences.[27]

The final, highest stage of *Gelassenheit* paradoxically incorporates both the sense of trust in God, that is, leaving oneself in God's hands, and that of abandonment, the feeling of having been left by God. Bernhardt demonstrates this multiplicity of the meanings of *Gelassenheit* and Seuse's practical understanding in an analysis of Seuse's lament over being accused of having impregnated a woman.[28] Noting that the term *lassen-gelassen-gelassenheit* permeates the passage, she shows that it is used even within the same sentence to mean both his abandonment by God and entrusting his troubles to God. In this semantically charged outcry, Seuse wears himself out and finally grasps true *Gelassenheit* when he stills himself, accepts his lot, and cites Christ: *fiat voluntas tua*.[29] As Bernhardt summarizes, "Gelassenheit wird semantisch entfaltet im Spektrum Gleichmut—Gottvertrauen—Gottverlassenheit sowie mit Geduld und natürlich mit Leiden in Beziehung gesetzt [*Gelassenheit* semantically unfolds along the spectrum: equanimity—trust in God—abandonment by God and is placed in relation to patience and, naturally, suffering]."[30] This coincidence of meanings must also be at work in the compressed statement in the *Little Book of Eternal Wisdom*: "Ein gelazenheit ob aller gelazenheit ist gelazen sin in gelazenheit [the greatest self-abnegation of all is being patient/humble/trusting when abandoned]."[31] Imitation of Christ in *Gelassenheit* does not necessarily entail physical suffering, but rather the patient acceptance of the will of God in whatever suffering is sent.

Seuse offers a deeper discussion of *Gelassenheit* in the *Little Book of Truth*, which recounts a philosophical dialogue between a disciple and the personified figure of Truth as she coaches him in the true spiritual way.[32] The work begins more or less at the same point as the conversion of the Servant in chapter 19 of the *Vita*. The disciple has long practiced the forms of asceticism common to beginners but knows that he is missing something, for he remains "ungeübt in sin selbs nehsten gelazenheit [unpracticed in his own innermost *Gelassenheit*]."[33] *Gelassenheit*, as Truth explains in Chapter 4, entails *sich lassen*, abnegation of the self.[34] However, Seuse intentionally softens Eckhart's philosophy of essential unity in the ground whereby the soul loses or destroys its created nature in order to be "one only one" with God.[35] Truth clarifies that *Gelassenheit* does not entail total annihilation of the self and indistinct union with God.[36] On the contrary, each person has five kinds of "self," and only the last is at issue. Each person possesses a being self, which stones also have; growing, which humans share with plants; feeling, which animals enjoy; human nature, which all humans share; and finally, individual personhood.[37] The middle three selves are identifiable as Aristotle's nutritive, sensitive, and rational souls.[38] All of these selves are created but nevertheless do not prevent perception of God in the divine ground; only the characteristics of individual personhood obstruct *Gelassenheit*. Even so, Truth specifies that these traits must not be destroyed but simply given up or despised (*ufgeben oder verahten*).[39] Here as in the *Vita*, self-denial, defined as the recognition of one's own powerlessness and the acceptance of suffering, allows one to un-become (*entwerden*) and unite with Christ in the divine ground. Truth summarizes, "dis gelassen sich wirt ein kristförmig ich [this *gelassen* self becomes an I according to Christ's form]."[40] Abandoning one's own identity, goals, aspirations, and practices produces a Christlike self through acceptance of God's will in suffering.

Tauler's understanding of *Gelassenheit* is similarly broad but often more abstract than Seuse's. In her systematic analysis of Tauler's use of *Gelassenheit* throughout the surviving sermons, Imke Früh notes that Tauler never explicitly defines *Gelassenheit* as Seuse does, so that the term comes to encompass a broad range of virtues, importantly including the monastic virtues of humility and obedience.[41] Moreover, although Tauler does also endorse contemplation and imitation of Christ's passion, suffering does not pervade his sermons as it does Seuse's writings. When he does speak of it, Tauler tends quickly to abstract the concept of *leiden* from the experience of pain to a state of passivity. As Alois Haas explains, "*Gotliden* meint die Absenz allen menschlichen *würkens* . . . und damit die schrankenlose Offenheit und Empfänglichkeit für die von Gott gewirkte Einigung des Menschen mit Gott [suffering God entails the absence of all human work . . . and therefore the unbounded openness and receptivity for the union of the person with God, effected through God himself]."[42] Früh also emphasizes passivity in Tauler's conception of *Gelassenheit*, noting that "leaving oneself" constitutes "weniger eine aktive Handlung als vielmehr einen Übergang in die Passivität [less an active deed than a transition into passivity]."[43] This passivity is not a form of quietism but rather a receptivity to the workings of God, who can only enter an

empty vessel. Achieving this state of receptivity ("reine Empfänglichkeit und
Bestimmbarkeit" in Markus Enders's words[44]) by preparing the ground of
the soul proves absolutely central to Tauler's concept of *Gelassenheit*.

This concept of *Gelassenheit* as receptive passivity is worked out in a
sermon for Christmas. Tauler explains that the three Masses celebrated on
Christmas day honor three different ways in which Christ is born. First, the
birth of the Son from the Father, second, the birth of Jesus from Mary, and
third, the eternal birth of God in the soul should be commemorated over the
course of the day. In explaining the first form of birth, Tauler draws on the
Johannine association of Christ with the Word of God. Echoing the inward
turn that he will argue the human soul must take, Tauler explains that God
turned inward to the abyss (*abgrund*) of his own being and, in pure understanding of himself, spoke himself out as a Word, that is, Christ the Son. If
one wishes to receive God in the soul, Tauler continues, one must be able to
hear the speaking of this Word.

> Wan wenne zwei súllent eins werden, so mûs sich daz eine halten
> lidende und daz ander wúrckende; sol min ouge enpfohen die bilde
> in der want oder waz es sehen sol, so mûs es an ime selber blos sin
> aller bilde, wan hette es ein einig bilde in ime einiger varwen, so
> gesehe es niemer kein varwe; oder hat daz ore ein getöne, so gehört
> es niemer enkein getöne; so welich ding enpfohen sol, das mûs itel,
> lidig und wan sin.[45]

> For if two should become one, then the one must stay passive and
> the other active; if my eye is to receive the images on the wall or
> whatever it is supposed to see, it must in itself be pure of all images,
> since if it even had one image in it of whatever color, it would never
> see any color; or if the ear had a tone, it would never hear any tone;
> so anything that should be receptive must be empty, passive, and
> pure.

According to medieval Aristotelian theories of perception, sense impressions
quite literally impressed the form of the object perceived into the soul's cog-
nitive faculty, causing that faculty momentarily to share the form of the
perceived object. In order for this object impression to operate correctly, the
faculty had to be itself formless and plastic, allowing it to receive foreign
forms easily.[46]

The natural receptivity of the soul's faculties is both an advantage and a disadvantage. If one turns inward, the soul will easily be able to receive (or conceive) God, but the faculties too often are oriented outward toward things in the world. These outer things occupy the soul and obstruct God's natural desire to pour himself out. "Und darumbe soltu swigen," Tauler explains, "so mag dis wort diser geburt in dich sprechen und in dir gehört werden; aber sicher, wiltu sprechen, so mûs er swigen [And for this reason, you should be silent: so that the Word of this birth should speak in you and be heard in you; but certainly, if you want to speak, he must be silent]."[47] The obstructive tones that may prevent an ear from hearing are here given a power that goes beyond inattention to full interruption. It is not merely that the soul cannot hear; unless silence is accomplished, God does not speak at all. In order passively to receive God's will, one must empty the soul of the world. McGinn concludes that debating whether *lidikeit* in Tauler's sermons should be translated as emptiness (*Ledigkeit*) or passivity (*Leidendheit*) argues a moot point: *lidikeit* represents a neologism that intentionally evokes both meanings.[48] Emptying out the soul prepares it for true passivity.

In order to undergird his association of Christmas with *Gelassenheit* with silence, Tauler cites Wisdom 18:14–15, signaling explicitly that the text serves as the Introit for Mass on the Sunday within the Octave of Christmas.[49] Because of its reference to the descent of the Word, the verse had long been used for the celebration of the Incarnation.[50] After translating the entirety of the Introit, Tauler expounds the mention of silence as the purification of the soul required for *Gelassenheit*.

> Hievon sol man singen in dem nehsten sunnendage in dem anhe-
> bende der messen: *dum medium silencium fieret*, do daz mittel swigen
> wart und alle ding in dem höhsten swigende worent und die naht
> iren louf vollebroht hette, herre, do kam dine almehtige rede von
> dem kúniglichen stûle, das waz daz ewige wort von dem vetterlichen
> hertzen. In disem mittel swigende, in disem do alle ding sint in dem
> höhsten swigende und ein wor *silencium* ist, denne wurt man dis
> wort in der worheit hörende; wan sol Got sprechen, du mûst swigen;
> sol Got ingon, alle ding müssent uzgon.[51]

One sings about this next Sunday at the beginning of Mass: *dum medium silencium fieret*, when the middle/medium was silent and all things were in the highest silence and the night had completed its

course, Lord, your almighty speech came from the royal seat, that
was the eternal word from the Fatherly heart. In this silent medium,
in this where all things are in the highest silence and there is a true
silencium, here one will hear the word in truth; since if God should
speak, you must be still; if God should go in, all things must go out.

By using the Introit for an upcoming Mass to illustrate his point, Tauler
prepares his audience to understand that feast in light of his spiritual philosophy. The Christmas season and its celebration of Mary's passive role should
lead one to reflect on one's own submission to God's will. However, identifying silence as the ethical concern of a liturgical text produces an interesting
paradox. Tauler urges his audience to consider their own pursuit of *Gelassenheit* while singing the Divine Office. This contemplative performance results
in a curious situation in which the singers ought to be striving for inner
silence, while they are singing outwardly. Seuse, with his greater attention to
the immediate liturgical contexts, deals with this paradox of passive performance more effectively than Tauler, who remains more interested in the theological significance of feasts than in the spiritual interpretation of individual
texts.

Liturgical Piety in the Global and the Particular

Tauler and Seuse deal with liturgical context in very different ways, which
are at least partly motivated by the difference in genre. As sermons, Tauler's
works were naturally embedded in the liturgical context during which they
would have been delivered. Although it is rarely explicitly noted, this context
can be recovered from his interpretations of the pericopes, scriptural passages
which rotated with the liturgical calendar. Finally, the manuscripts which
contain large collections of his sermons frequently organize them according
to the liturgical cycle rather than thematically. In contrast, Seuse contextualizes his visions and experiences within the liturgy through citation of Latin
Mass texts. Neither Seuse nor Tauler represents liturgical performance with
anything like the frequency or vividness of the sisterbooks. Moreover,
whereas the sisterbooks employ Office texts, Tauler and Seuse both rely more
heavily on the Mass for inspiration. Both friars also share an anxiety over
the disruptive behavior that experiencing divine insight during communal
celebration can cause.

Aside from the scriptural readings for a particular day, Tauler cites liturgical material less frequently and less systematically than even his prominent forebear Meister Eckhart.[52] Tauler rarely offers specific liturgical texts as devotional inspiration, and when he does, as in the sermon for Christmas, he casts his net more widely than the context of a particular feast. Indeed, Joachim Theisen admits to being initially disappointed by Tauler's apparent disregard for "the liturgical microcontext of the Mass."[53] Tauler does always explain the scriptural reading for the day, Theisen notes, but "läßt sich ansonsten jedoch nicht von den anderen Texten des Meßformulars leiten, sondern von den thematischen Vorgaben der liturgischen Zeit [otherwise is not directed by the other texts of the Mass formulary but rather by the thematic guidelines of the liturgical cycle]."[54] Thus in sermon Vetter 1, Tauler describes the three Masses for Christmas Day as three kinds of divine birth and even assigns spiritual meaning to the fact that one is sung in the dark, one at dawn, and one when it is light. Rather than dwelling on the specific texts for a specific Mass, Tauler invests the entire feast and all that pertains to its celebration with spiritual meaning.

This orientation is likely what made Tauler an attractive choice for table readings at St. Katherine's in Nürnberg.[55] Divorced from the context of its original delivery during a Mass and relocated to the refectory or chapter, a focused explication of liturgical texts would no longer be as significant or as relevant. Devotional interpretation of the feast within the context of the liturgical year, however, would be eminently useful in orienting the audience in an informed, orderly performance of the liturgical duties of that season. Tauler's sermons spiritualize the liturgy on a global scale, allegorizing large-scale practices such as the three Masses on Christmas Day. His interpretations prepare the audience especially for high times in the liturgical year, when the special feasts were celebrated with unique variations in the Rite. Tauler both provides theological explanations for these broader changes in liturgical practice and offers spiritual lessons which give the feasts personal import. However, Tauler is not sensitive to the devotional power of liturgical text within the context of its performance, something that inspires both Seuse and the women of the sisterbooks.

Liturgical performances certainly inspire many of Seuse's visions, and he also uses liturgical citations to comment on or gloss visionary experience. Although most studies focus on the role of images and visual piety in Seuse's devotional program,[56] Steven Rozenski has compellingly argued that "the auditory often occupies a place of privilege vis-à-vis the visual: music and voice are frequently treated as both more powerful and more trustworthy than images, visions, or texts."[57] Rozenski points out not only that hearing something can incite a visionary experience for Seuse, but that within such visions he often imagines himself rapt outside his body to some insubstantial place of angelic performance, where he sings along or dances to the tune. Although the Servant often hears instrumental dance music, liturgical song appears just as often in visions of musical performance. In contrast to Tauler's global interest in the devotional significance of liturgical feasts, Seuse uses particular liturgical texts as either inspirations for or explanations of visions which are often extracted from their context in the liturgical calendar.

Seuse's liturgical visions share many of the characteristics and functions such narratives display in the sisterbooks, with two signal differences pertaining on the one hand, to the meaning they produce and on the other, to the time and location of their occurrence. As I will show in the following chapter, the sisterbooks deploy liturgical citations as part of complex visions which either explore theological concepts or perform a sister's holiness by drawing her into association with a saint. Seuse prefers to use the genre of philosophical dialogue to tackle theological issues, but he does use liturgical visions to reflect on his own spiritual state or to communicate some devotional lesson. For example, Seuse recounts a curious nightmare in which he is selected as celebrant for Mass. Taking him by surprise, the choir sings an Introit of a Mass for martyrs.[58]

Die senger hůben an die messe von den martrern: *Multae tribulationes justorum* etc., daz da sait von menigvaltigem lidene gotesfründen. Daz horte er ungern und heti es gern gewendet und sprach also: 'wafen, wes töbent ir úns mit den martrern? War zů singent ir hůt von den martrern, und es hůt enkaines martrers tag ist, den wir begangen?' Sú sahen in an und zögtan mit den vingern uf in und sprachen: 'got der vindet sin martrer hůt an disem tage, als er sú ie vand. Berait dich núwan dur zů und sing fúr dich!'[59]

The singers began the Mass for Martyrs: *Multae tribulationes justorum etc.*, which handles the multifarious suffering of the friends of God. He did not like hearing this and wanted to change it, so he said: "hey, why are you blasting away about the martyrs? What are you singing about martyrs for, when we are not celebrating any martyr's feast?" They looked at him and pointed at him with their

fingers and said: "God will find his martyr on this day as he ever
found them. Prepare yourself for this alone and sing your own feast!"

Terrified by this prophecy, Seuse flips through the pages of the missal before
him, seeking the feast of some confessor or anything else. When he sees that
the missal contains nothing but martyrs, he resigns himself to his fate and
accepts the suffering he knows will come. By singing a Mass for martyrs on
his own behalf, Seuse interprets his own trials as martyrdom and assimilates
the narrative of his own life to their hagiographic *vitae*. His self-castigation
and his persecution at the hands of others are given both redemptive meaning
and exemplary status through Seuse's liturgical association with the Church's
martyrs.

   As I will discuss in more depth in the following chapter, the sisterbooks
also often deploy liturgical citations in order to reveal the spiritual state usually of a deceased sister. Seuse's nightmare resembles in particular a dream
granted to the Gotteszell sister Adelheit. She sees a recently deceased sister
dressed in rich robes, emblazoned with liturgical passages from Offices for
martyrs on the front and back: *Qui vult venire post me* and *Qui mihi minis-
trat*.[60] The similarity of the episodes brings important differences sharply into
focus. First of all, Seuse may arrogate to himself the honor due a martyr even
before he has earned it. Dominican sisters, in contrast, usually must wait
until after death for confirmation of their spiritual state. This difference
makes manifest some of the dynamics of gendered power which increasingly
meant that the only holy woman was a dead woman.[61] Second, Seuse and
the sisters experience the liturgy in different ways and with different intensit-
ies and therefore draw on different liturgical texts for their visions. The friar
Seuse hears an Introit for a Mass at which he himself is meant to preside.
The Gotteszell sister appears with the written texts of two antiphons for
Lauds, that is, excerpts from the hours. Seuse's vision of a martyr's Mass is
representative of his liturgical citations on the whole. Befitting his status as a
friar and priest, Seuse tends to cite from the Mass more often than from the
hours, which constituted the sisters' liturgical focus and their primary source
for visionary material. Comparing Seuse's dream with a similar vision from
the sisterbooks reveals significant manifestations of gender difference in access
to saintly status and in experience of the liturgy. Seuse's status as a male
Dominican allows him to celebrate his own blessedness more openly and
orients his use of liturgical material toward Mass texts over the hours. Nevertheless, the way in which Seuse reconfigures liturgical context to create meaning within his visions corresponds to the literary methods of the sisterbooks.

Arnold Angenendt has identified a further difference between Seuse's use of liturgical material and that of the sisterbooks. Whereas the visions of the sisterbooks are often inspired by a liturgical performance during which they occur, Angenendt notes that Seuse's visions have a sacramental character, and reproduce or reimagine liturgical celebrations but are detached from the performance itself. "Die erzielte Wirkung geschieht letztlich unabhängig von fester liturgischer Form, von sakraler Zeit und geweihtem Ort [The intended effect in the end is accomplished independently from strict liturgical form, from sacred time and holy place]."[62] Instead of seeing angels appear during the *Sanctus* or Mary in response to the *Salve regina*, Seuse tends to envision heavenly liturgical celebrations during private contemplation. For example, the Servant experiences a vision while meditating between the first two Masses on Christmas.

Des liehten morgens, do man daz frölich gesang von dem veterlichen glanz der ewigen wisheit solt singen ze messe: *Lux fulgebit*, do waz der diener des morgens in siner kapell in ein stilles rüwli siner ussren sinnen komen. Do waz im vor in einer gesicht, wie er wurdi gefüret in einen kor, da man mess sang.[63]

On the morning when the joyful song about the paternal radiance of Eternal Wisdom, *Lux fulgebit*, should be sung at Mass, in the morning in his chapel the Servant came into a quiet silence of his outer senses. It appeared to him in a vision that he was led into a choir where Mass was being sung.

In meditating on the upcoming liturgical service, Seuse envisions celebrating it with an angelic choir that performs music of untold beauty. He sings the *Sanctus* along with them, but when the *Benedictus qui venit* begins, he is so overpowered by the beauty of the music that he can no longer stand and sinks to the floor. He comes to as his body hits the ground. Still entranced by the melody, Seuse approaches the altar while singing the angelic *Benedictus* to himself under his breath. Although Seuse attends a visionary Mass, in reality he is alone in the church and the second Christmas Mass has not yet begun. He sings a *Sanctus* with the angels but not with his fellow friars. Since he is alone during this experience, his fall and the noise he makes singing to himself do not disturb any communal liturgical celebration.

The fact that Seuse's miraculous Mass and his uncontrollable response occur in between the communal celebrations on Christmas Day bears even greater significance than Angenendt ascribes to it. Namely, disruption of the communal liturgy by physical responses to divine experience proves a concern for both Tauler and Seuse. The majority of Seuse's visions end because "der krank lip nit me moht erliden [his frail body could no longer endure it],"[64] and he makes an involuntary physical gesture; for example, he sinks to his knees or places a hand over his heart, interrupting his prayer practice.[65] Tauler also speaks of people who are "als über gossen mit innerlicher fröide das der kranke licham die fröide nút enthalten enmag und bricht us mit eigener sunderlicher wise. Und tete er des nút, das blůt breche im lichte zů dem munde us [so overwhelmed by inner joy that the sick body cannot contain the joy and breaks out in strange ways. And if it did not, blood would probably pour out of the mouth]."[66] The overwhelming experience of divine joy results in actual physical pressure, which the body will purge in another way if it is not released through cries and wild laughter. Excessive spiritual experience overwhelms the soul and bursts out from the body in jubilation,[67] interrupting contemplative prayer or, worse, disrupting the communal liturgy.

These outbursts represent a correlative or even a consequence of the friars' rejection of quietism. That is to say, if access to God in the ground of the soul leads to virtuous living, then any disorder in this process will necessarily result in disordered behavior and disruption of prayer practice. Although they disapprove of these uncontrolled expressions in principle, Tauler and Seuse both acknowledge them as an initial phase in the slow development of spiritual perfection; for Seuse, it provides "ein reizlicher vorlof [an enticing prelude],"[68] and for Tauler, it represents "der erste grat eins inwendigen tugentlichen lebens [the first degree of an inner virtuous life]."[69] This disorderly behavior is acceptable for beginners but must be overcome in order to advance in spiritual perfection. Moving beyond this preliminary stage and developing the proper modes of behavior requires discernment.

Order and Discernment

Although the spiritual programs laid out by Tauler and Seuse display different characters, both insist that there is a wrong and a right way to seek spiritual perfection. As Bernhardt and Früh note separately, the two Dominicans both urge true detachment, *rechte Gelassenheit*, but never use negative adjectives to qualify this mystical virtue. The opposite vices are named rather as false freedom, false passivity, or even *Ungelassenheit*.[70] In order to avoid the disorder of false freedom, one must tread a careful path between outer actions and inner contemplation. Both outer and inner devotions serve the pursuit of true *Gelassenheit*, provided they are performed in an orderly manner governed by discernment, *bescheidenheit*.

In the Middle Ages, *bescheidenheit* meant not modesty but rather prudence, discernment, or discretion. It is etymologically related to *underscheidunge*, which in Middle High German signifies not only difference itself but also the ability to perceive differences. *Underscheidunge* would become the technical term for *discretio spirituum*, discernment of spirits, that is, the ability to tell whether a vision came from God or from the devil.[71] A vast literature on this subject would develop in the late fourteenth and the fifteenth century, but Tauler already uses the term *unterscheid* in discussing the discernment of spirits according to Paul in I Corinthians 12:10.[72] Neither Tauler nor Seuse, however, restricts the term to this particular meaning, but instead they associate *underscheidunge* and *bescheidenheit* more broadly with order and orderliness as the preconditions for true *Gelassenheit* and avoidance of heresy.

Seuse frequently associates *ordenunge* with *underscheid* and ascribes central importance to these qualities. Indeed, the prologue to the *Exemplar* states that Seuse's *Vita* provides instruction in precisely these virtues, because they are the most necessary but very often lacking. Without discernment and order, those who pursue mystical experience will go astray and become a danger to themselves. For this reason, the prologue tells us, "git es vil gůten underschaid warer und valscher vernúnftekeit und lert, wie man mit rehter ordenhafti zů der blossen warheit eins seligen volkomen lebens sol komen [it provides many good distinctions between true and false reasoning, and it teaches how one shall attain the pure truth of a blessed and perfect life through correct orderliness]."[73] The Servant's life provides a narrative, practical example of how to achieve *Gelassenheit* through discernment (*underschaid*) and order (*ordenhafti*).

These virtues also determine Seuse's mentorship of Elsbeth Stagel. In advising her to discontinue the ascetic practices she had taken up in imitation of the Desert Fathers and the Servant himself, he insists that prudence must govern ascetic zeal. "Gemeinlich ze sprechen so ist vil bessrer bescheiden strenkheit füren denn unbescheiden [In general, it is much better to pursue prudent than imprudent austerity]."[74] Such prudence is necessary because too quick an ascetic advance will result only in a relapse, "wan es geschiht dik, so man der natur ze vil unordenlich ab prichet, daz man ir och dur na ze vil müss unordenlich wider geben [for it often happens that if one withholds too much from one's nature in a disorderly manner, one must afterwards disorderly give back too much, as well]."[75] Only order and prudence lead to sustainable ascetic practice. The extreme castigation the Servant himself had pursued is unsuited to Elsbeth, "wan es diner fröwlichen krankheit und wol geordneten nature nit zů gehöret [because it is not appropriate for your feminine illness and well-ordered nature]."[76] Whether or not one agrees with David Tinsley that it is Elsbeth's frailty and not her gender that constitutes the first criterion,[77] the second point is clear. The self-castigation that the beginning Servant performs is meant to order his disordered nature. Imprudent asceticism can only bring Elsbeth's well-ordered soul into disorder, and the Servant must direct her down a different, prudent path.

This purpose is restated in the final chapter of the *Vita* as Stagel sums up the instruction she has received through his mentorship. Chapters 46 through 53, which Blank identified as representing the final stage of spiritual perfection, contain a series of theological questions posed by Elsbeth and answered by the Servant. He only permits her to ask them in the first place, because "du ordenlich dur dú rehten mitel bist gezogen [you have come in an orderly manner through the right means]."[78] Once all her curiosity has been satisfied, the daughter exclaims at the conclusion of the book:

> gelopt sie dú ewig warheit, daz ich von úweren wisen und leblichen worten so schon bewiset bin dez ersten beginnes eins anvahenden menschen, und der ordenlicher mitel midens und lidens und übens eins zůnemenden menschen, und mit gůtem underscheide in togenlicher wise der aller nehsten blossen warheit.[79]

> Praised be eternal Truth, that by your wise and vivid words I have been so well instructed about the first steps of a beginner, about the orderly means of renunciation, suffering, and the exercises of a progressing person, and, with good discernment, about the most perfect and bare truth in a mysterious way.

Stagel here sums up the didactic program of the *Vita*, emphasizing order as necessary for the path and discernment for the goal. Achievement of mystical perfection is a gradual process with various stages on the way—beginning, progressing, and perfect. Certain kinds of ascetic or devotional practices are appropriate for some levels of mystical achievement and not for others. True progression requires orderliness for the development of discernment, without which one cannot grasp the most hidden truth.

This final point is developed further in the *Little Book of Truth*, where *underscheit* also proves a structuring theme, in Susanne Köbele's words the "intellectual center"[80] of the work. As Loris Sturlese has shown, this dialogue systematically takes up and defends the propositions that were condemned in Eckhart's heresy trial.[81] Seuse largely accomplishes this by qualifying the statements as true only according to human perception, not in essence. Susanne Köbele argues that the primary thrust of the *Little Book of Truth* is to limit Eckhart's mystical-philosophical language, which operated analogically, by reintroducing difference (*underscheit*) and thus blocking the heretical movement toward indistinct union.[82]

Köbele's argument that *underscheit* drives the *Little Book of Truth* is corroborated by two further observations. Namely, the disciple defends this very principle by differentiating between different kinds of difference and stating that the object motivating the discussion of distinction is right order. Although most of the work recounts conversations in which Seuse as the "disciple" interrogates the allegorical figure of Truth, in one chapter Seuse himself is put to the test by a sentient image (*ein vernünftiges bilde*) that identifies itself as the Nameless Wild One (*daz namelos wilde*). The dialogue begins when the disciple asks this figure, "wa lendet din bescheidenheit? [where does your discernment lead?]" and receives the answer, "in lediger friheit [to unencumbered freedom]."[83] To argue against the false freedom and misdirected *bescheidenheit* of this strange figure, the disciple differentiates between *underscheit* as good judgment or discernment, *underschidunge* as separation or disjuncture, and *underscheidenheit* as distinction between things that may be conjoined.[84] Body and soul are *underscheiden*, since they are not the same thing, but they cannot exist in *underschidunge* if the person is to be alive. This distinction between the two different kinds of distinction is important, because it also describes the relationship between the three persons of the Godhead. Furthermore, and most importantly for the disciple's argument, the difference between *underscheidenheit* and *underschidunge* justifies how a human soul can be united with God but remain distinct. The heretical Nameless Wild One thinks that it becomes God in *Gelassenheit*. It does not possess the *underscheit* to see the difference between *underschidunge* and *underscheidenheit*.

Lack of discernment is the root of all problems for the Nameless Wild One, because without *underscheit* there can be no order, and disorder is the root of all evil. Reversing the relationship posited by Stagel, the disciple explains that "swem underscheides gebristet, dem gebristet ordenunge, und waz ane reht ordenunge ist, daz ist böse und gebreste [whoever lacks discernment, lacks order. And whatever is without correct order is evil and defective]."[85] The Nameless Wild One is not content with this and asks him how he defines order. The disciple responds, "ich heis daz ordenhaft, wenn alles daz, daz der sache zůgehörlich ist von innen ald von ussen nút underwegen blibet unangesehen in dem uswúrkenne ["orderly" is when everything that pertains to a matter, both interiorly and exteriorly, is not left out of consideration in carrying it out]."[86] Order is not merely a matter of spiritual rectitude or correct devotional disposition. Order is completed in well-considered action, indeed in the performance of duty: that is, everything that pertains (*zugehörlich ist*) to a given circumstance. Order thus provides an important counterargument both to the charge of quietism and to the Nameless Wild One, who had argued that his unencumbered freedom (*ledige friheit*) authorized following his own inclination (*můtwillen*).

Tauler does not pair order and discernment as consistently as Seuse does, but he does define prudence as the ability to regulate, that is, order, one's own behavior.[87] In this vein, he mentions *Bescheidenheit* in several sermons as the crowning virtue or the highest faculty of the soul. For example, in a sermon on preparing for divine grace, Tauler wishes his audience to note "wie der heilige geist danne die obersten krefte zieret mit göttelichen tugenden, und wie dis mit der bescheidenheit sol als gericht und geordenieret werden [how the Holy Spirit decorates the highest faculties with divine virtues and how these should be regulated and ordered by prudence]."[88] In several sermons Tauler expresses similar positions on the role of prudence in ordering both inner and outer works. In sermon Vetter 60h, for example, he asserts that three virtues are absolutely indispensable for spiritual perfection: humility, love, and prudence. He goes so far as to claim that anything without prudence is neither good nor pleasing to God.[89] Just as the disciple explains to the Nameless Wild One that discernment orders one's works and that disorder is evil, Tauler also exhorts his audience that prudence must order and govern virtuous practice.

Tauler takes up the issue of quietism and objections to outer works as well. In sermon Vetter 74 Tauler condemns those who believe that all outer works hinder spiritual perfection and that all inner contemplation advances it. Works of love are not inherently bad and distracting, but are only so if they become an end in themselves. Similarly, some are drawn astray by inner contemplation, because they stick to their devotional images "also der bere an dem honige [like a bear to honey]." Tauler counters that everything must be done in an orderly manner.

> Nu us disen beden werken, usserlich und innerlich, ob sú mit ordenunge gewúrket sint, so wurt geborn daz edel luter gût, die innerlich raste do man mit eime stillen swigende aller bilde und formen kummet in daz götliche vinsternisse, do man rastet und gebruchet mit ime.[90]

> Now from these two works, outer and inner, if they are done in an orderly manner, is born the pure, noble good, the inner peace where one comes through a quiet silence of all images and forms into the divine darkness where one rests and delights with him.

Tauler links this inner silence with *Gelassenheit* and the birth of God in the soul by referring here as well to *Dum medium silencium*, insisting that all works, both inner and outer, should foster this noble silence.[91] Ordered practice entrains a disposition of virtue that, far from obstructing or distracting, furthers the pursuit of *Gelassenheit*.

In another sermon, Tauler uses the image of the Body of the Church to argue that each person is ordained to certain kinds of work, which one should not neglect in favor of contemplation. He accuses his audience of laziness in an amusing metaphor: "Nu wellent ir echt ledig sin. Es kumet sere von tragheit: ieklichs wil ein ouge sin und wellent alle schouwen und nút wúrken [So you want to be truly empty. That mostly comes from laziness: everybody wants to be an eye and to see and not to work]."[92] Against the objection that duties (*amt*) cannot be ordained by God, because God would not impose hindrances to mystical union, Tauler argues that his audience has mistaken the cause of their dissatisfaction. "Was dir disen unfriden machet, das entûnt nút die werk, nein nút, es tût din unordenunge, die du hast in den werken [What is causing you this distress is not the works, no, it is the disorder that you have in the works]."[93] Order, however, is not miraculously obtained but must be developed through practice.[94] Tauler concludes the sermon by asserting that even the discernment of spirits (*underscheit der geiste*) is not a divine gift, but an ability developed through trial. Those who have been tested and tormented by spirits have learned to know which are evil.[95] Spiritual perfection, therefore, can only be attained through orderly works, both inner and outer. Far from hindering *Gelassenheit*, orderly works prepare the soul.

Order Within the Order

A closer look at Tauler's use of *ordenunge* shows that he links orderliness, not only etymologically but also conceptually, to the Dominican order in particular and further to any religious order in general. As I have just established, *ordenunge* in external works is not simply something that results from divinely granted prudence or the achievement of *Gelassenheit*. Orderliness constitutes a set of difficult practices with manifold variations, all of which are meant to foster the internal order that culminates in *Gelassenheit*. The best place to practice order, Tauler assures, is in an order.

> Dis meinent und diseme dienent alle die wisen und alle die werg
> und übungen die wir hant in unserm heilgen ordene, und alle andere
> ordenunge . . . das er in uns hochgezit mache und wir mit ime
> habent ein unbekumberten grunt, der nút inne enhabe denne Got
> luterlichen.[96]

> All the methods and all the works and practices that we have in our
> holy order and in all other orders intend and serve this . . . that He
> make a feast day in us and that we have with him an untroubled
> ground that has nothing in it but God alone.

In consonance with Tauler's injunction not to wait for God to endow one with virtue, this passage concisely presents Tauler's formulation of the usefulness of a Rule. Contrary to Zekorn's dismissive statement that Tauler sees no value in the order's precepts,[97] Tauler states explicitly here that one observes the order to prepare the ground of the soul for the divine feast. *Hochgezit* must not be mistranslated as "wedding," since the term referred to any special liturgical feast. Although the connotation of bridal mysticism remains, the *hochgezit* is first and foremost a period of intensified liturgical activity. Fulfilling the obligations of the order produces an ordered ground, in which God himself can celebrate his own liturgy.

Heinrich Seuse also considers pursuance of the order's statutes as one of the requisite tasks for the quickest path to *Gelassenheit*. In a letter to a spiritual daughter, perhaps also Stagel, Seuse claims that his own personal experience has led him to the conclusion that nothing better serves mystical fulfillment than renouncing all things. However, he qualifies this renunciation by describing what kinds of outer practices it entails.

> Ich han nach miner wise vil gestudieret und vinde nút nehers, denne daz sich ein mensche wislich und ordenlich allen dingen, als verre er mag, entsage . . . und dar zů höret stille swigen und hoch betrahten, wenig wort und vil strenger werk . . . sinen orden strenklich halten.[98]

> I have studied much in my own way and find nothing quicker than that a person renounce all things wisely and in an orderly way, insofar as he is able . . . this includes silence and high contemplation, few words and much hard work . . . strictly observing one's order.

We will see this celebration of strict observance of the order echoed in the sisterbooks. Although Seuse uses vocabulary associated with *Gelassenheit* and mystical un-becoming (that is, *entsagen*/renunciation and the quickest path), he also immediately reminds the reader that this mystical renunciation does not take the form of inactivity or quietism. Seuse encourages not only orderly renunciation but renunciation into an order, framing withdrawal from the world as enclosure in a convent.

The first aspect of regular life that Seuse highlights in this passage is the practice of silence. Spiritual silence served as a metaphor for *Gelassenheit*, but both Seuse and Tauler also hold that external silence produces internal mystical silence and urge their Dominican audience to observe the silence of the order. Both the Constitutions for friars and those for sisters devote an entire chapter to silence. Dominican men and women were obliged to remain silent at all times in the cloister, in the dormitory, in cells, in the refectory, and in oratories. Indeed, even outside of these areas, for the most part they required permission to speak at all.[99]

In accord with the importance of silence to daily life in the order, Seuse devoted an entire chapter of his *Vita* to "the useful virtue, which is called silence."[100] He happily claims that he never broke silence at table except once in thirty years. Tauler also encourages silence, while contextualizing it as an essential practice of the order.

Ich enheischen von úch kein grosse volkomenheit noch heilikeit, denne das ir minne habent zů úwerem heiligen orden, und die minnekliche gesetzde meinent ze haltende als verre als ir múgent, und úwer swigen gerne haltent uf allen den stetten do es gebotten ist, und aller meist ob dem tische und in dem kore.[101]

I expect no greater perfection or holiness from you than that you love your holy order and intend to observe its sweet statutes as far as you can. Gladly observe silence in all the places where it is commanded, particularly at table and in the choir.

Tauler repudiates supererogatory asceticism and encourages only strict observance, in which context silence is to be understood. Nevertheless, *swigen* and *stillekeit* also appear outside the context of the statutes, among lists of ideal virtues in Tauler's sermons. For example, he attributes it to Christ and thereby assimilates silence into the project of *imitatio Christi*.[102] The external practice required by the order thus has both symbolic and pragmatic value. In sum, observing silence outwardly fosters spiritual silence.

As with silence, prayer also must not become an end in itself, but rather serve the end of *Gelassenheit*. Indeed, for Tauler, true prayer may just as easily be experienced in silence as in speech, since he adopts the definition of prayer as ascent of the mind to God.[103] He describes this ascent with a metaphor of incense: burning incense represents outer prayer practices and the smoke is the mind ascending in true prayer, released from the kernel in which it had been trapped. Burning incense serves the sole purpose of releasing smoke, and similarly outer prayer practices serve no other purpose than releasing the mind.

Also ist ussewendig gebet nút me nútze denne also verre als es zů diser edelen andaht den menschen reisset, und dannan uzbrichet der edel rouch; wanne der denne uskummet, so la das gebet des mundes künliche varn.[104]

Thus external prayer is only useful insofar as it draws the person to this noble contemplation, and from thence the noble smoke breaks out; when that comes out, so leave off the prayer of the mouth.

Prayer practices are useful because, but only insofar as, they create the proper disposition for "noble contemplation," the ascent of the mind to God in

Gelassenheit. Tauler therefore discourages the practice of reciting ever greater numbers of prayers, and repudiates the idea that prayers could "buy" spiritual effects. He may have had in mind visionary claims, such as the notion that reciting the psalter or *Pater noster* a certain number of times released an equivalent number of souls from purgatory. However, he also explicitly denigrates the practice of endowing memorial services.[105] The act of mouthing prayers earns nothing from God in a mercantile exchange but rather serves only to promote a contemplative disposition, which of itself constitutes "true" prayer. If one allows external prayer to become an end in itself or even approaches it as the means to any particular end, self-will infects the practice and precludes abandoning one's will to God. For this reason, Tauler authorizes his audience to desist from reciting prayers if and when this practice begins to obstruct the empty *Gelassenheit* that fosters divine intimacy.

Tauler's admonitions concerning external prayer, however, always introduce an important qualification that makes it clear he is referring only to paraliturgical or private contemplative practices that do not form part of the Divine Office according to the Dominican Rite. The person seeking *Gelassenheit* should desist from any prayers or works that interfere with devout contemplation, "usgenomen das gezit alleine die das schuldig sint von ordenunge der heiligen kilchen; ane das so los künlichen varn so was anders dich hindert an dem woren weselichen gebette [except only for the hours which are required by the order of the holy church; except for this, forget about anything else that hinders you in true and essential prayer]."[106] One should only recite supererogatory prayers to the extent that they aid devotion and should stop if they do not. The Office, however, is obligatory, and religious must cultivate true prayer as best they can while performing the prayers prescribed by the Church and their orders.

Tauler reassures his audience in another sermon that the Dominican Rite is already structured with this principle in mind.

> Nu tůnt die pfaffen also in der vasten: so lesen wir so vil der salmen und vil wisen; ze ostern so slahen wir ab und lesen denne ein lange wile dri salmen, ein antiphone und ein collecte. Als hochgezit ist, so slahen wir ab unser frouwen zit und preces. Also, liebes kint, als das hochgezit mag gesin eines innerlichen keres, so slahe das uswendige künlich ab, ob es dich dises hindert.[107]

> Now the priests do this during Lent: we read so and so many of the psalms and many melodies. At Easter, we cut down on these and

then read for a while three psalms, an antiphon, and a collect. During Eastertide we leave out the hours of the Virgin and the preces.
Thus, dear child, so that you may have the Feast of an inward turn,
wisely leave out the outward prayers if they hinder you.

Tauler was not the first to claim significance for the abbreviated Easter liturgy, as we shall see in Chapter 5 regarding the German translation of William Durandus's *Rationale divinorum officiorum*. According to Tauler, the
Dominicans incorporated extra time for contemplation into the cycle of their
Rite by abridging the liturgy for the days when particular devotion is encouraged. For the Dominican women hearing or reading this sermon, reduction
of the Eastertide liturgy is both a real requirement and an allegorical lesson.
Just as the Dominican Rite relaxes liturgical obligations to celebrate the
important feast, so too should all Dominicans relax external prayer practices
to welcome the feast in the ground of the soul. Yet neither in the real Easter
liturgy nor in its allegorized spiritual correlative are the obligations ever fully
dissolved.

Canonical prayer and supererogatory prayer thus possess radically different status within Tauler's model of spiritual practice. One should desist from
"manig salter und vigilien gelesen und manig messe gelesen und gesungen
und manig gros oppher geophert [many psalters and vigils read, many Masses
read and sung, many great sacrifices made]"[108] if such distract from true
contemplation. Liturgical prayer, however, not only remains obligatory
regardless of devotional concentration but, to return to the principle of order,
cannot obstruct *Gelassenheit*. Tauler reprimands those who would claim that
observing the order draws them away from spiritual perfection. "Dunket dich
das dich dise uswendigen werk hinderen, als kor gan und dienstliche werk
der gehorsamkeit: liebes kint, die werk die enhinderent dich nút, sunder dine
unordenunge in den werken die hinderent dich [It seems to you that you are
hindered by outer works, such as going to choir and works of obedient service? Dear child, the works do not hinder you, but rather your disorder in
the works hinders you]."[109] The Office, like all the practices of the order, is
intended to order the spirit and thereby prepare the ground of the soul for
Gelassenheit. If it seems to obstruct this aim, that does not indicate a flaw in
the order but rather a greater disorder within the self.

Seuse similarly confirms that external prayer is worthwhile, but again
only insofar as it promotes a devotional attitude and inspires inner pursuit of

Gelassenheit. In the *Little Book of Eternal Wisdom*, for example, the Servant explicitly asks his divine interlocutor whether external praise is useful.

> Herr, ist daz uzzer lob, daz man mit worten und gesange tût, icht
> vúrderlich? *Entwúrt der Ewigen Wisheit:* Es ist wol vúrderlich, und
> sunderlich, als vil es den inren menschen gereizen mag, der vil dike
> da von gereizet wirt, und sunderlich an anvahenden menschen.[110]

> Lord, is the external praise one renders in words and songs at all
> beneficial? Response of Eternal Wisdom: It is beneficial, especially
> insofar as it can urge on the inner person, which is often urged on
> by it, especially in the case of beginners.

Although a state of continual inner praise represents the spiritual goal, external prayers and songs are not detrimental. Instead such outward practices assist by inspiring the inner person, particularly in the beginning stages of one's spiritual journey. Nevertheless, Eternal Wisdom does not say that external prayer is only useful for beginners, just that it is particularly useful for them. People at all stages of their spiritual progression may be incited to greater fervor by external praise, and there seems to be no point at which it should be abandoned. External prayer practices ought to ground and inspire spiritual fervor throughout one's path.

The Song from the Ground

Among these inspiring prayer practices, the Divine Office holds pride of place. The second letter of Seuse's *Great Book of Letters* addresses the virtues and behavior appropriate to a nun. Seuse opens the letter by praising enclosure and the abandonment of worldly love for love of Christ, but then proceeds to a series of more specific directives. Foreshadowing the visitation letters of Observant reformers, Seuse places devotion to the Office foremost among practices of the order that foster spiritual perfection.[111]

> Min kint, du solt dich flissen gemeiner haltung dines ordens, und
> vor allen dingen solt du dich flissen, daz du zitlich zů kor gangest
> und zúhteklich da standest mit ernst und mit andaht, und nút dicke
> us louffest; du solt dich selben negeln in den stůl, voll us ze stenne,

und sunderlich die messe in der minne, als Cristus voll us stůnt an
dem krútze. Du solt under dannen nit anders tůn, so du nit siech
bist, denne daz ouch der covente tůt an singen und an lesen, daz du
dinú zit denne mit sprechist, daz du dar nach deste lediger siest,
noch kein ander langes gebet tůn, daz dich des singens möhte
ierren.[112]

My child, you should be diligent in common observance of your
order. Above all, you should endeavor to go to choir punctually and
to stand there, well-behaved in seriousness and devotion, and not to
run out all the time. You should nail yourself to your chair and
endure it to the end, particularly the Mass, in contemplation of how
Christ endured the cross to the end. Unless you are ill, you should
do nothing other than what the convent does with regard to
singing or reading. You should say your hours with [the rest of the
convent] and be that much more free afterward. Do not do any
other kind of long prayer that would draw you away from this
singing.

Seuse places the primary emphasis on observance of the order's practices. I
will discuss this at greater length in the following chapter, but for Seuse as
for the sisterbooks this strict observance prominently includes simple attendance at the canonical hours and performance of the order's prescribed
Office. The sisterbooks develop this liturgical potential further, but Seuse also
gestures toward the possibility of imbuing scrupulous practice with spiritual
meaning without deviating from the common directives. The impatience one
feels during long hours should be converted through contemplation into the
patience of the suffering Christ. What I have translated as "free" here is *ledig*,
one of the key terms associated with *Gelassenheit*. Being *lediger* after attending
the Office hours does not mean that one has more free time. It suggests
instead that humble observance of the Office performs the work of asceticism
in emptying the soul of worldly concerns.

Tauler proposes a similar form of contemplative *imitatio Christi* that can
be performed during the Office without distracting from or interrupting it.
In sermon Vetter 47 he urges his audience to keep Christ's suffering before
them in all they do. When they eat, they should imagine that every bite they
take has been pressed into his wounds, and "als unsere swestern ir salmen
singent, so súllent si einen ieklichen salmen legen in sine sunderliche wunden

mit underscheide. Alsus bild in in dich und dich in in [as our sisters sing their psalms, they should lay each of their psalms in a particular one of his wounds with discernment. In this manner, form him in yourself and yourself in him]."[113] This form of contemplation accompanies but does not disrupt one's regular activities, banal as they may be. Imagining the bread and the psalms in one's mouth as soaked in Christ's blood imbues these routine practices with spiritual meaning.

Both friars claim that learning to integrate pursuit of *Gelassenheit* with liturgical practice results in exceptional spiritual performances. An anecdote from Seuse's *Vita* reveals the positive ways in which such experiences could affect participation in worship. Far from interrupting his liturgical duties, the inner experience expresses itself in a way that enhances the devotion of those around him through his mediation. In chapter 9 of the *Vita*, the Servant is asked what he was contemplating while singing the *Sursum corda*, because the grace of his experience was evident in his voice.

> Dú wort giengen im als recht begirlich uss sinem munde, daz dú menschen, dú es hortan, einen sundern andaht dar ab möhtin han genomen. Diser frage entwúrt er mit einem inneklichen súfzen und sprach also: 'wenn ich dú selben lobrichú wort *Sursum corda* sang in der messe, so geschah gemeinlich, daz min herz und sele zerflussen von götlichem jamer und begirde, die min herz uss im selb an der stunde verflögten.[114]

> The words left his mouth so full of longing that those who heard it could have received a special spirit of devotion. He answered the question with a deep sigh and said, 'When I sang those venerable words *sursum corda* at Mass, it usually happened that my heart and my soul dissolved in tearful longing for God, a longing that immediately caused my heart to flee out of itself.

The language of this passage echoes those in which he must place his hand over his chest as his spiritual joy pours through his heart into his body. In the context of the Mass liturgy, the sensation of his heart flying away is given special significance; in the moment that he sings *sursum corda* (lift up your hearts) his heart indeed rises to God. Unlike the angelic Christmas Mass, however, the only physical manifestation of his inner experience is that his voice is so much more beautiful than usual that those listening are called to greater devotion.

This story recalls that of the Engelthal song mistress Hailrat singing a responsory so sweetly that her community falls senseless.[115] The two anecdotes share the premise that the voice of the one presiding over liturgical ritual mediates his or her own spiritual experience to others. However, several divergent characteristics of the two episodes allow me to summarize important differences between Seuse's representations of liturgical devotion and those of the sisterbooks, upon which the following chapter will expand. First, unlike the ecstatic sisters at Hailrat's matins service, neither Seuse nor his congregation exhibit physical symptoms, and the Mass is not disrupted. Seuse prioritizes orderly performance, whereas in the Engelthal sisterbook the very disruption signals the greatness of the experience. This difference, however, produces the second, namely, that Seuse remains exceptional and his experience private, whereas Hailrat's devotion explodes the Office into communal rapture. Both stories feature a liturgical soloist inspiring the other participants, but the difference in degree introduces a wholly new quality to the communal piety in Engelthal. Finally, Hailrat's devotion is to the Office and to the Dominican Office in particular, since the event occurs during the first Advent celebrated according to the order. In contrast, Seuse's devotion is to the canon of the Mass, which is introduced by the *sursum corda*. Both Seuse and the Engelthal sisters represent liturgical practice as foundation and inspiration for extraordinary piety, yet the differences in expression, in degree of communal participation, and in the liturgical texts chosen mark some of the divergences, which I explore further in the next chapter.

In light of the emphasis on the order as a way to access the empty ground of the soul, the phrase which I chose as this chapter's epigraph takes on its full significance. Tauler also praises the effects of liturgical song performed while in a state of *Gelassenheit*. He allows that a sister might excuse herself from the Office if she is unable to control herself and is likely to disrupt the others in their worship. Better yet, Tauler explains, would be if she could receive the spiritual experience while continuing to participate in the communal liturgy.

> Und geviele das eine swester stünde in dem kore und súnge und
> befúnde das das si Got manete sich in ze kerende und si das gûte
> werk des hindert, des inkeres: si solte den sang lossen sinken unde
> volgen Gotte und lossen die anderen gar vaste singen. Mer möchte

sis beide getûn, das uswendig mit dem inwendigen, das were besser.
Der sang us dem grunde der gienge gar hoch.[116]

And if it so happened that a sister stood in the choir and sang and
felt that God moved her to turn inward, and if the good work hindered her in this, the turn inward: she should let the song be and
follow God and let the others continue to sing. It would be better if
she did both, the outer with the inner. The song from the ground
would rise high indeed.

The ground of the soul functions similarly here to the heart in Seuse's writings. For Seuse, the heart represents the juncture of the soul and body which
allows divine experience to spill over into physical gesture. In Tauler, the
ground of the soul is the place where the mystery of God pours itself out into
the human. The highest form of *Gelassenheit*, for Tauler, allows a person to
fulfill the works of the order from out of a pure ground. The ultimate goal
of *Gelassenheit* is to dispose oneself such that all the banal rituals of daily life,
all the duties of degrading service, all the unembellished chants of Humbert's
Office are performed from out of this ground, channeling the divine through
the order.

A century later, both Johannes Tauler and Heinrich Seuse would be read,
propagated, and revered by the men and women of the Dominican Observant movement.[117] This fact should no longer surprise, given their shared
insistence upon adherence to the order. Tauler and Seuse are both able to
redirect spiritual pursuit in the wake of Eckhart away from the suspicions of
quietism or libertinism. They integrate the cultivation of divine union in the
ground with observance of one's duties, that is, the Dominican *forma vitae*
and all that pertains to the life under the order, including the liturgy. This
ordered practice provides a framework that helps the contemplative free the
soul through discernment and renders praise to God, lifting the self from out
of the pure ground back into its own abyss. While the works of these two
friars provide the groundwork for a spirituality rooted in the order and its
Office, the sisterbooks illustrate the blossoming of this liturgical devotion.

CHAPTER 3

Liturgical Devotion and Visionary Order in the Fourteenth-Century Sisterbooks

Da mit wir an ir hailig leben gemanet werdent, da von schribent wir
von etlichen die vor úns warent [We write about those who came
before us, so that we might be admonished by their holy lives].
—Prologue to the Töss Sisterbook

The earliest of the texts now known as "sisterbooks" were compiled in the first half of the fourteenth century in Dominican convents in Southern Germany and Switzerland.[1] They comprise collections of miracles and visions granted to the sisters of a particular convent, as well as accounts of their devotional practices and virtues. The sisterbooks of Unterlinden and Adelhausen were originally written in Latin (although later translated), and the other seven (Weiler, Kirchberg, Gotteszell, Töss, St. Katharinental, Oetenbach, and Engelthal) in German. Some bear the names of authors or first-person editorial comments. The Töss sisterbook, for example, was ascribed to Elsbeth Stagel, Unterlinden to Katharina von Gueberschwihr, Adelhausen to Anna von Munzingen, Engelthal to Christine Ebner, and Kirchberg to a sister Elisabeth.[2] Even when the intervention of a single hand is fairly likely, the authors rely on earlier writings or the stories of older nuns as well as their own experience. These works, however, do not simply record the past, but present it to new readers as exemplary. The sisterbooks held the mirror of the past up to the future; they were a collaborative effort by women to memorialize their forebears and thereby to instruct and edify their future sisters.

When the sisterbooks appeared on the modern scholarly scene in the nineteenth century, their accounts of miraculous experience were read as evidence of feminine hysteria. If one reads the narratives without taking into account literary conventions and their spiritual and liturgical backdrop, the *vitae* do indeed provide rich fodder for arguing that medieval women's spirituality was unlearned, immediate, and bodily, in the sense that the weakness of women's bodies made them susceptible to mystical fantasies.[3] Feminist currents in twentieth-century scholarship made it possible to recognize women writers as literary agents with conscious compositional programs, even if the resulting text is often still evaluated as having more practical than aesthetic merit.[4] Although some scholars have persisted in trying to glean information about the real lives of medieval nuns from the accounts,[5] the sisterbooks are now generally treated as literary creations which draw on the conventions of hagiography to promote their community, celebrate exemplary figures, and reach out to teach the future.[6]

An aura of feminine hysteria, however, continues to haunt the sisterbooks. Even after the "literary turn" in their analysis, arguments persist which oppose the extreme asceticism and bodily affectivity of the female spirituality exemplified in the *vitae* to the rational and heady male theology of, for example, the Dominican philosopher Meister Eckhart. Still, in a recent essay which concerns Eckhart's engagement with female spirituality, Lydia Wegener introduces the sisterbooks as describing "a specific kind of spirituality that is both abhorrent and fascinating at the same time."[7] This devaluation owes some of its staying power to the fact that it coincides with and supports modern versions of the historiographical arc of decline in the fourteenth century and renewal in the fifteenth. The violent asceticism and visionary raptures of these texts are adduced as proof that the Dominicans had fallen from their initial staid and scholarly devotion.

Although there is some historical validity to the narrative of late fourteenth-century decay in the Dominican order, the absorption of the sisterbooks into that narrative is a purely modern invention, as may be deduced from the energetic reception of this literature by Observants. The seven collections that were originally in German were all owned by St. Katherine's in Nürnberg, a model Observant convent. Three of the sisterbooks (Töss, St. Katharinental, and Oetenbach) were copied by the Nürnberg sisters as an omnibus sisterbook collection edited by reformer Johannes Meyer. The exemplar for this manuscript arrived in St. Katherine's after Kunigunde Niklas's death in 1457, along with Meyer's practical treatise, the *Book of*

Duties, which I address in Chapter 6. St. Katherine's also possessed the sister-books of Weiler, Kirchberg, Gotteszell, and Engelthal in unedited versions. Chapter 6 treats the sisterbooks Meyer composed and his promotion of Observant women, but to bring that analysis to its fullest conclusion, I first argue for an understanding of the fourteenth-century sisterbooks that accounts for their inherent appeal to both the reformers and reformed, without assuming that fifteenth-century readers would be wary of the same elements that disturb modern readers.

If we read the sisterbooks in their own right, obedience and regular observance, that is, adherence to Dominican legislation, surface as major themes, representing a continuity with rather than divergence from the advice of such friars as Johannes Tauler and Heinrich Seuse. In the sisterbooks, even the most awful mortifications are presented as part of a divine ordinance that supplements but never supplants their vows to the Dominican order. Far from celebrating extra-ordinary exceptionalism, the narratives in the sister-books continually privilege observance of the Rule and Constitutions, as well as devotion to the Divine Office. With regard to the latter, it has long been recognized that the visionary lives of thirteenth- and fourteenth-century religious women revolved with the cycle of the liturgical calendar. Many of the lives in the sisterbooks, however, also model precisely the kind of intellectual, creative engagement with Latin liturgical texts prescribed by the Constitutions. Far from subverting the Dominican *forma vitae*, the sisterbooks promote and model a life of strict observance and intelligent liturgical piety.

Reading the Sisterbooks with the Observance

Nevertheless, for most of their modern scholarly career, the sisterbooks have been read as a deviation from the norm of male Dominican theology and have been compared to the work of contemporary fourteenth-century friars, such as Heinrich Seuse and Johannes Tauler. In the previous chapter I engaged in such comparison in order to present the sisterbooks in a more positive light and to gesture toward the kind of analysis I perform in this chapter. Recently, however, the fifteenth-century Observant literature has increasingly served as the foil against which the sisterbooks have been read. Werner Williams-Krapp is the most prolific scholar to argue that fourteenth-century spiritual literature was considered dangerous material by the

fifteenth-century reformers. In a series of short essays and articles, he interprets the "explosion" of manuscripts containing German vernacular devotional literature as an effect of the Observant reform.[8] His evidence for this
argument is provided by the provenance of surviving manuscripts, which
show that convent libraries grew rapidly after undergoing Observant reform
and that spiritual works both old and new were transmitted through Observant networks.[9] He further argues that the Observant reform had consciously
and decisively shaped the tenor of fifteenth-century spiritual literature by
censoring the works of the previous century. He suggests that the reformers
considered the exceptional lives of mystical visionaries dangerous, because
they promoted a spirituality independent from ecclesial hierarchies and networks of control, such as confession.[10] The Observants walked a thin line
between reviving devotion and keeping the sisters under their thumb. The
"egocentric radical piety"[11] portrayed in the lives of fourteenth-century
women could be edifying for fifteenth-century readers only if first censored
for extreme or heretical episodes and relativized by prologues and epilogues
warning against spiritual pride and the tricks of the devil.

William-Krapp's thesis has been received in Anglophone scholarship via
the final chapters of Jeffrey Hamburger's *The Visual and the Visionary*, which
are devoted to spiritual literature from St. Katherine's in Nürnberg and
Johannes Meyer's engagement with the genre of the sisterbooks. Paraphrasing
Williams-Krapp, Hamburger writes, "the tension between two different paradigms, the first upholding exceptional individual experience, the second,
championing self-sacrifice and conformity to strict communal standards . . .
represents the difficulty inherent in reconciling two different visions of religious life."[12] Focusing on the treatment of devotional images, Hamburger
argues that Meyer pursued a program of elimination and containment in
editing and excising devotion to works of art and sacred objects out of the
sisterbooks. He focuses on the radically abbreviated Adelhausen text in order
to argue that Meyer brutally excised visionary material from his source texts.[13]

With this understanding of the Observance as a point of departure,
scholars who valorize the bodily and visionary aspects of the sisterbooks as
subversive resistance to male authority have trouble reconciling their own
interpretation of the fourteenth-century *vitae* with Meyer's minimal intervention in the sisterbooks of Töss, St. Katharinental, and Oetenbach. Of these
three, Meyer seems to have altered Töss most, but his interventions are limited to replacing the prologue, adding *vitae* of Elsbeth Stagel and Heinrich

Seuse's mother, and moving the life of Mechthild von Stans to the front.[14] Yet in a recent essay on the illuminations of the sisterbook manuscript produced by the women of St. Katherine's in Nürnberg, Jane Carroll writes that "the contents of *Töß* run counter to some of the primary goals of the reform, such as its emphasis on community, skepticism about female mysticism, and containment of women within the rules of the Order."[15] Meyer, she muses, must have found the celebration of community so important that he overlooked the visions and miracles when deciding to edit and propagate this sisterbook.[16] I concur with Carroll's (and Hamburger's) argument that community is an overriding concern for Meyer and will argue this in Chapter 6. Yet it seems incongruent to me that, if Meyer were passionate enough about restricting visions to censor the Adelhausen sisterbook so cruelly, he should simply reorganize Töss. This interpretive paradigm does not fully account for Meyer's reception of the sisterbooks.

The ways scholars have responded to Williams-Krapp's characterization of Observant reception help to adjust our paradigm by acknowledging women's own engagement in reform and literary reception.[17] Several scholars have been able to demonstrate that Williams-Krapp overstated the interference of male Observant reformers in the fifteenth-century dissemination of fourteenth-century mystical literature. Sabine Jansen notes that, apart from the one collection edited by Meyer, the other four sisterbooks owned by St. Katherine's in Nürnberg were unredacted.[18] Antje Willing observes that the library catalog of St. Katherine's (in which the male superiors had no hand) consistently leaves out texts associated with Meister Eckhart, whose writings are supposed to have been too difficult for women and laypeople to understand. Poor reception of Eckhart does not seem to have been the result of male supervision; the women owned these texts but did not value them enough to make them easy to find in the library.[19] Balázs Nemes illustrates another form of Eckhart reception, describing how a collection from St. Katherine's in Nürnberg "displaces" and "mutilates" an Eckhart sermon by softening the language of indistinct union (as Tauler and Seuse had done) and recontextualizing *Gelassenheit* within "kirchlich sanktionierte Wege der Reinigung [ecclesiastically approved paths to purification]."[20] Anne Winston-Allen characterizes the Observance as a literary florescence for women, in which their active participation in the reform and the increasing use of the vernacular "produced a new form of agency by enabling participation in literate discourse on a larger scale and in wider networks than previously."[21]

The reception and circulation of particular texts and kinds of texts through female Observant networks must be read as reflecting the women's own concerns and preferences at least as much as the guiding hand of the male reformers.

Just as Williams-Krapp has placed too much weight on the interference of male reformers in Observant women's literary interest, Jeffrey Hamburger and, following him, Jane Carroll overstate Johannes Meyer's antagonism toward fourteenth-century female spirituality. Meyer and his Observant Dominican colleagues did indeed discourage radical asceticism and the desire for ecstatic experience and visions, as the letters of Nürnberg prior Eberhard Mardach and others testify.[22] Yet Meyer's supposed redaction of the Adelhausen sisterbook is not one; it is an alphabetical necrology updated to 1482 and supplemented with information, mostly from the sisterbook but from other sources, as well.[23] For example, the fourteenth-century sisterbook can hardly have contained the following entry: "Edelin de Ow, priorissa, do man die beschlötzt vnd die gemein hie anvieng. Anno D. 1465 [Edelin of Au, prioress when enclosure and common property were instituted here in the year 1465]."[24] Given the formal distance between the fourteenth-century sisterbook and Meyer's alphabetical register, one must exercise extreme caution in drawing conclusions about Meyer's attitudes toward the sisterbooks from it.

The Oetenbach sisterbook provides the best case study of Meyer's editorial engagement with women's writing. Here, Meyer supplemented the fourteenth-century collection with a new *vita* he composed from material sent to him by the Oetenbach nuns: the life of Margarethe Stülinger. Her *vita* differs markedly in character and orientation from the earlier lives in that it displays no interest in the asceticism of suffering that permeates the rest.[25] Wolfram Schneider-Lastin, however, notes that large portions of the life of Oetenbach sister Elsbeth von Oye contained within this manuscript correspond to the autograph manuscript of her visions.[26] It is impossible to know whether the lack of interest in asceticism within Stülinger's life belonged to Meyer, to the fifteenth-century Oetenbach sisters who supplied him with information about their sister, or to Margarethe Stülinger herself. It is demonstrable, however, that Meyer did not substantially censor the violence of Elsbeth von Oye's text.

The sisterbooks were inherently of interest to Observant friars and nuns alike; censorship and cautionary prologues were not a necessary condition of their reception. I concur with Sabine Jansen, who suggests that reading the sisterbooks as dangerous and potentially subversive to the goals of the reform ascribes a character to them that they do not in fact possess.[27] In order to understand their appeal to the fifteenth-century Observance, we must take the sisterbooks on their own terms, reading them as literary creations oriented toward the future even as they celebrated the past. Within these works, the past represents a fertile ground in which the future must remain rooted if it is to blossom to its fullest extent. The Observants understood themselves to be this future and the project of the sisterbooks to be the same as their own. Namely, just as the illustrious past grounded a devout future, so too should the Dominican *forma vitae* provide the earth out from which the women's spiritual lives might flower.

Indeed, the narratives in the sisterbooks continually privilege observance of the Rule and Constitutions as well as devotion to the Divine Office, which held the status of legislation. In the previous chapter I showed how the Dominican friars and spiritual advisors Tauler and Seuse reconfigured the concept of the ground of the soul to represent adherence to the order as a component of mystical pursuit and ascetic practice. This chapter builds on the former to follow the spiritual progression from ground to blossom—from strict adherence to the order, through observance of the Dominican Office, to devotional engagement with liturgical text and the attendant visionary experience. This progression should be envisioned not as a journey toward a goal but as the construction of a tower; the earlier stages cannot be left behind. Far from rebelling against the restrictions of the order, the sisterbooks present the Dominican *forma vitae* as the ground from which liturgical piety grows.

As a final preliminary comment, I remind the reader that these stories are exemplary, and their relationship to a real lived past is irrecoverable. The sisterbooks do not represent historical realities but rather historical ideals. I invoke the caveat with which Richard Kieckhefer introduced *Unquiet Souls*, his classic study on fourteenth-century saints' lives.

> It is usually impossible to determine the extent of the sources' historical accuracy, so we must ultimately bracket out the question of historicity and focus on the texts themselves. The central question is not why the saints were as they appear in the sources; they may or may not in fact have been so. The fruitful question is why their biographers represented them as they did—why they recognized certain traits and not others as integral to sanctity.[28]

The sisterbooks are no more a dispassionate record of fourteenth-century religious practice than the saints' lives and canonization proceedings which form the basis of Kieckhefer's study. Moreover, I am less interested in how fourteenth-century nuns actually lived or even what fourteenth-century Dominicans valued than I am in what attracted fifteenth-century Observants to these texts, that is, how the idealized accounts in these fourteenth-century narratives resonated with the goals and ideals of reform a century later. Yet, as Kieckhefer also notes, it would become rhetorically unwieldy to hedge each and every anecdote with "Sister X is said to have done Y." I have chosen to use the present tense to summarize the stories in order to nudge the reader toward understanding them more as literature than as history, but I also simply ask that one bear this caveat in mind.

The Most Pleasing Life of Obedience

The forms of spirituality celebrated in the *vitae* differ in character from convent to convent,[29] but despite these variations, obedience to the order and observance of the Dominican *forma vitae* remain foundational concerns. Gertrud Jaron Lewis calls praise for adherence to the order a "leitmotif" in the sisterbooks, and Leonard Hindsley notes that "each nun was often portrayed as a heroine of observance."[30] Rebecca Garber also remarks upon the variety of spiritual expression in the sisterbooks as a contrast to the consistency in portrayals of office-holders. She ascribes this continuity to Dominican legislation, writing that "due to the (hopefully) assiduous obedience to the Dominican Rule, *Constitutiones, Consuetudo,* and *Admonitiones* within the respective convents, the monastic authority and rank inherent in the roles of the officers remains consistent."[31] Strict observance of the order and its practices represents a point of consistency across the works. Nevertheless, the superiority of life under the order is not always treated as a foregone conclusion, and some *vitae* explicitly acknowledge a sister's doubts over her calling. These narratives illuminate why life within the Dominican order is superior to that of a beguine or anchoress. The advantage lies neither in the safety of strict enclosure nor in the time spent in prayer and contemplation. Instead, the sisterbooks emphasize obedience and submission to a Rule as the foundation of spiritual life.

The life of Oetenbach sister Adelheit von Freiburg makes it clear that the obedience (*gehorsam*) from which spiritual benefit derives is not submission to the will of another individual, nor service to the church, but rather pursuit of the *forma vitae* of the Dominican order. After being orphaned and dispossessed, Adelheit becomes a beguine and serves as sacristan in a parish church before working as a servant at the Adelhausen convent. She is devoted to this work, since she believes the life of active service to be most pleasing to God. One day, however, one of the enclosed Adelhausen sisters informs her that "das gehorsam leben got allerliebest ist [the life of obedience is dearest to God]."[32] Adelheit immediately snatches up a rock and bangs on the door of the convent, demanding entry. Obedience is not an attitude toward others, since Adelheit had long been faithfully serving others before officially joining the order. Rather it represents a formal aspect of regular life, one which is critical for developing spiritual grace. As shall become clear from the examples below, obedience still encompasses a wide range of aspects, from participating in the convent's daily routine, to fulfilling the responsibilities of an office-holder, to observing the Divine Office. All these activities serve the end of overcoming one's own will in order to follow God's.[33]

Adelheit's story is only the most prosaic (and most explicit) of similar stories that confirm the superiority of the order because of its demand for obedience. The most spectacular such tale is found in the St. Katharinental sisterbook. The professed sister Berta von Herten is unsure of her decision to join the order and wonders whether she might not be better suited to life in an anchorage. She knows an anchoress named Gût and admires her secluded life in the forest. In order to reassure her, Christ sends Berta a vision in which the walls of the convent are made of glass. She sits inside with Christ watching a desperate woman (the aforesaid Gût) try to penetrate the invisible barrier, while he explains to her that "das glas, das du sichst, daz zwúschen mir vnd ir ist, das ist der eigen wille, das si nit vnder gehorsami ist. Vnd da von mag si mir niemer als nahe komen als dv, won dv vnder gehorsami bist [the glass that you see between me and her is her willfulness that she is not under obedience. And for that reason she may never come as close to me as you, because you are under obedience]."[34] The affirmation of conventual life over life *in einer klausen*, in an anchorhold, highlights that the aspect of religious life that is most pleasing to God is not enclosure but obedience and submission to a Rule. The walls that should block the sisters from seeing and being seen by the outside world appear transparent, and, countering Berta's thoughts of leaving, the walls function not to keep her in but to keep the willful Gût out. Physical enclosure may help one avoid certain vices or temptations, but true walls are built by the spirit.[35] Only submission to an order helps to rid oneself of the self-will that obstructs intimacy with Christ.

Obedience and strict adherence to the order supersede not only service
and enclosure but also prayerful contemplation. Although the goal of the
sisters' lives is intimacy with God in prayer, these stories suggest that the
Dominican *forma vitae* is the path, and there are no shortcuts. Sisters often
receive greater spiritual rewards for leaving prayer than they if they had
stayed, including visions or messages from Christ. Weiler sister Heiltraut von
Bernhausen is called away from her prayer for duties pertaining to her office
as cellarer.

So sprach sie: "ach herr got, nu wer ich gern bey dir, so muß ich
mich durch gehorsam von dir scheyden." So sie denn hin wider kom
an ir gepet, so enpfant sie alz kreftiges würcken der gnaden und der
großen süßikait dez götlichen einflußes, daz ir ein sicher beizeichen
ward gegeben, daz er ir an der stat gebeytet het, biß daz sie geleistet
het ir gehorsam.³⁶

She spoke: "Ah, Lord God, I would rather be with you, but I must
leave you out of obedience." When she came back to her prayer, she
experienced such a powerful effect of grace and of the great sweet-
ness of divine inspiration that it was a sure sign that he had waited
for her in that place until she had fulfilled her obligation in
obedience.

Leaving contemplation out of obedience certainly delays Heiltraut's experience of grace, since she must return to her contemplation in the choir in
order to receive her spiritual reward. Still, fulfilling her duty does not preclude the experience and it may even intensify it. In a similar story, Oetenbach sister Elsbeth von Oye receives more direct confirmation that obedience
increases grace. She wishes to remain at prayer in the choir rather than going
to the common work hour, but Christ informs her, "ich pin alle zeit mit
dir nachjagende nach deinem heil, und wa ich das allerläutterlichest an dir
außwürcken mag, do ist dir mein minikliche beiwesen allergegenwürtigst [I
am always with you chasing after your salvation, and wherever I may work
most purely in you, there is my loving companionship most present]."³⁷ In
insisting upon her own desire to remain at prayer in the choir, Elsbeth would
paradoxically alienate Christ, who can only work in those who have given up
their own will. In going obediently to the workroom, an apparently less

sacred place, Elsbeth may remain closer to Christ in obedience than by willfully remaining at prayer.

The St. Katharinental sisterbook elevates obedience despite contemplative desires to the status of a major thematic focus. Numerous sisters are praised for leaving communal or private prayer in order to complete some task. Mechthilt von Eschenz is in the choir during Mass when the prioress tells her to go to the kitchen. As she leaves, Adelhait Ludwig sees her shining like crystal. When Adelhait later asks Mechthild what she had been thinking when she was asked to leave the choir, Mechthilt responds, "ich gedächt, das gehorsami besser were denn dehein ding, das ich möcht getůn [I was thinking that obedience was better than anything I could do]."[38] Obedience places Mechthilt into a shining state of grace that she had not been enjoying even in attendance at Mass.

Other St. Katharinental nuns are rewarded with visions that are at least equal to those they would have received if they had remained at prayer. Adelhait die Huterin, who held the office of cellarer, has a vision of the Christ child while praying after none. When the porter calls her away for some task, "do gedächt si: 'Herr, nv wil ich dich lässen in rechter gehorsami', vnd gieng vsser dem kor. Vnd do si in die kuchi kam, do sach si aber das kindli als vor in dem kor [she thought: "Lord, now I want to leave you in right obedience," and left the choir. But when she came into the kitchen, she saw the child again as she had before in the choir]."[39] Obedient fulfillment of her duty does not deprive Mechthild of her visionary experience. Rather, Christ follows her in her tasks, as he had similarly promised to Oetenbach sister Elsbeth von Oye.

The St. Katharinental sisterbook clearly valorizes obedience to duty equally with devout prayer, but even simple adherence to the convent's daily schedule is rewarded. After taking communion, Adelheit von Spiegelberg remains in the choir to pray and has a vision of the Christ child.

Vnd do si in dirr gesicht was, do lut man über tisch. Do gedächt si: "Ach herr, nv wil ich dich lässen dur dich in rechter gehorsami, das du dich niemer von mir gescheidist." Vnd also gieng si nach orden ze tisch. Vnd do sy in das reuenter kam, do kam das kindli vnd lúff ir vnder den mantel.[40]

And while she was in this vision, the bell rang for dinner. She thought: "Ah, Lord, now I want to leave you for your sake in right obedience, so that you will never depart from me." So she went to table according to the order, and when she came into the refectory, the child came and ran under her cloak.

An almost identical story is told of an anonymous sister, but here Christ speaks directly to confirm the message of the vision. "Mit der gehorsami vindest du mich, vnd mit gehorsami verlúrt mich nieman [In obedience you find me, and in obedience will no one lose me]."[41] Strict observance of the order, even of those mandates as simple as going to table at the appropriate time, is valued equally to or even above private devotion and prayer. As Amiri Ayanna notes, "both mundane convent tasks and devotional practice require a subsuming of the body to the spiritual needs of the order."[42] In these stories as well, banal service and everyday life do not obstruct intimacy with God; only stubborn insistence on self-will draws the sisters away from Christ. The duties and responsibilities of convent life provide Dominican women with an opportunity to divest themselves of their own self-interest and practice submitting to God's will by submitting to the order's *forma vitae*.

As Garber and Lewis have shown, the sisterbooks all celebrate observance of the regulated life of the order and obedient fulfillment of responsibilities, creating a strong continuity between texts that otherwise portray fairly different expressions of female spirituality. These virtues represent the *sine qua non* of spiritual life in the sisterbooks, because they allow one to practice self-abnegation and assumption of God's will. Otto Langer suggests that total subjection to obedience could itself become subversive. Total obedience would effect a self-abnegation that brings one into immediate contact with God and thus paradoxically grants one the authority to dispense with obedience to worldly superiors.[43] While it is possible to see this "dialectic of obedience" in a few isolated instances, it does not rise to the level of a broadly present theme. Obedient life in the order appears less as training wheels that should be shed by the experienced than as a foundation in which one must remain grounded. As Leonard Hindsley suggests in prefacing his study of the Engelthal sisterbook with a discussion of the Dominican Constitutions and conventual life, "the ideals of that life expressed in legal documents and in inspiring texts along with the lived regimen of Dominican monastic life foster an environment of intense spirituality and mystical experience."[44] The varied interests of the different sisterbooks represent unique expressions of spirituality that blossomed forth from the same regular ground. Indeed, the life set forth by the Constitutions not only fostered the necessary humility of spirit but moreover provided the form and tenor of the sisters' spiritual practices, even though taken up differently in their different communities. Of all the mandated practices of the order, the Divine Office consistently appears as the most fruitful and, although the beauty and contemplative potential of the liturgy certainly do not detract from it, the spiritual power of the Office also is rooted in its status as a compulsory element of the Dominican *forma vitae*.

Liturgical Order

The Divine Office proves the most important and frequently mentioned practice of the order that the sisters are praised for observing.[45] That liturgical observance is considered part of the order's obligations is clear from its frequent appearance as a specification after general statements of obedience. For just one example, Töss sister Elsbet von Cellinkon "hat och vor andren tugenden zů der gehorsami als grossen andacht und zů allen den stuken des ordens und sunderlich zů den zitten, das sy die in dem kor begieng [above her other virtues, also had great devotion to obedience and to each article of the order and especially to the hours, which she performed in the choir]."[46] The Divine Office appears here as the last in a list that is not additive but rather narrows and specifies its object. Obedience represents the broad commitment to the Dominican *forma vitae*; the articles of the order refer to its legislation, including most importantly the Rule and Constitutions but also the final element; the hours of the Office are compulsory for Dominican women. Elsbeth is particularly devoted to the hours, but her participation is not optional; rather, liturgical observance is one compulsory aspect of regular life, albeit a particularly fruitful one.

In the same sisterbook, the life of Ite von Wezzikon gives further detail concerning the kind of liturgical participation that is expected of Töss sisters. Beyond coming to the choir and singing with the community, observance of the Office entails following the rubrics regarding when to stand and when to bow or incline:

Sie hielt iren orden an allen dingen als volkumenlich als wir ie
dekain schwester sachent tůn; sy was vil die erst in dem kor und
hielt sich da mit grossem fliss an naigen, an ston, und das sy gar
endlich sang alles das sy kund, wie sy doch nit wol sang.[47]

> She observed the order in all things as completely as we have ever
> seen a sister do. She was often the first in the choir and comported
> herself with great diligence in inclining and standing. Finally, she
> sang everything she could, even though she did not sing well.

As in the *vita* of her colleague Elsbet, Ite's life associates zealous attendance
at the hours with strict adherence to the mandates of the order. Here as well,
liturgical observance comprises the most significant of a set of obligations
that Ite observes. Yet this passage further specifies what fulfillment of the
Office under the order requires; it entails not only attending and singing
correctly but also ritual fulfillment of the various movements, whether inclinations, standing, kneeling, procession, or prostration. These ritual performances were prescribed in the Ordinary compiled by Humbert of Romans,
which the Dominicans treated as legislation equal in status to the Constitutions, making performance of liturgical ritual a binding obligation under the
order.[48] The final clause of this passage, that Ite sang everything she could,
also recalls the admonition from a late thirteenth-century set of ordinances
for Dominican women in Teutonia, which enjoins that "quod cantare tenentur, non legant [what they are required to sing, they should not read]."[49]
Despite her lack of innate vocal ability, Ite observes the order and its Ordinary as far as is possible for her. In this context, her bad singing voice
becomes a broader example that is corroborated by the numerous tales of
sisters who come to choir in spite of illness: ineptitude or even debility does
not excuse one from one's duties to the Divine Office.

Other sisterbooks also narrate spiritual rewards received for zealous performance of liturgical ritual. Oetenbach sister Ita von Hutwil experiences
Christ's presence while performing the ritual inclinations. "So si sich im kor
neigte, so was ir, wie si sich auf in leite [When she inclined in choir, she felt
as if she were laying herself on him]."[50] An anonymous sister of Weiler also
sees this practice validated in a vision. While the convent is singing the *Salve
regina* after compline, Mary enters with Christ as a young child.

> Und da man sang dy wort: et Jesum benedictum fructum ventris
> tui, da ging ez für die swester hin und welhe alz tyff neyge, daz eß
> derlangen mocht, dy ving ez zertlichen zu ym mit seinen armen; dy
> aber nicht nach dem orden nyder nygen, so ez der niht erlangen
> mocht, so ging ez für und ließ sie mangeln seins ümvanges.[51]

And as they sang the words: *et Jesum benedictum fructum ventris tui*,
the child walked in front of the sisters and those who inclined deep
enough that he could reach he drew tenderly to him in his arms;
those, however, who did not incline according to the order, so that
he could not reach, he passed by and left them without his embrace.

This vision is embedded within and responds to a specific moment of the
liturgy, since Mary and Christ appear while the convent sings about them.
Yet it explicitly links Christ's pleasure with fulfillment of the rubrics, that is,
the ritual instructions concerning inclinations contained in the Ordinary and
the Constitutions. Visions of Christ as a baby or child are common in convent literature, but here the requirement to incline at specific moments is
creatively linked with the small size of the Christ child. Those who perform
the order's ritual gesture, humbling themselves in obedience, are rewarded
with Christ's embrace, and the disobedient or inobservant are passed over.
    This is also the context in which Erika Lauren Lindgren understands the
amusing story about Engelthal's Alheit von Trochau. Alheit has such devotion to the Office that she sings the verses for both sides of the choir when
they are supposed to alternate. The prioress scolds her, telling her that she is
acting like a goose and to sing only the verses she is supposed to sing. There-
upon Alheit literally begins acting like a goose, flapping her arms, until the
prioress backs down and says she is not a goose.[52] Alheit's *vita* is filled with
other virtues, visions, and miracles, but it is difficult to see where the exemplarity in this particular story lies. Nevertheless, Lindgren is certainly correct
in noting that "Alheit's fault lay not in the singing itself, but rather in not
observing the proper order and requirements of the singing."[53] Again, virtuous conduct during the Office entails more than presence and more than
participatory singing. One must also hold to the rubrics of the order.
    This anecdote about the prioress constraining Alheit to participate in the
liturgy in the prescribed manner conforms to Otto Langer's observation that
the sisterbooks often treat the Divine Office as an end in itself, rather than
only as a means to spiritual experience. He writes that the sisters acknowledge
"das liturgische Gebet als übergeordnete objektive Norm[,] deren Erfüllung
auch subjektiven Glückserfahrungen vorgezogen werden mußte [liturgical
prayer as an overriding objective norm, whose observance must be prioritized
over subjective experiences of joy]."[54] Whether Alheit experienced divine
grace from her singing or simply was enjoying herself, her personal desires
and pleasures must be subordinated to regulated performance according to

the prescriptions of the Ordinary. This status is not unique to the Office but, as I showed above in the discussion of obedience, is shared by all the order's legislation.

As a component of the whole Dominican *forma vitae*, the Divine Office shares not only its priority over private joys and self-will with the order's other practices, but also their spiritual objective. Namely, these practices aid one to overcome self-will in order to come closer to Christ, a project which occasionally requires apparently paradoxical behaviors such as leaving prayer for kitchen duty. In this vein, Peter Ochsenbein remarks that praiseworthy devotion to the Office often seems to have more to do with fulfilling obligation than with fostering contemplation or spiritual grace. He uses the example of Engelthal sister Hedwig von Regensburg, who entered the order late in life and had not learned Latin.

> Die wolt sich dez chors ab tun: si verstund sin niht. Da sprach ein stimme: "Ge hintz chor: du verstest ez hie auzzen als wenig als dinnen." Do gewan sie groz lib zu dem chor, daz sie emsiclich dar gink, wie kranch sie waz.[55]

> She wanted to dispense with the choir: she did not understand it. Then a voice spoke: "Go to the choir: you understand it just as little out here as in there." Then she gained such a great love for the choir that she eagerly went, no matter how sick she was.

Hedwig joins the ranks of sisters who continue attending the Office despite illness, but only after a conversion experience. She initially wishes to avoid choir, not because of sickness or strain, but because she does not understand the Latin and presumably therefore does not get anything out of the experience. The miraculous voice does not change her abilities but it does transform her attitude. As Ochsenbein concludes, Hedwig's story communicates "daß es nicht auf das persönliche Verständnis des Rezitierten ankomme, sondern auf die Erfüllung der aufgetragenen Pflichten [that it is not a matter of understanding what is recited but of fulfilling the assigned duties]."[56] Whether or not one's devotion may be increased by contemplation of liturgical text, attending the hours and performing the liturgy proves valuable in and of itself as an exercise in obedience—one that pays off for Hedwig. One day as the community filed into the choir for compline, "da sahen sie alle daz ir ir hertz schain als die sunne durch ir gewant, reht als sie tut durch daz glaz [all saw that her heart shone like the sun through her robes, just as through glass]."[57] Her devotion to the Office, even without understanding the Latin, places her in a state of spiritual grace. Like the other elements of life under the order, the obedience fostered through the Divine Office ideally leads to greater spiritual perfection and its attendant rewards.

Nevertheless, Hedwig ought to present an exception in at least one sense. Having entered the order older, as "ein vil alte swester," Hedwig either was exempt from learning Latin or was understandably unable to do so. Although liturgical piety in the sisterbooks begins with the steady attendance and precise observance of the rubrics, it should culminate in creative and visionary engagement with Latin liturgical text.

Understanding the Office

Ritual gestures were not the only requirements pertaining to performance of the Office that were laid out in the Dominican women's statutes. As I noted in Chapter 1, the Augustinian Rule, which served as the foundation of Dominican life, lacked specific liturgical regulations. It did, however, enjoin strict observance of whatever liturgy might be prescribed. The Rule also contained a further exhortation, in observance of which Dominican sisters would build further on the foundation of obedient attendance and pursuing the rubrics: that is, meditative concentration on the sung text. The chapter on prayer in the Rule commands, "psalmis et hymnis cum oratis deum, hoc uersetur in corde quod profertur in uoce [when you pray to God in psalms and hymns, consider in your heart what you offer with your voice]."[58] In addition to compulsory participation and strict adherence to the gestures, movements, and prayers laid out in the Dominican Ordinary, the sisters were also obligated to meditate on liturgical text during the performance of the Office.

This mandate of the Rule was supplemented by the chapter on novices in the Constitutions, the wording of which is fairly ambiguous. "Item nouicie et alie sorores que apte sunt in psalmodia et officio diuino studeant diligenter [Item, novices and other sisters who are fit should apply themselves diligently to psalmody and the Divine Office]."[59] I have translated *studeant* here and in Chapter 1 according to its broader meaning, leaving open the possibility that Dominican nuns would simply be expected to put their energy into learning to perform the chants of the Office. The term, however, is the same as that used to describe the efforts of the young friars, that is, *studentes*, in the male

Constitutions. At least some sisters understood their Constitutions to entail some form of liturgically oriented education, since the sisterbooks mention teaching and learning in conjunction with the Office. Engelthal sister Irmgart von Eichstätt, for example, "het die tugent, daz sie gern lert waz zu gotes dinst gehort [possessed the virtue of gladly learning what pertained to the Divine Office]."[60] Her colleague Cristin von Kornburg went zealously to choir and was diligent in everything pertaining to the Office, "mit lernunge und mit swigen und an allen ordenlichen dingen [including learning and with silence and in all things of the order]."[61] Learning formed part of regular devotion to the liturgy, at least in Engelthal.

The life of a sister Elsbetlein from Gotteszell portrays her educational zeal with an unusual amount of detail and depicts studying liturgical text in a scholarly sense, though not with a scholar's goals. Elsbetlein had been especially devoted to learning and reading from the time of her entrance to the convent at a young age. When other children went to play, she continued to study so that she eventually grasped the texts enough to understand whatever was sung or read.[62] As an adult, Elsbetlein is particularly devoted to the feast days throughout the year and prepares for them by reading prayers and psalms. Her contemplative preparation, however, serves a more precise goal than simply awakening a devout attitude, since she also reads the ancillary liturgical material in advance. "Zu den seltern laz sie die aussgesuchten ymnussen, respons, anthifen, der sie sich gefleissen kunde, und die sie aller meiste zu andacht bewegen mochten [With the psalms she read the chosen hymns, responsories, and antiphons to which she could apply herself and which would most greatly move her to devotion]."[63] The hymns, responsories, and antiphons for feast days were different from the usual ferial days and often unique to a single day in the entire liturgical year. Reading and meditating on this special liturgical material in advance allows Elsbetlein to experience the greatest devotion possible on the day itself. Her interest in the feast days led her to study, in the more restricted educational sense, the Office texts so that her devotion would be increased by her comprehension.

Both St. Katharinental sister Anne von Ramschwag and Oetenbach sister Elsbeth von Oye also model interpretive contemplation of liturgical text outside of the hours. After matins on Easter, Anne contemplates an image of the Resurrection while mulling over the words Christ spoke to his disciples, *data est michi omnis potestas in celo et in terra*, a text for the Friday after Easter.[64] Like Elsbetlein, Anne is preparing for liturgical celebration in advance. Elsbet von Oye's contemplations have been temporally decontextualized by the thematic reorganization of her text. It is therefore not possible to determine whether she contemplates a given text before, after, or during the hour in which it would have been sung, but she also explicitly meditates on the meaning of liturgical text, asking Christ for clarification.[65] These sisters exemplify intellectual contemplation of Latin liturgical text in service to pious devotion.

It is difficult to determine the form and degree of Latin fluency common in these convents, but it is worth addressing this question briefly here. A solid understanding of liturgical context and educational expectations must inform interpretation of Latin citations and their significance in the sisterbooks. In some cases, placing the tales in conversation with the expectations of the Dominican Constitutions restores their wondrous effect. In his study of fourteenth-century Dominican women's Latinity, Peter Ochsenbein relies solely on statements made internally to the sisterbooks and arrives at a rather dim view of their literacy. He writes, for example, about Töss laysister Adelheit von Lindau, who is miraculously taught the antiphon *Ave stella matutina* by the Virgin Mary herself, and after her death appears to a choir sister reciting a psalm verse. In surprise, the sister asks if she understands what she is singing, to which Adelheit replies that she does, because she is in a place where she has experienced it.[66] Ochsenbein concludes from the expression of surprise that it must have been unusual for Dominican women to have possessed a great degree of fluency in Latin, since "erst im Himmel versteht sie endlich, was sie ein Leben lang singen und rezitieren mußte [only in heaven does she finally understand what she had to sing and recite her whole life]."[67] Comprehension of Latin in this life must have been unusual if it is perceived as such a miraculous gift in the hereafter. However, attention to the status of the sisters in the story adds a significant qualification: Adelheit von Lindau is a laysister. As such, she would only have been expected to know the *Pater noster*, which laysisters repeated a given number of times in place of the various prayers recited by the choir sisters.[68] Although the choir sister to whom Adelheit appears would be expected to know the psalm verse, a laysister's knowledge and comprehension of it would indeed have been unusual and nonobligatory, and the surprise of the choir sister would be justified. Interpreting the sisterbooks in light of Dominican legislation helps clarify why and when certain uses of Latin liturgical citation are considered miraculous or signs of grace.

Erika Lauren Lindgren presents a more optimistic picture of the sisters' Latinity than Ochsenbein does. She argues that many of the Latin citations in the sisterbooks reveal engagement with nonliturgical Latin texts and prove that Dominican women could and did read Latin prose treatises and devotional literature or the Vulgate Bible. For example, she lists three passages in which sisters mention quotes from Augustine whose source has not been identified in his works. Lindgren argues that, although we cannot determine which of Augustine's texts the sisters had access to, they must have possessed and read some work of his.[69] The passages in the Unterlinden sisterbook give me no reason to doubt Lindgren's conclusion, but the citation in Töss has not been found in Augustine's writings, because it is not from Augustine at all. Instead of an Augustinian treatise, Mechthild von Stans cites a responsory from the third nocturn for the feast of Augustine.[70] Similarly, Lindgren notes that two Weiler sisters cite St. Paul on their deathbeds and concludes that they read the Vulgate Bible.[71] At least one of these passages also is liturgical: Elisabeth von Esslingen refers to the chapter reading for none on the Commemoration of Paul.[72] To be sure, religious women encountered scripture in other contexts, such as table readings and sermons, if not private reading.[73] Yet a far greater variety of Latin sources than merely the psalms were sung in the course of the hours. We must seek Latin citations in the liturgy before drawing conclusions about access to other Latin sources. More importantly, citations of Office texts carry with them intertextual significance derived from their liturgical context.

Liturgical Intertext and Spiritual Meaning

Once we recognize a broader array of these Latin citations as liturgical and place them in their proper context, the ways the texts are deployed within the narratives reveal much more about the extent to which Dominican women understood the language as well as what kind of spiritual meaning these citations bore. On the one hand, passages from the Office either inspire or explain the sisters' visions. On the other, these texts never have only superficial significance, but rather remain embedded in or refer back to the feasts from which they are drawn. The feast or the liturgical season, the literal meaning of the quoted text, and the actions or images presented in the vision all come together in a complex interplay of meanings, which bears on points of theological significance or comments on the spiritual state of a given sister.

It has long been recognized that texts of and about medieval religious women exhibit a predilection for visions of the saints on their own feast days, in particular during the liturgical celebration in their honor.[74] The sisterbooks, too, recount innumerable visions of Christ appearing at Christmas, Mary responding to the *Salve regina*, or the Holy Spirit descending as a dove during the *Veni creator*. Often, however, the saints do not remain a benevolent yet inactive presence but rather respond in some way to the context of the feast or a specific moment in the Office. Weiler prioress Gisela von Grüningen, for example, experiences a vision in which Mary appears during the antiphon *O virgo virginum*, which was sung at Saturday vespers during Advent.[75] When the sisters come to the line *Filiae Jerusalem*, Mary exposes her pregnant belly and addresses the community with the words of the antiphon: "quid me admiramini? Divinum est misterium hoc quod cernitis [why do you marvel at me? The mystery you see is divine]."[76] Mary's appearance indicates more than just the saint's approval of the community's celebration. Gisela brings the context of the liturgical year, that is, Advent, to bear on the antiphon's text and interprets the divine mystery to signify the virgin birth of Christ. The sisterbook does not present the vision as an interpretation of the antiphon or a revelation of its meaning; indeed, none of the meaning-producing elements is given priority. The antiphon text, the liturgical season, and Mary's pregnant body each comment upon and clarify the others in a complex network of referential meanings.

These complex visions inspired by liturgical celebration sometimes include details that only make sense when one both knows and understands the entirety of the text whose incipit is given. For example, during a matins responsory on the second Sunday in Advent (*Ecce dominus protector*),[77] St. Katharinental sister Adelheit Ritter experienced a vision of Christ in suffering with the crown of thorns upon his brow. As she watched, his body was transfigured and the crown transformed into a thing of beauty.[78] It would seem that this vision belongs in the context of Holy Week rather than Advent. Nevertheless, the responsory whose incipit she cites reads in its entirety: "Ecce dominus, protector noster, sanctus Israel, coronam regni habens in capite suo [Behold the Lord, our protector, the holy one of Israel, wearing the crown of the kingdom on his head]." Adelheit's vision is not a passion meditation enjoyed out of context. It is an allegorical commentary that interprets the crown mentioned in the Advent responsory as both the crown of suffering and the crown of glory, illustrating the theological paradox of exalting humiliation which begins with Christ's humble assumption of human form.

This vision surpasses the kind of practical-theological inquiry that Béatrice Acklin Zimmermann imputes to the sisterbooks, in arguing that they deploy figures from their daily routine in order to work through theological issues that have direct impact on their own spiritual lives.[79] The conclusions that Bruce Holsinger and Anna Harrison have drawn concerning the intellectual engagement of the Helfta nuns are more pertinent here. Holsinger argues against a scholarly tendency to see liturgical devotion as an inherently conservative aspect of medieval women's spirituality. On the contrary, the mysticism of the Helfta nuns "transforms the structure, practice, and meaning of Christian liturgy practically beyond recognition."[80] Their liturgical visions surpass mere illustrations of dogmatic content to perform independent and creative theological work. Adelheit's vision of the crowns clearly falls into this category of intellectual curiosity, since it provides a theological gloss of the liturgical text but lacks any of the images from daily convent life or personal relevance that Acklin Zimmermann describes as characteristic. Finally, the account of the vision anticipates that the reader will possess a high degree of both liturgical familiarity and Latin comprehension. The textual crown that inspires the vision is not cited in the narrative. In order for this vision to make sense, the reader must supply the remainder of the liturgical text herself, something the author clearly expected her audience to be able to do.

Engagement with complex theological issues in these liturgical visions does not preclude use of liturgical text to comment on or illustrate points of practical-theological import. Even in the visions which bear directly on the spiritual state of an individual nun, the liturgical context of the Latin citation contributes important additional significance. At a loss for something new or different to pray, Kirchberg sister Mechthild von Waldeck asks that the Lord work his will in her. Pleased with this prayer, Christ responds by offering her a divine kiss and loving intimacy, saying, "tota pulchra es amica mea et macula non est inte [sic]. Du pist gancz schon, mein freunddin, vnd kein mackel ist in dir [You are lovely, my friend, and there is no flaw in you]."[81] The citation from the Song of Songs reinforces the bridal imagery of the vision. Christ's response is inspired, however, by Mechthild's submission to his divine will. The liturgical context of this scriptural passage provides the missing link between Mechthild's humble devotion and Christ's loving answer. This verse from the Song of Songs supplies an antiphon for vespers on the vigil of the Assumption of Mary.[82] Mechthild's surrender to divine will resembles that of Mary, the quintessential handmaiden of the Lord. The scriptural context of the Latin phrase provides the tenor of Christ's response, but the Marian liturgical context is necessary to understand why Mechthild's prayer prompted such grace. Through the double scriptural and liturgical context of the Latin passage, Mechthild simultaneously participates in the tradition of bridal mysticism and is rewarded for her obedience with assimilation to the humble virgin Mary. More than simply asserting her blessedness, the citation draws Mechthild into a complex web of traditions regarding feminine perfection and service.

A similar vision is granted to this same Mechthild on her deathbed. When she was about to die, she heard the angels sweetly singing the word *veni* with Christ chiming in to sing *electa mea* and *intra thalamum sponsi tui*.[83] This vision also thematizes bridal imagery derived from the Song of Songs, but the text itself is the end of the antiphon *Vox de caelis* from the feast of Catherine of Alexandria.[84] The layers of meaning in this passage function similarly to the vision discussed above. Mechthild is represented as a bride of Christ through the scriptural citation and as a quasi-saint, since the words the angels sing over her are the same as those the community sings over St. Catherine. As in the visions that handle theological concerns, these passages also deploy visionary experience, Latin text, and the context of the liturgical feast to produce a complex web of meaning. Yet the visions of this Kirchberg sister further include elements that draw on the citation's place in scripture in addition to the nexus of liturgical contexts.

Mechthild von Waldeck is not the only woman whose deathbed scene deploys liturgical text to comment on the sister's holiness. When an anonymous St. Katharinental sister dies, her sisters carry her into the choir, where a voice speaks from the shrine: *Veni in ortum meum, soror mea sponsa*.[85] As with Mechthild's first vision, this text is both a citation from the Song of Songs and an antiphon for the third nocturn of the Marian feast of the Purification.[86] As Weiler sister Elisabeth von Esslingen is about to die, the sisters watching over her hear her recite the chapter reading for the Commemoration of Paul: "bonum certamen certavi, cursum consumavi, fidem servavi, etc., ich han gestriten ein guten streyt, ich han verendet den lauff, ich han behalden den glauben, mir ist behalden dy ewig kron [I have fought the good fight, I have finished the race, I have upheld the faith, mine is the eternal crown]."[87] Beyond summarizing her own life and accomplishments, Elisabeth equates the form of life of Dominican women with the apostolate by speaking Paul's words as her own. In these accounts as well, the scriptural context of the citation marks the sisters as paragons of either the contemplative life (in the bridal tradition of the Song of Songs) or the active life (in the evangelical tradition of the apostle),[88] while the liturgical context validates celebration of these women as quasi-saints.

One of the more complex visions of this type is recounted in the Gotteszell sisterbook. After her death, a sister Heilwig appeared to Adelheit von Hiltegarthausen dressed in glorious robes.

> Sunderlich hette sie durch den rucken einen strich mit guldein buchstaben, und vorn an dem herczen ein creucz mit guldein puchstaben, und an dem striche durch den rucke da sprachen die guldein buchstaben also: Qui vult venire post me, abneget semetipsum. Da sprachen die buchstaben vorn an dem herczen: Qui mihi ministrat, me sequatur et sub etc. Und da die heilig Adelheit so wunderlich zirde sach an der seligen Heilwigen, da sprach sie: Vil liebe swester meine, mit welcher zirde hastu verdint die edeln schöne, die du durch deinen rücke hast? Da sprach sie: Das han ich von der betrubde, die ich erliden han an alle schulde, als du wol weiste, die dranck so tieffe in gotes herz, das er mirs lonen wil von eben zu eben.[89]

> She especially had a stripe along the back with golden letters and in front over the heart a cross with golden letters. In the stripe on the back the golden letters said thus: *Qui vult venire post me, abneget semetipsum.* The letters in the front on the heart said: *Qui mihi ministrat, me sequatur et sub etc.* When the saintly Adelheit saw such marvelous ornaments on the blessed Heilwig, she spoke: dear sister mine, with what ornament have you earned the noble beauty that you bear on your back? She spoke: I have that for the sorrow, which I suffered without guilt, as you well know. It penetrated so deep into God's heart that He wants to repay me from age to age.

Innocently suffering undeserved sorrow in this life, Heilwig's imitation of Christ has earned her an eternal reward. Yet Adelheit does not enumerate gemstones and ornaments which represent the various misfortunes, illnesses, or insults suffered by Heilwig during her life. Instead, Heilwig is clothed in golden letters which display words Christ spoke to his disciples, marking her as one who follows after Christ.[90] Again, however, the scriptural context of these citations does not exhaust their meaning, since both passages are used in offices for one martyr.[91] Heilwig's suffering may not have earned her a crown, but she does attain a place among the martyrs and the appropriate liturgical commemoration.[92] The Latin citations which appear in Adelheit's vision perform a double function. Their scriptural context comments on the form of Heilwig's service during her life, while their liturgical context reveals the state of her soul and the reward that her discipleship earned her in heaven.

Augustine's Wounded Heart

Far from reveling in uncontrolled ecstasy, the sisterbooks celebrate and encourage dedication to the life of order, from the required ascetic practices such as discipline and fasting to avid devotion to the Divine Office. For the choir sisters, if not for the laysisters, fulfilling their statutes entailed not just regular attendance in the choir but also studious preparation of and intelligent attention to the Latin liturgical text. Although the sisterbooks do display different interests and themes, all include visions and narratives that both demonstrate understanding of the literal meaning of Latin citations and require knowledge of liturgical context in order to grasp the full significance of the texts chosen. German translations of Latin Office passages do not necessarily indicate low levels of Latin fluency, but participate in the creation of surplus meaning. The authors of the sisterbooks must have mastered many of the forms of literacy that various scholars have proposed for medieval nuns, that is, the phonetic literacy needed to decode writing, the musical literacy necessary for singing from a book, and the comprehension literacy of understanding the Latin language.[93]

Although the authors of the sisterbooks may not have attained a level of literacy that permitted independent composition of new texts in Latin, they do model another higher form of liturgical literacy. This ability was similar to the theological literacy of the *Mosaiktraktat*, the mosaic tract, which constituted a new work of theological or devotional literature cobbled together out of sections or even individual sentences of other works.[94] These Dominican women, namely, commanded a broader liturgical fluency that would allow them not only to understand the literal meaning of the liturgical citations but also to identify their place in the Office and to draw their liturgical context into the process of meaning-production. Even if they do not produce new Latin text, they utilize liturgical Latin to produce new senses through its reconfiguration. In addition to presenting avid attendance and language learning as exemplary behaviors, the sisterbooks model an intellectual and devotional engagement with the Office which deploys both liturgical texts and liturgical contexts in the creation of new spiritual meaning. This creative, intellectual engagement was not subversive to the order but rather a zealous expansion upon the mandates of the Constitutions.

The life of Töss sister Mechthild von Stans exemplifies the various characteristics of the sisterbooks that I have discussed in this chapter. Namely, Mechthild obediently observes the order, participates zealously in the hours, and deploys liturgical text in a rich vision that celebrates her own piety and devotion to Dominican life. When he edited his collection of sisterbooks, Johannes Meyer moved the life of Mechthild von Stans from its place toward the end of the Töss sisterbook to the opening position, right after his newly composed life of Elsbeth Stagel. Jane Carroll comments that "this change allowed the St. Katharine's *Töß* to open with a story whose theme of piety rewarded clearly reflected the messages of the fifteenth-century reform of the Order."[95] Certainly, Mechthild's life opens with a veritable résumé of the habits conforming to the order: she obediently performs all tasks assigned to her; she never misses the Office hours unless sick; she eagerly goes to the workroom when it is time, and when the bell rings for refectory or choir she hurries to the appropriate place; she prostrates herself on bare knees; she keeps silence in all the required times and places.[96] Mechthild is represented as a true paragon of observance.

Carroll also draws attention to the historiated initial that opens Mechthild's life in the manuscript produced by the Observant women of St. Katherine's in Nürnberg. In the illumination, Mechthild stands with an angel kneeling before her holding a heart in a cloth. Carroll interprets this image as the common mystical motif of the "exchange of hearts," in which the contemplative asks to relieve Christ's suffering by exchanging his wounded heart with her whole one. She further connects this motif specifically with the Observance through one of its celebrated saints, noting that "in making her petition, Mechthilt took St. Catherine of Siena (1347–1380), the most famous Dominican Tertiary, as her model."[97] This comparison may have been alive for the illuminators and readers of the St. Katherine's manuscript, and the image might bear comparison with the illuminations which decorate the *Vita* of Catherine of Siena in manuscripts from other fifteenth-century Dominican convents.⁹⁸ The Töss sisterbook, however, predates Catherine of Siena, and the vision selected as Mechthild's signature draws on a much older model.

Mechthild von Stans does not request an exchange of hearts, but rather asks for the five stigmata, in order to relieve Christ's pain through her compassion. In an elaborate vision of white-clad souls frolicking in a field, Mechthild is informed that God has decided to grant her request, but only partially. She will not receive all five stigmata, but only the one in the heart. The wound is inflicted upon her immediately, and blood and water begin streaming out of her chest. Dismayed, Mechthild pleads with God that the wound be only internal, so that she will be able to bear this grace privately. The subject of the illumination follows: "Und zehand do sy das begert, do knúwet ain engel vor ir und hat ain himelfarwes werkli in siner hand und lait ir es gar zartlich in die wunden, und recht zehand do was die wund ussnen zemal hail. Aber das scharf ser belaib ir untz an iren tod [As soon as she desired this, an angel knelt before her with a heavenly tool in his hand and he laid it tenderly in the wound. Right away the wound was healed on the outside, but the sharp pain remained until her death]."⁹⁹ The angel in the illumination is not delivering Christ's heart to her but closing up the stigmatic wound to her own heart. The episode asserts Christ's favor for Mechthild while allowing her to demonstrate the virtue of humility, which for the Observance was a crucial element in ascertaining that a sister was divinely rather than demonically inspired.

Up to this point, Mechthild's *vita* follows a fairly standard narrative arc, employing pastoral imagery that Carroll rightly compares with Heinrich Seuse. Following Francis of Assisi, requests for the five stigmata prove quite common a theme in late medieval spiritual literature. In Mechthild's story, however, the aftermath of this grace draws together a truly remarkable network of images, references, and creative liturgical piety. The life does indeed compare Mechthild directly with a saint, although not Catherine of Siena. As Mechthild awakens from her vision of the angelic field, the bell for matins rings, and the pain in her heart becomes so unbearable that she screams, bringing several sisters running. They help her back to her bed where she lies, blessedly lovesick.

Won Christus hat ir hertz enzúndet inbrúnsteklich mit sinem gótlichen hertzen. Das mag man offenlich merken das sy wol mocht

sprechen das, das man von dem hochen lerer Sant Augustinus liset:
Vulneraverat caritas Christi cor meum:
> Die min Christi hat min hertz verwunt,
> und ich wird niemer me gesund
> e ich getrink von dem götlichen runs,
> da die lebenden brunnen fliessent
> und sich alle minende hertzen ergiessent
> die sich im alain gebent:
> den git er hie fröd und dert ewig leben.[100]

For Christ had ardently inflamed her heart with his divine heart.
One can clearly see that well may she say that which is read about
the high teacher Saint Augustine: *Vulneraverat caritas Christi cor
meum*:
> Christ's love has wounded my heart,
> and I will never be well again
> until I drink from the divine brook
> where the living wellsprings flow
> and all loving hearts pour themselves out.
> To those who give themselves to him alone,
> he gives peace here and there eternal life.

Like the living springs and loving hearts of the poem, this passage brims over
with meaning. Mechthild's physical pain is given a spiritual cause, and the
sisters will later call a doctor to confirm that she is merely lovesick and not
suffering from a disease. As with many of the other visions, her condition is
explained or glossed through the citation of liturgical text, although after
rendering the incipit the translation bursts into an independent song. Here,
too, it is possible that the chant inspired the vision or informed Mechthild's
desire. Mechthild prayed for all five stigmata but only received a wound to
the heart, the organ mentioned in the chant. The passage furthermore explicitly contextualizes the liturgical material as pertaining to Augustine. The
Latin phrase *Vulneraverat caritas christi cor meum* is the incipit of a responsory
for third nocturn on the feast of St. Augustine.[101] The liturgical text is drawn
from a passage of the *Confessions* and, as Barbara Newman has observed,
made its way not only into the Office for Augustine but also into Jacobus de
Voragine's *vita* of Augustine in his *Legenda aurea*.[102] Achieving broad reception through these two avenues, the phrase proved a popular inspiration for

iconography of the saint, who is often portrayed with a pierced heart as his identifying attribute.[103] As Mechthild von Waldeck was associated with Catherine of Alexandria by quoting her Office and Elisabeth von Esslingen with Paul, Mechthild von Stans is likened to the great patristic authority, even sharing iconographic representation, as she also appears in the miniature with her wounded heart.

Dominican women, however, experienced Augustine not primarily as a theological authority, but as the founder of their Rule. All official documents referred to them as Augustinian sisters under the care of the Friars Preachers. At least ideally, they frequently read and listened to the Augustinian Rule at collation or chapter and strove to foster the religious disposition it propounded. Associating Mechthild von Stans with Augustine through liturgical citation thus doubly grounds her spirituality in the order, by tying it simultaneously to the Office and to the father of the Rule. Just as the Latin liturgical text grounds and inspires the effusive German poem, the statutes of the order provide the foundation and framework for spiritual experience.[104] The Rule, the order, and the Office are not restrictive bonds to be broken but living wellsprings from which the sisters drink.

Not all the spiritual literature of the fourteenth century found a warm reception in the fifteenth. For example, although Heinrich von Nördlingen recommended Mechthild von Magdeburg's mystical masterpiece, the *Flowing Light of the Godhead*, as spiritual reading for Dominican nuns in the fourteenth century, this work did not enjoy Observant rediscovery as did the sisterbooks.[105] Such differences in reception highlight that the sisterbooks emphasized values and virtues shared by the Observance. In the sermons, treatises, and *vitae* that they composed and propagated, the fifteenth-century reformers urged their Dominican brothers and sisters to revive a spirituality grounded in the practices of the order. This battle was not fought only in didactic literature; the Observants sought to realize their vision by means of legislation, as well.

CHAPTER 4

The Office in Dominican Legislation, 1388–1475

Imprimis divinorum cultui intendentes, volumus et ordinamus,
quod [. . .] divinum officium secundum constituciones et rubricas
precise observetur [First of all, we being zealous for the worship of
divine things, wish and command that (. . .) the Divine Office be
observed according to the Constitutions and the Ordinary].
— Acts of the 1397 General Chapter in Frankfurt

Histories of the Dominican order long presented a grand historical narrative
of a Golden Age at the order's founding in the thirteenth century, decline
in the fourteenth, and vibrant renewal in the fifteenth century. Although
scholarship and poverty are most commonly plotted along this course, liturgical devotion is associated with this historical arc, as well. William Bonniwell,
for example, opened his *History of the Dominican Liturgy* by explicitly linking
liturgical piety to the health of the order. "When the Dominican life was
strong and vigorous, the liturgy held an honored place in Dominican priories;
on the other hand, in those unfortunate periods of decline, which tend to
mar the history of a Religious Order, it is found that the liturgy had fallen
from its proud place."[1] Bonniwell presents the triumph of Humbert's Rite
and the development of the *Salve regina* procession in the thirteenth century
as high points in the order's history, followed by a creeping decay which set
in around 1300. In his account, the mid-fourteenth-century Plague seems to
have hit only the virtuous, giving "lazy and worldly friars" free rein. Master
General Raymond of Capua (1330?–1399), filled with "bitter grief" at the state

of his order, instituted the Observant reform. As a result of his "manful" efforts, "the entire liturgical service of the Order was fulfilled in all its primitive fervor and glory."² The early piety and practice of the Dominicans, destroyed by the trials of the fourteenth century, was restored by the glorious Observants.

Bonniwell does not stand alone in perpetuating this historiographical tradition into the twentieth century.³ Indeed, although the depravity of the fourteenth century has been greatly exaggerated, not least by the Observant reformers themselves,⁴ the decline seems to be less of a fiction than the Golden Age, at least for the Dominican order. Well before 1300, the flexible statutes that propelled the first generation of Dominicans to success had proven filled with loopholes and easily exploited by friars not committed to religious austerity.⁵ Although the Mendicants had never truly fulfilled their ideal of poverty, the fiscal excesses of many convents increasingly inspired outrage from secular clerics, as well as fellow religious.⁶ After 1378, the Papal Schism divided Western Christendom, bifurcating not only the secular ecclesiastical hierarchy but the religious orders, as well.⁷ At the end of the fourteenth century, the Dominicans were only one branch of a Church and Empire suffering widespread organizational disruption that required decades and multiple councils to resolve.⁸

Bonniwell's depiction of fourteenth-century liturgical decline is visible in Dominican records. The General Chapter of Ferrara in 1362 released a lengthy diatribe on the lax pursuance of the Constitutions and the Office.

Cum cunctis pateat evidenter a recta via vivendi quomodolibet declinari [et] dampnabiliter obliquari, certa quoque nos docuerit experiencia fratres nostros a nostris constitucionibus et regula sanctissimis declinasse, mandamus et imponimus districtius, iniungendo prioribus provincialibus universis ac eorum vicariis quibuscumque necnon et singulis presidentibus conventuum singulorum sub pena absolucionis ab officio ac privacionis omnium ordinis graciarum, quatenus ad observancias regulares secundum formam nostrarum constitucionum et regule realiter et de facto reducere satagant. . . . Specialiter autem studeant reducere semetipsos et fratres alios ad sequendum nocte dieque chorum, et ibidem divinum officium celebrandum secundum modum fratribus per reverendum magistrum ordinis in alio capitulo cunctis datum.⁹

Since it is manifest to everybody that the brethren have culpably
turned away from the right manner of living, and reliable experience
has shown that our brothers have strayed from our most holy Constitutions and Rule, we strictly command all provincials, vicars, and
heads of convents, under penalty of removal from office and the loss
of every benefit of the order, that they strive to bring back themselves and their subjects to regular observance according to the form
of our Constitutions and Rule. . . . In particular, they should strive
towards choir attendance both day and night, and to the celebration
of the Divine Office in the manner the Master General laid down
for the friars in another chapter.[10]

Among a host of problems, liturgical observance receives special attention.
Some friars were apparently not observing all hours in the choir, and those
who did come were not singing the Dominican Office. The remonstrations
of the General Chapter do not seem to have had an appreciable effect. Fourteen years later, Master General Elias Raymond of Toulouse (served 1367–
1380) sent an encyclical to the entire order decrying the great laziness that
had befallen the friars, such that those who actually observed ecclesiastical
ceremony were considered "singular."[11] In the same year (1376), the General
Chapter commanded all priors to correct their missals and Constitutions
within a year on pain of being removed from office, an injunction repeated
in 1378.[12] Several feasts had been added to the Dominican calendar over the
course of the previous century, for example, Thomas Aquinas and Corpus
Christi,[13] and the order struggled to enforce global adoption. In the second
half of the fourteenth century, liturgical observance in the Dominican order
was affected both by lax participation and by a failure of uniformity, the
latter problem greatly aggravated by the Schism.

    Although a reform movement had already begun among the Italian Fran-
ciscans in 1368,[14] the Dominicans did not see the beginnings of a similar
reform until twenty years later, when it took root in the province of Teutonia.
During the chapter of faults at the General Chapter of the Roman Obedience
held 1388 in Vienna, Friar Conrad of Prussia stood before the assembled
brethren with a rope around his neck, crying that he was worthy to be hanged
by it for his failure to uphold the Dominican Constitutions.[15] A year later,
in the summer of 1389, Conrad received the commission to create a reformed
cloister at an existing house in Colmar directly from the Master General,
Raymond of Capua, formerly confessor to the reformer and mystic Catherine

of Siena. Raymond forcibly deposed the prior and subprior, and Conrad installed himself in the Colmar house with thirty zealously observant brothers. A female Observant community was founded in an abandoned convent at nearby Schönensteinbach eight years later, in 1397.[16]

In November 1390 Raymond commanded the provinces under his jurisdiction to establish one house each in which friars might pursue strict Observance, a directive confirmed by papal bull in January 1391.[17] Nevertheless, very little progress was made, even in Teutonia, where Conrad of Prussia awakened fervor both for and against the reform. Only the Nürnberg friary was successfully reformed, upon the request of the city council, when in 1396 Raymond of Capua sent Conrad to oversee the process.[18] However, his attempt in 1398 to reform St. Katherine's in Nürnberg was a resounding failure, and Raymond officially capitulated to the recalcitrant Dominican women in December that year.[19] He died a year later, in October 1399, while visiting the Nürnberg friars, and was buried in their church before the altar.

After Raymond's death, the Observant movement in Germany stagnated until 1426, when Bartholomew Texery was elected master general and Nicolaus Notel provincial prior of Teutonia. Shortly thereafter Johannes Nider, who had spent his novitiate under Conrad of Prussia in Colmar, was appointed special vicar over the reformed houses in Teutonia and prior of the friary in Nürnberg.[20] Under the leadership of these three men, the Observant movement started on its path to eventual success. With the direct support of Texery, Nider undertook in 1428 a second, this time successful, reform of St. Katherine's. This convent became possibly the most important center of reform in Teutonia, bringing the Observance to numerous convents through both parties of reforming sisters and dissemination of Observant devotional literature. Texery served as Master General until 1449, nurturing the Observance into a healthy strength that would continue to grow throughout the fifteenth century. Around 1465, Observants started electing their own provincial vicars, and in 1475 the complete province of Teutonia came into Observant hands when the Observant candidate was elected provincial prior.[21]

Recent scholarship has examined the controversial attempts to revive the practice of poverty and the Observant ambivalence toward higher education when it eclipsed the purpose of preaching.[22] The reformers saw themselves surrounded by heinous infractions in these areas, and their goal was self-evidently to lead the order back to observance of its Constitutions. This goal was undergirded by a conviction that regular life was not an end in itself but a path to spiritual growth and increased devotion.[23] The reformers believed that the practices had been instituted in order to foster a spiritual way of life that would allow the Preachers to lead the people by example as well as by words.

Although the revived importance of the Augustinian Rule and the Constitutions in the project of reform has long been recognized, scholars of the Observance have overlooked the role of Humbert's Rite.[24] Yet it was, along with the Constitutions and the Augustinian Rule, one of the three foundational documents laying out the Dominican *forma vitae*, and the Observants held it in equal esteem. Indeed, during the fifteenth century almost every single General Chapter of the Roman Obedience, and after 1417 of the reunited order, began the injunctive portion of the acts (now called *ordinaciones*) with instructions concerning the Divine Office.[25] The contents of these ordinances vary, but all either command the brothers to attend all the canonical hours, enjoin the friars to sing according to Humbert's Office, or both. The 1397 General Chapter in Frankfurt repeated an ordinance from the previous assembly in Venice (not extant), that the Divine Office "secundum constituciones et rubricas precise observetur [be observed precisely according to the Constitutions and rubrics]."[26] The 1401 General Chapter specifies that if twelve or more brothers are present, the entire Office must be sung. If a prior fails to enforce this, he may be removed from his post and, more remarkably, if a brother neglects the Office, he should be punished by having to recite the hours before all his confrères while sitting on the floor.[27] Such injunctions were repeated in the 1405 General Chapter in Nürnberg, with the addition that priors must obtain corrections for their Constitutions, ordinaries, missals, and other books under pain of similar punishment.[28] The 1410 General Chapter in Bologna repeated the injunctions and punishments from the previous chapters and added that no one was to change anything in the Divine Office, since this could only be done by the General Chapter.[29] Late in the century, friars who do not have their own breviary are ordered to obtain one within six months.[30] The General Chapters in 1417, 1426, 1428, 1431, 1434, 1437, 1442, 1450, 1456, 1459, 1465, 1468, 1470, 1474, 1478, 1481, 1484, 1491, 1494, and 1498 all begin their ordinances either with repetitions of the above, sometimes word for word and sometimes explicitly referencing the acts of previous chapters, or with enjoinders that cite the chapter of the Constitutions that handles the Divine Office.[31] Indeed, since the General Chapters only met every two or three years, it would have been more expedient, if less rhetorically striking, for me to list the very few that lack an ordinance concerning the Office. Furthermore, this number would likely be even smaller, since some of the acts are incomplete, and later chapters refer to injunctions concerning the Office made in chapters from which none are extant.[32]

It is difficult to know how to interpret the consistency with which the General Chapters urged observance of the Office according to the *nota ordinis*, the *constituciones*, and/or the *rubricas ordinis*, which last refers to the instructions concerning performance of the rituals which accompany the chants in Humbert's Rite. In addition to the differences between Observant and unreformed convents, the expense of replacing corrupted liturgical books must have played a role, as it had in the thirteenth-century resistance to Humbert's revised liturgy. Several chapters required priors to obtain corrected Office books and friars accurate breviaries. Furthermore, the 1431 General Chapter in London entrusted Johannes Nider and future Master General Guido Flamochetti with a task reminiscent of that delegated to the Four Friars in 1245.

> Committimus magistro Ioanni Nider, priori Basiliensi provincie Theutonie, et magistro Guidoni Flamocheti priori Cambriaci provincie Francie, quod super diversitate rubricarum et constitucionum usque ad sequens capitulum videant, dissonancias concordent, et teneantur presentare diffinitoribus capituli generalis.[33]

> We commit to master Johannes Nider, prior of Basel in the province of Teutonia, and to master Guido Flamochetti, prior of Cambrai in the province of France, that before the next chapter they review the diversity of the rubrics and the constitutions, harmonize the dissonances, and present [their work] to the diffinitors of the General Chapter.

The problem was therefore not simply that most of the friars either did not show up or did what they liked rather than following the Office of the order. Over the centuries, changes had crept into the liturgical books themselves, whether by intention or scribal error. Furthermore, the Roman and Avignonese Obediences had continued to pass legislation and changes independently of each other during the Schism, producing the dissonances that now needed resolving. It was, however, no longer possible to correct the rubrics according to Humbert's exemplar, since several feasts had been added and others elevated in status.[34] Nider and Flamochetti were therefore tasked with unifying the Rite and determining the authoritative updated version of the order's legislation. Unfortunately, although the acts of the 1434 General Chapter in Colmar preserve an injunction that priors bring their books of Constitutions to the next assembly for correction, the revision of the liturgy never seems to have been completed.[35]

The ordinances and visitation letters of Observant reformers carefully attend to liturgical performance. For example, Bartholomew Texery's ordinances for reform of the men's house in Basel in 1429 begin with a series of injunctions concerning the Divine Office that echo the General Chapters with remarkable exactitude. Texery begins by insisting that the night offices be performed with the same diligence, solemnity, and attendance as the daytime services, and quotes the passage from the Constitutions enjoining a pause in the middle of each verse. Texery elaborates on the injunctions of the chapters and revives the thirteenth-century prohibition on singing in multiple voice parts, or indeed "in any way other than what is contained in the notation of the order."[36] For the Master General, as for the General Chapter, reform of the order required diligent and devout communal observance of the Office. Given the changes and feasts introduced over the last two centuries, some of it would no longer be Humbert's, but even the new material was to conform with the intention and spirit of his authoritative Office.

Observance and Liturgy Among Dominican Women

The Observant reformers thus displayed significant interest in reforming the Office in the male branch of the order, where it had been considered an important component of Dominican legislation but of secondary importance to preaching and study. In light of this, it is much to be expected that the Observance would emphasize liturgical reform even more strongly for Dominican women, since the Office was their primary obligation and occupation. Although strict enclosure seems to have eclipsed devotion to the liturgy among the reformers' concerns, they did make the restoration of communal piety in liturgical worship one of their primary goals in reforming women's houses.

In fact, Bartholomew Texery's ordinances from January 1429 for St. Katherine's in Nürnberg anticipate his similar instructions for the reformation of the men's house in Basel. In this earlier letter, too, he begins his injunctions with directives concerning the Divine Office. Where in ordinances for Basel he quotes the Constitutions, Texery introduces the ordinances for St. Katherine's with a citation of the Augustinian Rule:

Des ersten, wann vnszer heiliger vater sant Augustin spricht also in vnszer regel: *ir sölt dem gepet beigesten zu gesaczten zeiten und stunden, und bey nichten singen denn das ir lest daz ze singen sey,* dar umb wil ich, daz die syben zeit alle in dem kor gesungen werden nach ewer statuten lauten.[37]

First, since our holy father Saint Augustine says thus in our Rule: *you should attend to prayer at appointed times and hours and by no means sing anything other than what you read is to be sung.* For this reason, I want the seven [canonical] hours all to be sung in the choir in accordance with your statutes.

Texery emphasizes the importance of liturgical observance by reminding the sisters that it is required in both of the institutional documents by which they are bound, that is, the Augustinian Rule as well as the Dominican Constitutions. He continues with a lengthy series of instructions reminiscent of the fifteenth-century General Chapters, with specific punishments enjoined for certain infractions, while the penalties for others are left up to the prioress.

Other reforming documents for the sisters contain similar instructions regarding the Divine Office and its effective and accurate observance. Johannes Nider's 1436 visitation letter to the convent of Unterlinden devotes the majority of space to detailing errors to be corrected in the rubrics of their choir books. Reform was accomplished by ousting convent leadership and installing nuns transferred from an Observant house who would teach the reformed way of life. Records of reform show that these parties of Observant nuns brought liturgical books with them, either to replace or to correct the liturgy in use in their new home.[38] To Nider's 1437 visitation letter to Schönensteinbach provincial prior Nicolaus Notel added that neither the speaking nor the confessional windows were to be used during Mass or the canonical hours, and furthermore that the cantrices, or choir mistresses, were not to hold other posts simultaneously.[39] The instructions for the women, then, are of the same nature as those for the men: they must attend, pay attention, and obtain corrected books from which to perform.

Even documents from convents that successfully resisted reform reveal the importance of liturgical observance to this enterprise. Evidently fearing such a foreign takeover, the prioress of Oetenbach wrote in 1466 to the provincial prior Peter Wellen. He responded with a letter reassuring the community that they need not fear an externally imposed reform, provided that they

strictly observe the hours, live peacefully with each other, maintain claustration, and enforce honorable behavior among the young.[40] As in the acts of
the General Chapters and the letters of visitation, liturgical observance stands
at the forefront of reforming concerns. Similarly, in 1512 the prioress of Engelthal indignantly denied that her convent required reform, even though they
did not maintain enclosure. Her sisters had intentionally entered a community that was unenclosed, she argued, and besides, they observed the statutes
"mit allem zustandt als Singen und Lesen sambt anderm bey tag und nacht
ufrichttig und volkomenlich, nichts weniger den die, so reformirt und in den
versperten clostern sein [with all that pertains such as singing and reading
and other things, by day and night, earnestly and completely, no less than
those who are reformed and live in enclosed convents]."[41] Whether or not
her male superiors agreed, Engelthal's prioress clearly regarded complete and
attentive performance of the Office to be the most important aspect of Dominican convent life, even superseding enclosure. At the very least, she believed
that it was important enough to the Observant reformers that they might not
press for enclosure, provided the women's current practice did not disrupt or
distract from the liturgy.[42]

The Dominican women did, however, give cause for an additional concern
that was not considered applicable to the friars. In order to celebrate the Office
in accord with the Rule and their own Constitutions, the sisters needed to be
capable of active engagement with the Latin liturgical texts. Since the liturgy
was supposed to be the most important source of devotional and contemplative
text for the women, it was imperative that they understand it. This kind
of worry about female literacy represents a departure from the early statutes.
Thirteenth-century legislators had been more invested in preventing women
from studying theology than in compelling them to learn liturgical Latin, such
that the most positive encouragement is an absence of constraint. In contrast,
fifteenth-century friars were deeply concerned by the idea that the nuns were
merely parroting sounds without comprehending the text of the psalms, and
that the time spent in liturgical worship might be wasted.

This anxiety finds exemplary expression in a sermon delivered by a certain Friar Alanus and copied in 1454 by Katharina Holzschuher in the Dominican convent of St. Katherine's in Nürnberg.[43] Relying heavily and
explicitly on Dialogues 9 and 10 on prayer in the *Conferences* of patristic
author John Cassian, Alanus preached a sermon "zu uerstëeung vnd fleißiger
petung des psalters vnd zü frölicher psalm singung got zü lobe [on comprehension and zealous recitation of the psalter and on joyful psalm singing in

praise of God]." (fol. 1r) Much of the sermon concerns the value of the psalms not just as meditative texts but also as apotropaic mantras protecting against the devil. Alanus opens by asserting, however, that in order to profit from the power of the psalms, one must understand the words. "Darumb ist es nütze vnd heilsam züuerstëen das man alle tag list und pet," he explains "wann die verstantnüße meret die süssen andacht Vnd wenn man verstet daz man singt, so außlaufft nit daz gemüte durch unzimlich züfell [It is useful and salutary to understand what you read and pray every day, since understanding increases the sweet devotion, and when you understand what you sing, you don't lose your concentration to inappropriate thoughts]." (fol. 1r–1v) A wandering mind is almost inevitable when singing what amounts to nonsense syllables.[44] Since the choir nuns spent a hefty portion of the day singing the psalms in the canonical hours, it was critical that this time be well spent in informed and understanding contemplation rather than bored and mechanical rote performance.

Various strategies were employed to redress the problem of poor comprehension, most prominently translation of liturgical and regular texts into German. These translations could be studied privately, but were also read communally. At the close of his ordinances for St. Katherine's, Texery specifies the frequency with which the regular texts should be read at collation.

Aber dar vmb, daz ir nit wider die regel vnd statuten von vnwissende sundend, so will ich, daz euch ewer regel alle wochen einest werd gelesen vnd ewer statuten in czweyen monoten einest vnd disz ordenung, die ausser den vorgenanten statuten vnd auszer der regel genomen sind, all monott einest gelesen werd, vnd die auszlegung der regel einest im jar.[45]

But so that you do not sin against the Rule and Statutes out of ignorance, I want your Rule to be read once a week and your Statutes once every two months and this ordinance, which is taken from the Statutes and the Rule, once every month and the Interpretation of the Rule once a year.

All of these texts were originally in Latin, but Texery had permitted earlier in the ordinance that the table readings be delivered mostly in German.[46] The nuns accordingly possessed translations of the necessary texts. These German-language versions of Texery's ordinances for St. Katherine's are preserved in

manuscripts that also contain German translations of the Augustinian Rule
and the Constitutions for Dominican Sisters. St. Katherine's owned not only
a German translation of Humbert of Romans's Commentary on the Augustinian Rule but also that of Pseudo-Hugh of St. Victor. The library catalogs
of St. Katherine's in Nürnberg and their correspondence with St. Katherine's
convent in St. Gallen show that the nuns also used German translations and
commentaries at collation to expand upon the Latin liturgical texts performed in that day's services.[47]

In addition to the translations and manuscripts intended for table reading, numerous translations were available for private perusal, as well. In her
study of a fifteenth-century psalter translation from the Dominican convent
of Sylo in Sélestat near Strasbourg, Marianne Wallach-Faller, for example,
concludes that the German translation was used to aid the nuns who could
sing the Latin psalter but did not fully understand it.[48] I have elsewhere
argued that hymn translations did not devotionally replace the Latin hymns
of the Office, but instead were used pedagogically for Latin language instruction.[49] Many of the manuscripts containing such translations are laid out to
connect manageable blocks of German text easily back to the Latin original.
Such translations of liturgical texts did not supplant the Latin but supplemented it, making German available for private reading so the Latin would
be more accessible during the communal Office. Through study of the translation either in private or in the refectory, the nuns developed their understanding of the Latin and their ability to engage textually in the liturgy.

Finally, Observant reformers made foundational works of Dominican edification and spirituality available for the reformed sisters. In addition to the
commentaries mentioned above, German translations exist of Dietrich of Apol-
da's *Life of Dominic*, Raymond of Capua's *Life of Catherine of Siena*, and
Humbert of Romans's *On the three vows of religious*. Johannes Meyer, who
provides the subject of my final chapter, undertook to complete the canon by
translating the *Lives of the Brethren* and Humbert of Romans's *Book of Duties*,
among other things. In addition to translations of Latin works, the most vibrant
reception of German Dominican mysticism blossomed in the Observant
houses. These texts also supported the Observant goal of returning to a devotional Golden Age, since certain of the fourteenth-century texts (such as Tauler,
Seuse, and the sisterbooks) shared the concern of the later reformers to ground
Dominican spirituality in the Rule, Constitutions, and liturgy of the order.
The Observant interest in recovering a religious Golden Age reached even
farther back, prompting a vernacular reception of the desert fathers.

CHAPTER 5

Contemplative Visualization Versus Liturgical Piety in Johannes Nider

Laß die gedechtnüße dises verslein stetticklichen in deinem herczen sein in lieb vnd in leyt. Trag es pey dir in allen deinen wercken. In allen diensten vnd auff allem wege singe es in deinem herczen [Let the memory of this verse constantly be in your heart, in joy and in pain. Carry it with you in all your works. In all duties and on every path, sing it in your heart].

—High German Cassian Translation

Johannes Nider (1380?–1438) belonged to the second generation of Dominican Observant reformers and was instrumental in spurring the movement to its first success in his home province of Teutonia. Today Nider is remembered mostly for his service at the Council of Basel, as a delegate to the Hussites, and for his magnum opus, the *Formicarius*, and its influence on later witchcraft literature. He is important to this study, however, as the friar who reformed St. Katherine's in Nürnberg. The Dominican Observance had begun in 1389 with the take-over of the Colmar house by friar Conrad of Prussia. When Nider entered the Dominican order around 1402, he chose Colmar as the place of his novitiate.[1] After studying and serving briefly as magister and lector at the University of Vienna, late in 1427 Nider was appointed vicar of the Observant houses in Teutonia and prior of the friary in Nürnberg.[2] Between his assumption of this post and his appointment as prior of Basel in April 1429, Nider oversaw the reform of St. Katherine's.

Sometime during his tenure in Nürnberg, Nider delivered a sermon cycle, later reworked as a treatise, which took its point of departure from the *Conferences* of the patristic author John Cassian (d. mid-fifth century). The late antique series of dialogues with desert Abbas had long been a foundational text for religious life. The Benedictine Rule named Cassian's *Conferences* as recommended reading for monks, and in his *Book of Offices* Humbert of Romans endorsed the text for the Dominican order, both as devotional reading for novices and as table reading before the assembled friars.[3] In service to a movement that looked back not only to Humbert as the culmination of the order's origins but even further to the first archetypes of regular life, Nider seized upon a text that reflected both ideals.

His treatise, *Die vierundzwanzig goldenen Harfen (The Twenty-Four Golden Harps)*, consists of twenty-four chapters that follow the themes and topics of Cassian's twenty-four dialogues but deviate widely from them in content. Using the *Conferences* as an inspiration, Nider promoted his own vision of a religious life that would culminate in continuous prayer. Religious life, however, did not necessarily entail religious vocation for Nider.[4] Despite, or perhaps because of, his deep commitment to the Observant reform of the Dominican order, Nider exhibited a profound appreciation for the devout laity, who comprised the initial, although not exclusive, audience of the *Harps*. Shortly after composing the *Harps*, Nider also commissioned a direct and remarkably faithful translation of the *Conferences* into German, whose surviving manuscript witnesses suggest a reception limited to Observant mendicant women.

The differences in content and reception history of these two versions of the *Conferences* reveal two kinds of piety, one appropriate outside the order and the other necessary under it. The prayer practice that Nider presents in the *Harps* relies on visionary contemplation, while the translation promotes scriptural prayer within the context of the liturgy. The former was received by a wide audience, composed of the laity as well as religious women. However, the few surviving manuscripts show that, when Observant women shared the *Harps* with another community, they passed on the translation, as well. Observant Dominican women treated the translation and its liturgically oriented devotion as a necessary supplement for the visual piety of the *Harps*.

Absent a comparison of the *Harps* with the translation, it is reasonable to conclude, as many scholars have, that Nider excised mystical passages from Cassian so as not to give Dominican nuns fuel for their mystical fires. Yet for Cassian, spiritual ascent is inextricably bound to liturgical prayer and scriptural reading. When one removes the mysticism, so too the liturgy. While the

Harps provided edifying reading for all, the very broadness of the audience demanded a decontextualization of the contemplative practices so that any and all might find something useful in them. Observant Dominican women, however, additionally needed instruction in reviving not only their personal devotion but also their commitment to the regimen of the order and their engagement in the liturgy. In this context, the Cassian translation appears as one element of a much broader program of liturgical education aimed at a respiritualization of the Office.

Transmission and Reading Publics

Nider's *Harps* and the Cassian translation reveal more when placed in conversation than when considered separately, a procedure justified by their closely linked origins and diverging reception histories. Both works began their transmission histories within the walls of St. Katherine's convent in Nürnberg. From this point of origin both were circulated among reading populations, presumably with less or no facility in Latin, who participated in the reform and spiritual renewal movements of the fifteenth century. Nider's *Harps*, however, was also received by monastic men and the laity, whereas the Cassian translation seems only ever to have circulated in women's Observant mendicant convents. The breadth of the transmission differs dramatically, as well. Nider's treatise survives in entirety in twenty-seven manuscripts and went through seven print editions, whereas the Cassian translation survives completely only in three manuscripts. These transmission histories seem to reflect Nider's intentions for the texts, as well. The treatise was developed from publicly delivered sermons for an audience composed of both religious and lay readers, whereas the Cassian translation was commissioned and sent privately to the sisters of St. Katherine's. These differing communities of reception correspond to the different forms of prayer promoted in the texts. Visual contemplation was accessible and beneficial to all, whereas liturgical prayer was required only of the professed religious.

The *Harps* seems to have been both aimed at a broad audience and divorced from liturgical context from its beginning as a sermon cycle. Most sermons departed from interpretation of pericopes, scriptural readings that corresponded to particular days in the liturgical year. As I noted in Chapter 2, Tauler's sermons follow this common structure, which embeds them within the liturgical calendar and allowed Nürnberg librarian Kunigunde

Niklas to easily create a schedule of readings. The chapters of the *Harps*, however, lack these scriptural citations and hence any connection to the liturgical calendar. Stefan Abel suggests that the original sermons were delivered during Lent, a period of increased devotional activity but few specific feasts. Any such localization of the sermons within the liturgical year must remain speculative, because it is not inherent to the texts. Such thematic (rather than liturgical) sermon cycles were often delivered independent of Mass but coordinated with the schedule of Mass in the parish church, so that the laity might attend both.[5] The *Harps* originated as a series of independent preaching events supplementing the usual worship practices as an extra devotional option. Disconnected from both the liturgical calendar and the liturgical event of the Mass, they would have been more a lecture series than a component of communal worship.

As public events, Nider's initial sermons would have been open to both men and women of various states. This breadth of target audience was maintained for the treatise, although laywomen provided the catalyst for its composition. The prologue states that Nider had written his sermon cycle up as a treatise "durch bete vnd liebe ersammer burgerin [at the request and for love of honorable women]"[6] from the patrician families of Nürnberg. Through this dedicatory note in the prologue, laywomen remained marked as a particular target audience in the transmission. Still, both the topics addressed and certain formulations within the text suggest that Nider intended the treatise to serve a dual audience of both devout laity and professed religious. On the one hand, he refers to craftsmanship and decries dealing with money on Sundays or feast days, concerns relevant to lay merchants and artisans. On the other hand, he also urges religious to direct to God the love they would have had for biological children if they had stayed in the world.[7] Through the wide array of issues and concerns, the *Harps* proved relevant for religious and lay audiences of both genders.

That Nider delivered his sermons prior to the reform of St. Katherine's is evident from the earliest manuscript witness of the treatise. The codex Nürnberg, Stadtbibliothek, Cent. IV, 14, bearing the convent library call number J VIII, first belonged to a woman of the Nürnberg patriciate named Kunigunde Schreiber.[8] The manuscript is one of nineteen that she brought with her when she entered the convent as a widow after the 1428 reform.[9] Nürnberg at the beginning of the fifteenth century had a culture of laywomen interested in strict religious practice and pursuing devotional life and literature even outside the convent walls. Indeed, the convent's reform appears to

have been instigated not from within the order but by Nürnberg's city council, which had successfully imposed the reform of the men's house in 1396.[10]
According to Johannes Meyer's account, Schreiber's husband had recognized
her great piety and agreed to make his fortune over to whichever convent she
wished to enter upon his death. Apparently following in the footsteps of a
number of other devout women of the Nürnberg elite, Kunigunde Schreiber
made arrangements to enter the convent at Schönensteinbach, which had by
then already pursued the Observance for three decades. The city council
balked at seeing wealth drained from the city yet again and wrote to the
Dominican officials requesting a reform of St. Katherine's.[11] The Schreiber
fortune was used to underwrite the cost of the reform, and Kunigunde
entered the newly Observant convent with her collection of religious literature in 1429.[12]

Since Nider delivered the sermons after his arrival in Nürnberg, in the
late fall of 1427, and Kunigunde Schreiber already owned the manuscript
with Nider's *Twenty-Four Golden Harps* before entering the convent in 1429,
the manuscript must have been produced very close to the composition of
the treatise. It is reasonable to imagine Schreiber as one of the *ersame burgerin*
who had requested its transcription.[13] While she was perhaps exceptionally
wealthy, Schreiber was not unique among Nürnberg women with regard to
her devotion or even her manuscript collection. The convent library of St.
Katherine's also benefited enormously from the profession of another Nürnberg widow, Katharina Tucher, who not only brought twenty-four manuscripts with religious and mystical content into the convent but also recorded
her own visions.[14] In his *Formicarius* Nider himself would later represent the
laywomen in and around Nürnberg as extraordinarily pious.[15] Nevertheless,
the forms of piety in which laywomen engaged were qualitatively different
from those required of Observant Dominican nuns.

The contrasting production history of the Cassian translation suggests
that both Nider and the women of St. Katherine's considered it an important
supplement to the *Harps* treatise. While the *Harps* was produced before the
convent's reform and initially targeted a mixed audience of religious and
laypeople, the direct translation of the *Conferences* was completed afterward
and sent to St. Katherine's as a gift. It seems that Nider's sermon cycle and
the *Harps* treatise had awakened enough interest in the source text to justify
providing the sisters with a copy of Cassian's work that they could access
more readily than the Latin original. Nider commissioned a German translation of the *Conferences* upon his arrival in Basel in 1429 or shortly thereafter

and had it sent back to the women of St. Katherine's in Nürnberg.[16] The
library catalog of the convent reveals an interested reception. The convent
owned two copies of the translation under the shelf marks J VI and J VII.

> VI. Item ein puch; das helt in im die XXIIII collacion der heiligen
> altveter, die uns unser erwirdiger vater, maister Johannes Nyder, ließ
> schreiben zu Pasel. VII. Item ein puch; das helt in im die XXIIII
> collacion der heiligen altveter. Das puch hat swester Küngunt
> Niklasin geschriben.[17]

> VI. Item, a book that contains the twenty-four dialogues of the holy
> desert fathers, which our honorable father, Meister Johannes Nider,
> commissioned in Basel. VII. Item, a book that contains the twenty-
> four dialogues of the holy desert fathers. Sister Kunigunde Niklas
> wrote this book.

Kunigunde Niklas not only was the most productive scribe of the years following the convent's reform, but also compiled the catalog herself after being
appointed librarian in 1455. Her work for the convent reveals a focused interest in copying and acquiring devotional tracts and texts appropriate for table
reading.[18] She used an existing manuscript to draw up the cycle of table
readings from Tauler's sermons, but, together with Margreth Scheurer,
Niklas copied the massive three-volume German translation of William Durandus's *Rationale divinorum officiorum,* which provided spiritual interpretations of every element of liturgical ceremony from vestments to chants.[19] It
seems the Cassian translation enjoyed enough continued interest within the
convent and was aligned enough with the goals of the Observance to compel
Kunigunde Niklas to produce a second copy.

Beyond the reception within St. Katherine's, the further transmission of
the Cassian translation also reveals the interest of Observant women.
Although the original manuscript of the Cassian translation out of Basel is
now lost, three complete copies of this translation still survive, including
Kunigunde Niklas's copy.[20] Prague National Museum Cod. XIII C 20
belonged to the Dominican convent Maria Medingen. It was copied in 1476
by Magdalena Toppler, who moved from St. Katherine's in Nürnberg upon
the reform of Maria Medingen in 1472.[21] As the reforming subprioress, Toppler borrowed books from St. Katherine's as well as other convents, copied

them for Maria Medingen's use, and sent them back.[22] Maria Medingen also owned a copy of the *Harps* likewise produced in 1476, although this manuscript is now lost.[23] Magdalena Toppler's targeted acquisition of the Cassian translation for her new home signals that she considered the text an important enough source of devotional inspiration for the Observance to be worth the investment. Moreover, the acquisition of the *Harps* in the same year reveals that the Observant women did not consider the translation to supersede the treatise, but rather treated the texts as complementary.

The third surviving complete copy of the translation, from the Clarissan convent of Söflingen near Ulm, also shortly postdates that convent's reform in 1484. The manuscript (Bayerische Staatsbibliothek, cgm 6940) was copied in 1493 by "Cordula von reischach vnd Cristina keckin von nüremberg."[24] If not through the potential direct connection via Christina Keck, the manuscript may have come to Söflingen through their reform relationship with Pfullingen, which itself had been reformed by the Clarissan house in Nürnberg.[25] Although no copy of the Cassian translation in the Clarissan convents of Nürnberg or Pfullingen is attested, the Dominican and Clarissan convents within Nürnberg did exchange and copy each other's books.[26] Although it jumps to another order, this branch of the transmission also witnesses to the interest of Observant reforming women, who brought increased book production in their wake.

The survival of the Cassian translation in these few manuscripts from Observant female mendicant houses contrasts sharply with the extraordinarily broad reach of Nider's *Harps* treatise. Although the *Harps* was also primarily received by reformed houses, its dissemination reached across various orders in both men's and women's houses, particularly within orders that maintained libraries for *conversi*, the Latin-illiterate brothers who performed manual labor rather than the Divine Office.[27] The treatise found its way, for example, into the Benedictine monastery of Melk and from there into monasteries belonging to Melk's reform movement, such as Tegernsee.[28] In keeping with the original intent of the treatise, though, the *Harps* was also broadly received by devout laity of the urban elite, particularly once print editions went into production.[29] The most curious reception of the *Harps* is the *Buch der göttlichen Liebe* (*Book of Divine Love*) by the Constance patrician Dorothea von Hof, a mosaic treatise which she composed by cobbling together brief excerpts from other religious works. Next to Heinrich Seuse's *Little Book of Eternal Wisdom*, Nider's *Harps* provides the most material for the book.[30] Like the translation, Nider's *Harps* was transmitted through networks of religious reform and renewal. The *Harps*, however, enjoyed reception among the pious laity and male religious; there is no evidence that the Cassian translation was received by these communities.

Nider's doubled engagement with Cassian's *Conferences* in two very different treatments with different reception histories raises certain questions. Namely, what does the Cassian translation do that the *Harps* treatise does not, and vice versa? What makes one text appropriate for a broad audience of both genders and various religious estates and restricts the other to reception among mendicant women? Why send a literal translation of the source text to a community that already owns the updated and expanded adaptation? Even if Nider had commissioned the translation only at the request of the Nürnberg nuns and their new member, Kunigunde Schreiber, without the conviction that it held particular value, the nuns themselves certainly did not treat the translation as superfluous to the *Harps*. Both works were sent to Maria Medingen and copied for their post-reform use. For female religious, the advantage of the translation lies at least partially in the different ways the two texts handle prayer. The *Harps* promotes contemplative visualization of Christ and Mary as the true spiritual path. It lacks any discussion of oral recitation of scripture, the form of liturgical prayer on which Cassian focuses and which was required of religious women.

Previous scholarship on Nider's Cassian reception has treated nuns, *conversi*, and the pious laity together as a uniform target audience defined by their limited degree of Latin literacy. A wide variety of explanations have been presented for Nider's editorial choices in the *Harps*, but most of these come down to misogyny and social control as motivating factors. Nider's programmatic deviations from Cassian's ideal devotion supposedly derive from Nider's concern to provide nuns and devout laity (that is, all Latin-illiterate) with pragmatic directives for their daily lives while still denying them intellectual independence.[31] Ulla Williams points out that both Cassian and Seuse, as mystical teachers, composed their texts to guide the reader to independent contemplation, whereas Nider aims to maintain hierarchical order and withhold hermeneutic self-sufficiency from the Latin-illiterate, including nuns.[32] Karl-Heinz Steinmetz similarly reads Nider's university-oriented version of Conference 14 (discussed in more detail later) as a way of throwing the *simplices* a bone while reserving the pearl of scriptural exegesis for confessors and preachers.[33] Both approaches treat religious women and the pious laity together as a single readership with uniform devotional needs and intellectual handicaps, occupying the same place in the social order of the Church hierarchy.

Although these conclusions are incontestable on the basis of the *Harps* alone, the commissioning and reception history of the Cassian translation fail to corroborate that nuns were not permitted access to Cassian's dangerous original *Conferences*. If Nider had been concerned with preventing the Dominican women of St. Katherine's from interpreting scripture on their own, he failed spectacularly. In Kunigunde Niklas's library catalog, shelf mark A is devoted entirely to German translations of Biblical books, six of which Niklas copied herself.[34] These translated scriptural works were supplemented by shelf marks C and D, which contained German-language psalters and lectionaries, respectively.[35] The sisters not only engaged actively in scriptural reading, but crucially, this reading was in the vernacular. Even without strong fluency in Latin, access to Cassian's *Conferences* and to scripture in the vernacular opened up to the women of St. Katherine's the possibility of scriptural exegesis without the immediate oversight of confessors.[36]

Beyond maintaining clerical control by restricting access to literacy, Stefan Abel further posits a second potential area of concern that particularly affects religious women. He writes that in composing the *Harps* Nider systematically removed mystical material from the *Conferences* as a response to the female ecstatic spirituality and mystical exceptionalism of the fourteenth century. "Mit seinem Verzicht auf solche mystischen Anklänge entsprach Nider den Forderungen der Ordensreform nach einer Eindämmung mystischer Bestrebungen in den Klöstern zugunsten einer wiederzubelebenden *vita communis* [In foregoing such mystical overtones Nider met the demands of the reform for a containment of mystical endeavors in the convents in favor of re-enlivening a *vita communis*]."[37] Nider was clearly uncomfortable with mysticism, as his oft-cited skeptical treatment of Magdalena Beutler of Freiburg in the *Formicarius* makes evident.[38] Nevertheless, I have already shown that such assertions rest on a faulty understanding of the spirituality promoted in the fourteenth-century sisterbooks. As I showed in Chapter 3, these fourteenth-century works represented spiritual experience as rooted in the order's *forma vitae*, in a way fully consonant with the goals of the Observance. In any case, it makes little sense for Nider to have censored Cassian's text so severely out of concern for Dominican women and then to turn around and send them a complete and accurate German translation.[39] Whatever Nider's reasons were for excising so much material from his adaptation of Cassian, it can hardly have been that he did not want nuns to read it.

The discrepancy in the reception of the translation also calls for a recon-
sideration of the oft-repeated truism of Nider scholarship that he was pro-
grammatically engaged in an effort to monasticize the laity.[40] This
monasticization entailed certain ascetic practices that scholars judge to be
normal parts of religious life (thus appropriate for nuns and *conversi*) but
unreasonable to expect of laypeople. For example, Nider encourages the laity
to avoid sensual pleasures of all kinds, including comfortable bedding, soft
clothes, and rich food. Nider also discourages frequent bathing and other
hygienic care pursued out of vanity and not health. Foremost, however, he
advocates for the so-called *Josephsehe*, or chaste marriage, arguing that even
within a sanctioned marital union sexual activity leads one into sin.[41]
Granted, each of these ascetic practices, inspired by the widespread late
medieval admiration of the early desert fathers,[42] indeed represents an originally monastic ideal transported artificially into lay life. However, the most
central element of religious practice is conspicuously absent, that is, the
liturgy.

Religious women and the devout laity cannot be lumped together as a
single community of reception defined by low status in intellectual hierarchies and correspondingly low levels of Latin competency. Putting aside
objections to the blanket assumption about low female literacy, it is evident
from the transmission histories that Observant mendicant women represented a distinct audience and reading community, which joined the laity
and *conversi* in reception of the *Harps* but proved a unique target for the
translation. The devout laity did not need Cassian's discussions of communal
recitation and scriptural prayer, because lay prayer in southern Germany in
the early fifteenth century did not rely heavily on a monastically inspired
cycle of the hours.[43] Observant nuns required the translation as well as the
Harps, because they were obligated by the order to a program of liturgical
prayer similar to the one Cassian's Abbas explain and promote.

Religious Regimen and Spiritual Perfection
in the Cassian Translation

Nider's *Harps* diverges so greatly from its patristic inspiration that it is better
considered an original work than an adaptation.[44] In contrast, the translation
both follows the chapter structure precisely and pursues a word-for-word
rendering as far as comprehensibility and the capacity of the translator

allowed. Somewhat remarkably for medieval translations, which often adapt and update their sources liberally, it offers a fairly accurate rendering of Cassian's text and the form of life he promotes. Importantly for its use as Observant reform propaganda, the *Conferences* advocates cenobitic life as the best path to spiritual fulfillment. In a vision of regular life that is wholly in line with Johannes Tauler and Heinrich Seuse, Cassian's Abbas consistently identify continual prayer as the ultimate purpose of religious life and its rituals as the necessary means to this end. Although the prayers of the desert fathers and thus of Cassian's *Conferences* lack the elaborate specificity of medieval Rites, the Abbas nevertheless place ritualized recitation of scripture at the center of ordered religious life.

The *Conferences* promotes the forms of spirituality urged by the Observance through its focus on ascetic regimen, life in common, and liturgical prayer. The Abbas lay religious life and its practices as the foundation of spiritual perfection from the very beginning. In the first conference, Abba Moyses establishes the kingdom of heaven as the goal toward which monks (*müniche*) strive and purity of heart as the target on which efforts to achieve this aim must be focused. Furthermore, all the practices of religious life serve this end.

> Umb diser lautterkeit vnd reinikeit willen des herczen, sullen wir nu alle ding piten vnd begeren vnd tun vnd lassen—in vasten, in wachen, in die wüst gen, in arbeiten, in übunge des leichnams, in armut, in lesen—also dz wir mit solchen tugenden mugen gewynnen vnd behalten ein vnbetrübtes hercz vor allen schedlichen sachen. (9rb)[45]

> For the sake of this purity and cleanness of heart, we should beg for and desire all things, do and leave off all things. Fasting, vigils, going into the wilderness, work, chastising the body, poverty, reading, all so that through such virtues we may acquire and maintain a heart untroubled by harmful things.

The external practices of religious life are necessary for achieving purity of heart and serve to help direct the mind (here also rendered as *gemüt*) toward God rather than toward worldly things. Rather like Tauler's image of the mind as a keg that can be filled with either God or the world, Abba Moyses likens the mind to a mill that constantly grinds whatever the miller throws on it. The regulations of religious life direct the outward senses so that the mind is given only spiritual grist. Vigils and fasting turn the mind away from earthly pleasures, and contemplating scripture brings holy thoughts. Finally, "darvmb lesent wir die psalm vnd singent wir emsiclichen dz götliche lob, auff das, dz wir da von beweget werden [for this reason we read the psalms and zealously sing divine praise so that we will be moved by it]" (14vb). In order to develop spiritual purity and a habit of devotion, religious persons continually recite the scriptural texts that they want to hold continually in the heart. All the external practices of religious life, from fasting to the liturgy, are designed to purify the mind and focus it on God. The Abba's emphasis on regimen and ritual as the path toward spiritual purity falls wholly in line with Tauler and Seuse, who see the Dominican *forma vitae* as fostering *Gelassenheit*, as well as with the Observant revival and spiritualization of the order's practices.

Abba Moyses does not stand alone; several Abbas repeat the message that spiritual perfection may only be sought within the strictures of religious life. In Conference 14, for example, Abba Nesteros treats the interpretation of scripture but claims that true understanding is only accessible to those who have prepared themselves in ascetic virtue. He begins, however, by explaining that every craft (*kunst*) has its own order and method. The spiritual craft (*geistliche kunst*) has two paths of knowledge.

> Die erst ist ein würckliche weißheyt, durch die die siten des men-
> schen geregiret werdent vnd der mensch von seinen sünden gereyni-
> get wirt. Die ander ist ein smeckliche oder ein weseliche weißheyt,
> die do in der schawunge götlicher ding vnd in der bekantnüße der
> heiligen synnen gelegen ist. (124vb)

> The first is a practical wisdom, through which the habits of a person
> are governed and the person is cleaned of his sins. The other is a
> tasting or an essential wisdom, which lies in the contemplation of
> divine things and the recognition of holy meanings.

The goal of religious life is to achieve this essential knowledge, whose immediacy the translator expresses by rendering Cassian's Greek loan word, *theoretike*, with the metaphor of taste. In employing this metaphor to mark contemplative knowledge as experiential, the translator draws on a tradition of Latin exegesis that reads *sapientia* (wisdom) as etymologically derived from *sapor* (taste).[46] This unmediated tasting wisdom, however, does not arise of itself or through divine grace alone; rather it must be sought by pursuing practical wisdom first, "wann der geist gottes fleühet den gleichsner vnd wirt nicht wonen in dem leib, der den sunden vntertenig ist [for the spirit of God flees the hypocrite and will not live in a body subject to sin]." (125ra) Although Abba Nesteros does explain the fourfold method of scriptural exegesis, he concludes by urging his audience to persist in virtue. The practiced person attains tasting wisdom "nicht allein von ander lewt worten, mer von eygner volkumenheyt [not only through the words of others but rather through one's own perfection]." (127rb) Scriptural understanding must be sought through the practice of virtue, which purifies the heart and prepares it to receive divine knowledge. Abba Nesteros reframes Abba Moyses's teaching but retains the basic structure: regimented ascetic practice is a prerequisite for divine insight.

Where Moyses and Nesteros promote the same general idealization of religious order, Abba Isaac provides the most detailed treatment of prayer and its role in religious life. In Conferences 9 and 10, Abba Isaac identifies continual prayer as the end of the monk, citing Paul's command to pray without ceasing (1 Thes. 5:17). Isaac outlines various forms of prayer, such as supplication and thanksgiving, and provides an allegorical reading of the *Pater noster*. Most importantly, Isaac also argues that perfect prayer can only be attained through virtuous practice. "Als man die gestille des gepetes, von dem wir nu redent, nicht gewynnen mag on die vor gesagten tugentlichen übunge, also mag man auch die tugent on stet gepet nicht gewynnen [Just as one cannot achieve the tranquility of prayer about which we now speak without the afore-mentioned virtuous exercise, neither can one achieve virtue without constant prayer]." (84ra) The perpetual prayer that represents the goal of regular life must be pursued in tandem with physical and mental devotional exercise. Virtuous practice orients the mind away from the world, while prayer imbues outer works with spiritual meaning. Isaac's conferences also accord with the Observant conviction that a religious *forma vitae* fosters spiritual purity and devotion.

Abba Isaac applies Nesteros's argument regarding scriptural understanding to the verse he recommends as universally suitable for prayer, Psalm 69:2 (*Deus in adiutorium meum intende*, "Oh God, come to my assistance"). Isaac explains that "dises verslein ist nicht vmb sust aus aller heiligen geschrifft geczogen, wann es hat in im begriffen alle die begirde, die do in den menschen kumen mag [out of all holy scripture, this verse has not been selected

at random, for it contains all the desires that may enter a person]." (98ra)
Whatever comes to pass, one ought always to request the help of God. Importantly for the Observant reception context, many of the temptations Isaac
mentions represent struggles to observe the rigor of convent life. If one desires
richer food than is allowed, wishes to eat outside the permitted times, falls
asleep during communal worship, or is angered by another brother, one
should call upon the help of God. This continual prayer instills a disposition
of spiritual poverty, explained in terms reminiscent of Eckhart's Sermon 52
as "der do warlichen bekennet, dz er nicht hat vnd nicht vermage [he who
truly recognizes that he has nothing and is capable of nothing]."[47] (99vb)
Drawing on terms from the vocabulary of the fourteenth-century friars
(*bescheidenheit* and the *grunt*), the Cassian translation explains further:

> Wer von disem stat also für sich get vnd zu nymet, der besiczet nicht
> allein den stat der vnschult vnd der einfaltikeyt, mer er ist auch mit
> der tugent der bescheydenheyt gewappnet. . . . So wirt er alle die
> synne der psalm in im selben begreyffen vnd also über gen, das er
> sie mit grüntlicher bewegung wirt aus sprechen, recht als ob sie nicht
> von dem propheten, mer als von im selbs vnd als ob sie sein eygen
> gepet weren. (100rb)

> Whoever proceeds and advances from this state possesses not only
> the state of innocence and simplicity but also is armored with the
> virtue of discernment. . . . Thus will he grasp all the meanings of
> the psalms in himself and will surpass them such that he will recite
> them with a movement of the ground just as if they were not from
> the prophet but rather from himself and as if they were his own
> prayer.

One must subject oneself to the requirements of religious life and humbly
recognize that these mandates can only be fulfilled with God's aid. This
recognition instills a spiritual poverty graced with simplicity and discernment, by which one not only understands the meaning of the psalms, but
also prays them as if they were one's own words, arising, in accordance with
Tauler and Seuse, from one's own ground. This intimate understanding of
the psalms cannot be gained through exegetical casuistry, but only by entrusting oneself wholly to God and preparing the heart through religious practice.

Also in line with Observant interests, Abba Isaac presents scriptural prayer and religious regimen as the twin pillars of spiritual perfection.

Finally, Abba Isaac provides the fullest treatment of ecstatic experience, but grounds it also in the rituals of communal worship. Persistence in ascetically prepared recitation of the psalms renders one worthy of the highest form of ineffable continual prayer. One will achieve an understanding of God so immediate that it surpasses all earthly modes of representation.

> Also mag vnser gemüt zu dem warlichen steten gepet kumen, von dem wir gesprochen hant, vnd in dem also auff klymen, das es nicht allein nicht bekümert wirt mit sichtigen pilden vnd fanthasien, mer auch mit keinem vnterscheyde der stymme oder wort vnd des, dz da mit volpracht wirt. Wann die hiczige meynunge des gemütes sol danne also durch vnaußsprechenliche über trettung des herczen vnd in vnbeweisenlicher frewde des geistes über sich klymen vnd mit vnaußsprechenlichen seüfczen zu dem herren reden, wz es wil. (100vb–100ra)

> And so may our mind attain the true continual prayer of which we have spoken and may rise in it such that it is encumbered neither by visible images and fantasies nor by distinction of the voice or words or of anything accomplished by them. For the fiery thought of the mind should then, from ineffable excess of the heart and in unspeakable joy of spirit, climb above itself and with ineffable sighs speak to the Lord what it will.

At the final stage of spiritual perfection, neither images nor words can contain what is given to the heart to understand. This knowledge overflows the heart and manifests in wordless sighs, by which the mind freed from human discourse sends up unmediated prayer to God. As for Tauler and Seuse, Isaac's ineffable prayer results from inner joy that overflows into uncontrollable outbursts. Unlike the two friars, he makes this form of prayer the pinnacle of spiritual perfection rather than a disruptive beginning. Isaac makes clear, however, that this unmediated prayer is not sustainable in this life but will come and go with the experiences that inspire it. Although the death of a brother or the thoughts of one's own sins can incite such a reaction, these stimuli are above all liturgical, arising "aus einem verslein des psalmes, den wir singent; etwen aus einem andechtigen vnd einem heiligen gesange der prüder in dem götlichen ampte [from a verse of the psalm we are singing, sometimes from a devout and holy song of the brothers in the Divine Office]" (91va). The most intimate knowledge of the ineffable God must be prepared through the orderly ascetic practices of communal religious life (fasting, vigils, etc.) but sought in scriptural prayer and experienced in moments of grace.

The mystical practice described in Cassian's ninth and tenth conferences is as far from promoting ecstatic exceptionalism as it is from condemning ecstatic prayer. Rather, Abba Isaac represents mystical understanding as being deeply embedded in the communal experience of psalmody and liturgical song. Furthermore, the semi-Pelagian passages in the translation are marked in the margins with a red *Caue*, but no such warnings appear in Conferences 9 and 10 on prayer. The marginalia in these conferences tend rather to attract attention to precisely these "suspicious" passages by means of a *nota bene* abbreviation. These mystical teachings are absolutely appropriate for Observant nuns, but they would be irrelevant to laypeople.

The Cassian translation concurs with Tauler, Seuse, and the sisterbooks in presenting religious life under vows as the proper way to achieve spiritual perfection. Divine understanding and perfect prayer are pursued not through scholarly study or quietistic contemplation, but through the practice of virtue within the constraints of regular life. Moreover, the message was not lost on the translator, since the idea that outer practice paves the road to inner enlightenment crowns the translation's prologue.

> Wer aber ir synne warlichen versten will, auch das selbe befinden an im, das sy befunden hant, der sol sich fleissen eines solchen lebens als sie, haben einen sölchen guten willen als sie, vnd besiczen ein solche lauterkeit vnd abgescheydenheit als sie warent. So wirt ym müglichen als in, was im nu peinlichen vnd vnmüglichen bedunckt sein. (3vb–4ra)

> Whoever wishes to truly understand their [the Abbas'] meaning and to experience in himself what they experienced must endeavor to live as they lived, to will as they willed, and to possess such purity and detachment as they had. In this way, that will become possible for him as it was for them, which now seems painful and impossible.

Although it refers not to scripture but to the words of the Abbas, the prologue enjoins the reader to pursue the virtuous life the desert fathers modelled in order to access the inner truth they understood. Standing at the very end of the prologue, this admonition determines interpretation of the entire work. The *Conferences* imparts knowledge not in straight information but through the way of life of the Abbas, a life regulated by moderate ascetic practice and prayer in common, just as that of the Observant Dominicans should be. Despite the constant references to monks and brothers, it is easy to see how the *Conferences* would provide appropriate reading for reformed nuns adapting to new demands on observance, personal devotion, and liturgical piety. Cassian's Abbas both promote and model a purity of heart pursued in orderly communal asceticism and liturgical prayer and rewarded with unmediated experience of the kingdom of heaven here on earth. The consistent emphasis on ascetic regimen, scriptural prayer, and religious community brings the *Conferences* in line with Observant reforming interests. These aspects, however, are precisely what the *Harps* lacks.

Visual Piety in Nider's *Harps*

The broader audience of the *Harps* is reflected in the reorientation and decontextualization of the contemplative practices it promotes. Cassian's dialogues and the translation were directed toward religious communities, and accordingly dealt with aspects central to life in an order, including fasting, vigils, and poverty, in addition to communal prayer. None of these practices, including scriptural prayer, were required of the laity, but some method of developing spiritual focus was still needed. Nider accordingly excised devotional engagement with the Divine Office from his Cassian adaptation in order to make room for his program of visual contemplation in the *Harps*.

Thomas Lentes describes imaginative contemplation as characteristic of Observant piety. In an essay on Johannes Meyer (the subject of Chapter 6), Lentes places Meyer's treatment of visual piety in the context of other Observant German reformers of the Dominican as well as other orders.[48] He identifies a widespread attempt to control religious women's private devotion to statues, icons, paintings, and other art objects. The male reformers often confiscated private devotional images and placed them at the disposal of the entire community.[49] Further, they encouraged religious women to replace devotion to images with pious imagination; Meyer praises a sister Elisabeth Griss for her contemplative practice of imagining that each of her prayers represented a stitch in a garment she was imaginatively sewing for St.

Anthony. Lentes notes that "wesentlich häufiger als Gebete vor Bildern schildert Meyer entsprechend ein Beten in Bildern [much more frequently than prayers before images, Meyer depicts praying in images]."[50] These creative devotional practices were intended to focus the spirit in prayerful contemplation, while preventing the theologically unsophisticated women from treating objects as idols. This practice is not incompatible with liturgical devotion, but neither are the two forms of piety mutually necessary. Nider's *Harps* treatise presents an exemplary instance of this form of imaginative devotion, while excising ordered practice and liturgical prayer.

The relationship of Nider's *Harps* to Cassian's *Conferences* varies from chapter to chapter, sometimes remaining thematically close to Cassian and sometimes greatly digressing.[51] The fourteenth "harp," for example, retains almost nothing from Abba Nesteros's discussion of scriptural exegesis. On the other hand, Stefan Abel singles out Abba Isaac's Conference 10 as an example where Nider holds very closely to Cassian's text, both refraining from adding extraneous material and, in places, translating the Latin almost word for word.[52] Nevertheless, closer comparison of the *Harps* to the translation reveals that, even when Nider did not introduce a significant amount of new material, he excised enough of Cassian's text to create a very different form of devotion, one practiced through contemplative visualization rather than regular life and scriptural prayer. This reorientation of Cassian's spiritual program was appropriate for a broad audience of lay and religious readers but insufficient for Observant Dominican women, who were bound by the order to the daily cycle of liturgical prayer.

Like Cassian's Abba Moyses, Nider expounds purity of heart in the first chapter of the *Harps*, but he reverses the relationship between ascetic practice and spiritual state. Abba Moyses argues that devout practices are not virtues in and of themselves but rather the means to the end of purity of heart. For Nider, however, the value of the works depends not on their usefulness for the development of virtue but on the intentions and inner state of the one who performs them. He claims, "die ding sein an in selber niht tugunt, den als vil sie geen aus eim guten hertzen. Die ding mugen die posen als wol thün als die guten [the things are not virtues in themselves, except insofar as they come from a good heart. Bad people can do these things just as much as good people]."[53] Although both Nider and Cassian place purity of heart at the center of the conference, Cassian regards inner purity as the end of virtuous living, while Nider speaks of purity of heart as a prerequisite for good works.[54] Gone is the idea that religious regimen and ordered practice direct the mind toward God.

Nider also does not necessarily encourage focused contemplation as a daily activity, but merely notes that it is obligatory on Sundays and holidays and while at Mass.[55] Yet even the devotion Nider requires on feast days is different in character from the contemplative recitation of scripture enjoined by Cassian's Abbas. Nider never suggests that participating in liturgical ceremony or ritual prayer helps orient the mind toward God. Instead, he recommends a number of exercises that should put one in the correct frame of mind for private prayer or attendance at Mass. Aside from avoiding temptation and examining one's own conscience, chief among these is imagining Christ bodily before oneself.

> Wenn ein mensch peten wil, so soll er niht als pald anfahen mit dem munde. Er sol sein hertz vor zu got keren vnd sol Cristum Iesum fur die augen der vernuft pilden, als ob er leiplich vor im stund oder als in Maria leiplich trug vnter irem reinen hertzen.[56]

> When a person wishes to pray, he should not start right off with the mouth. He should first turn his heart to God and should imagine Christ Jesus before the eyes of reason, as if He stood bodily before him or as Maria bore Him bodily under her pure heart.

Nider privileges imaginative visualization over both ascetic practice and the prayerful recitation of scripture. In the *Harps* the activities that promote contemplative prayer are purely mental exercises of visual piety, instead of the religious life encouraged by Cassian. Nider even warns his audience that sins often masquerade as virtue, so if one wishes to achieve purity of heart, "so müs er pild haben vor den augen der sel. Das ist daz leben vnd ler Cristi vnd auch der seligen heiligen, die vor dir gelebt haben, vnd auch predig [he must have images before the eyes of the soul. These are the life and teachings of Christ and the blessed saints who lived before you and also sermons]."[57] The ascetic practices and communal prayer of religious life are wholly replaced by visual meditations and rumination on sermons.

This displacement of regular life continues in Conference 14, which has received the most scholarly attention, because it deviates so dramatically from Cassian's text and bears the most obvious influence of Nider's university training.[58] Even in replacing scriptural interpretation with a description of university disciplines, however, Nider does not update intellectual methods, but rather provides devotional scaffolding of the same visual character. In Conference 14, Nider excises the entire discussion concerning fourfold scriptural exegesis in favor of a practical-devotional reading of a dream vision from Heinrich Seuse's *Horologium sapientiae*.[59] In the vision Seuse progresses through a series of schools or classrooms which represent each of the disciplines, from the liberal arts all the way through medicine, law, and theology. For Seuse, the final and highest of these is the School of Eternal Wisdom, in which the eyes of the students are finally unbound and their thirst for knowledge is quenched.[60] Having briefly recounted Seuse's vision, Nider repeats the hierarchical journey, this time through the disciplines derived from Heinrich von Langenstein's vision for the faculties at the University of Vienna, where Nider had been trained.[61] In this lengthy disquisition, Nider both explains the areas covered by each discipline in fact and proposes spiritual interpretations of their content which provide devotional material for the uneducated.

For example, Nider explains that Grammatica teaches the alphabet, the grammatical tables, and the rules of syntax. The alphabet represents "den rehten glauben [the true faith]" without which no one may learn anything good. The tables represent the ten commandments and syntax proper and modest speech.[62] Surgery (*die wunden artzneyen*) similarly involves knowing anatomy, identifying the wound type, and making appropriate bandages.[63] Nider informs his reader that one must know the soul's anatomy in order to understand one's faults and that good works are the bandages that heal the wounds of sin. Furthermore, Christ is the ultimate surgeon, who healed the wounds of our souls with the wounds of his body. "Dar vmb sih den verwunten Cristum am kreutz an, so werden alle deyn wunt der sel geheilt [Therefore contemplate the wounded Christ on the cross. This will heal all the wounds of your soul]."[64] Nider does summarize more or less accurately the area of knowledge covered by each discipline at the university. The lessons he imparts to his audience, however, exclusively convey practical devotional advice for the Latin-illiterate. Cassian's primary concern in the fourteenth conference, interpretation of scripture, has no place in Nider's lay university.[65] Instead, Nider offers up visual imagination of Christ as a spiritual panacea.

This emphasis on the imagination and the contemplation of images runs directly counter to Cassian's recommendations, as becomes abundantly clear in the treatment of Abba Isaac's Conferences 9 and 10. Not only does Nider remove the discussions of liturgical prayer which are so central to Cassian's vision of spiritual life, he replaces them with visual piety, which Cassian explicitly rejects. Although Nider superficially preserves some of the content of the ninth conference, Abba Isaac's interpretation of the *Pater noster* as a claim to a filial relationship with God is removed, as is most of the discussion of fiery prayer, mentioned only briefly as a tearful longing for God. As had Tauler, Nider identifies the highest prayer as the ascent of the mind to God (*aufgank des gemütz zu got*), but strips this of mystical meaning, saying, "wenn du fleiß hast, gute pild vnd, was du predigen horst, das du das in dein dehtnüß heltest, so get dz gemüt auf zw got [when you endeavor to hold good images and what you have heard preached in your memory, then the mind ascends to God]."[66] Such a practice has no place in Cassian, whose devotions are focused on meditative oral prayer and physical asceticism. Indeed, Nider's repeated admonitions to pay close attention to sermons seem to contradict Abba Nesteros's warning that one cannot only learn "von ander lewt worten [from the words of others]." In directing his treatise toward a broader lay audience, Nider completely reverses the spiritual priorities of Cassian's work.

More strangely, Nider preserves the troubling story of Serapion at the beginning of Conference 10, but leaves out the conclusion of the story that makes it relevant to prayer. According to Cassian, Serapion was a very old monk and a model of virtuous living but nevertheless fell victim to the anthropomorphite heresy, that is, he understood God to have possessed human form before the Incarnation. A younger, but learned, deacon managed to convince Serapion of his error through theological arguments, with evidence drawn from scripture. Nider's version of the story ends with this success and the simple query why God had let the virtuous old man be led into error for so long and whether the devil was responsible. Cassian and his German translator continue with the disturbing account that upon attempting to praise God for his correction, Serapion discovered that he was no longer able to pray.

> Vnd wann aber diser alt man vor mals got in seinem gepet in
> menschlichem pilde vnd form für sich seczte, vnd also sich dar ynne
> übte, vnd nu gewar wart, dz das selb gewönliche pild gancz aus
> seinem herczen gestossen was, da wart er in im selbs also geschendet,
> dz er nider auff die erden viel vnd schrey peinlichen mit grossem

seüffczen: We mir vnseligem manne. Sie haben mir meinen got ge-
numen. Nu han ich nyemant, an den ich mich halten mag. Nu han
ich nyemant an zu peten. Wen ich fürpas an rüffen sol, das weis ich
nicht. (95va)

Yet since this old man had previously in his prayers set God before
himself in human image and form and had exercised himself in this,
when he realized that that same familiar image had been completely
banished from his heart, he was so disgraced within himself that he
fell down to the earth and cried pitiably with great sighs: Woe is me,
unfortunate man. They have taken my God from me. Now I have
no one to hold myself to. Now I have no one to pray to. Whom I
should now call upon, I do not know.

For Cassian and his translator, the story conveys a frightening lesson about
the dangers of relying on visual imagination for prayer. Such mental images
are idols and drive the contemplative away from the intimate relationship
established through religious ritual and virtuous recitation of the *Pater noster*
and the psalms. Nider, on the other hand, cannot include the conclusion of
this story in the *Harps*, because he is attempting to promote precisely this
practice, that is, praying not with words but with imaginations of Christ or
Mary as bodily present. Nider's treatment of Serapion in Conference 10 is
only the most egregious example of a consistent program of replacing ascetic
practice and liturgical prayer with imaginative visual contemplation.

Even in the conferences to which Nider adds little, his deletions are
severe enough to alter the encouraged form of prayer radically. For Cassian,
wordless and imageless prayer is the pinnacle of the religious form of life, the
reward given to a person who has prepared herself through the pursuit of
virtue and regular practice, including prominently the liturgical recitation of
scripture. The purpose of Nider's image-dependent devotional practice is
presumably to include the laity, that is, those with no access to the Latin text
of scripture and no vow to observe religious practice. This qualification
applies to those living in the world, as well as the *conversi*, who were associated with religious houses but did not participate in the Latin-language Office
and were often excused from the rigors of an order's diet and daily regimen.
Nider has almost nothing to say about religious ritual, and his preferred
form of prayer is visual imagination—a practice Cassian decries not merely
as undesirable, but as heresy.

The extreme privilege of visualization over scriptural prayer has a particularly ironic effect in Conference 10, which Cassian concludes by noting that the flexibility of the single psalm verse "*Deus in adiutorium meum*" (Oh God, come to my assistance) makes the practice he promotes accessible even to the illiterate.[67] Whereas Cassian promotes regular life as the path to scriptural understanding and inner spiritual perfection, Nider both universalizes devotional practice by transferring contemplative focus to images and controls it by urging attention to sermons. Anxiety about the mystical content may indeed have motivated Nider's choice to abbreviate Conference 10 so radically in the *Harps*, but the transmission of the translation reveals that this anxiety cannot have been inspired by the poor education of the nuns or the excesses of their private devotion. Despite the fundamental disagreement over the role of images in prayer, the Cassian translation did not replace the *Harps* but rather, as the transmission history shows, supplemented it in the libraries of Observant mendicant women. The *Harps* still provided a basic guide to beginning contemplation, but given the strictures of regular life and the importance the Observant reformers placed on the Office in convent practice and piety, the nuns of St. Katherine's needed a copy of Cassian's *Conferences* that preserved the spiritual, allegorical, performative, and devotional approaches to scriptural prayer.

Revitalizing the Office

Differentiating between the Cassian received by Observant nuns and the Cassian of Nider's devout laity highlights the importance of liturgical prayer to the Dominican *forma vitae* under the Observance. This interest in liturgical observance adds a layer to our picture of Nider as a reformer. Working primarily from the *Formicarius*, Michael Bailey concludes that Nider envisioned a reform that would encompass the universal church by re-enlivening the spiritual devotion of each individual Christian. The institutional reforms of a given order, "to which he actually gave rather scant attention, merely facilitated personal spiritual repentance and renewal."[68] Rules, regulations, and liturgical ritual were secondary to the private piety Nider prioritized. While it is certainly true that Nider's ultimate goal was a widespread renewal of individual devotion, Bailey downplays institutional reforms in a way that is not borne out in the sources that pertain to women's convents. Male Dominican houses certainly faced numerous challenges to their reform, and the pious laity needed more flexible and generalizable paths to virtue and devotion. For Dominican women, however, the practice of communal virtue and devotion and the observance of their Rule, Constitutions, and Office were the indispensable means to the end of renewed piety. Nider's letters to Dominican women demonstrate the importance that he attached to correct, informed, and considered performance of the Office. The library holdings and table readings of St. Katherine's likewise portray the sisters' zeal for finding devotional meaning in their way of life. The assumption that Nider's devotional and reform program for nuns and laity was one and the same disintegrates under this evidence.

Retraining the Divine Office was the first step in the reform of a female convent. Nider's letter to Schönensteinbach, in which he requests that they send a contingent of reforming sisters to St. Katherine's in Nürnberg, informs the Alsatian convent that the friars have already begun reeducating their Franconian sisters "mit singen und lesen [in singing and reading]."[69] He urges the Schönensteinbach women to send help in the form of nuns prepared to occupy the offices (prioress, subprioress, cantrix, etc.), so that the promising beginning may be brought to a good end. Nider also requests that the nuns bring their books with them, assuring them that these possessions will be sent back to Schönensteinbach after their deaths, a promise that the Nürnberg nuns never fulfilled.[70] Initial transfers of vernacular works seem to have been haphazard and the useful or necessary works acquired afterward, as Magdalena Toppler sought out the Cassian translation in the years after Maria Medingen had been reformed.[71] In contrast, updated liturgical codices were purposefully sent with reforming parties.[72] When St. Katherine's in Nürnberg took on in turn the duty of reforming other convents, they provided first and foremost Latin liturgical manuscripts. Christine Sauer describes how the Nürnberg sisters recycled and updated old missals to send to the Heilig-Grab convent in Bamberg.[73] Karin Schneider and Anja Freckmann describe how the local saints of Nürnberg were crossed out of the copies that St. Katherine's sent to Altenhohenau.[74] Writing about the exchange between the nuns of St. Katherine's in Nürnberg and in St. Gallen, Ehrenschwendtner remarks that borrowing and copying liturgical books was a central component of Observant reform. "Es war also allgemein eine Voraussetzung und Folge der Übernahme der Reform, daß die neu hinzutretenden Konvente von den bereits erfahrenen auch in diesem Punkt Hilfestellung erhielten [It was generally a prerequisite and consequence of reform that the convents joining the reform would receive help from the already experienced in this point, as well]."[75] The first step in the Observant reform of a convent was the correction of the liturgy; acquisition of appropriate vernacular devotional literature was a secondary concern.

Liturgical reform receives similar attention in the ordinances of male Observant reformers for the female convents they oversaw. After reviewing the practices and way of life in the reformed Alsatian convents in his capacity as Observant provincial vicar, Nider summarized his recommendations and requirements in visitation letters. The bulk of Nider's letter to Unterlinden deals with errors in the legislative and liturgical manuscripts that needed to be corrected in order to bring the convent's practice into line with the Observance.[76] Although Nider does not dwell on liturgical issues in his visitation letter to Schönensteinbach, Nicolaus Notel's appendix to Nider's letter includes the interesting injunction that the cantrices should not be burdened with additional duties.[77] These women were to focus on teaching their sisters correct liturgical performance and should not be distracted by other concerns. The emphasis on correct liturgical practice is also reflected in the reform *ordinatio* written by Master General Bartholomew Texery. This missive was sent to the nuns of St. Katherine's in Nürnberg in January 1429, immediately after their reform and before Nider had left for Basel. In this document Texery highlights the most important areas of convent life to maintain in the reform, as well as suggestions regarding how to punish those who fall short of the new demands. The very first item on his list is universal and orderly participation in the Office.

> Dar umb wil ich, daz die syben zeit alle in dem kor gesungen werden nach ewer statuten lauten, und daz da gegenwürtig seynd all swestren, ausz genumen die krancken vnd den die ze not denn müstend ir ampt ausz warten vnder ettlichen zeiten des tags.[78]

> Therefore, I want that all seven hours be sung in the choir according to the directives of your statutes and that all sisters be present, except for the sick and those who by necessity must perform their duties during certain hours of the day.

Texery places the performance of the liturgical hours before all other aspects of reformed behavior, including other rites such as Mass and confession. Except in cases of illness or (prioress-approved) necessity, each and every nun was to participate in this ritual in the choir in the manner specified in the

Constitution. The *ordinatio* and visitation letters demonstrate that the regulated and proper performance of the Office was of paramount importance for the Dominican Observant reformers, including Nider himself.

The reason for this importance lay in the idea that liturgical ritual fostered and supported the virtue, contemplative devotion, and piety of those who participated. As Cassian had argued, the rituals and practices were not ends in themselves but means to the end of purity of heart and spiritual renewal. Beyond simply insisting that the sisters fulfill the liturgical demands of the Constitution, the reformers worked to ensure that the nuns also grasped the reason for this emphasis and understood liturgical ritual as spiritually significant. Texery's *ordinatio* declares that the women of St. Katherine's should read "die auszlegung der regel einest im jar [the exposition of the Rule once a year]."[79] Although it took the nuns many years to build their library up to include all the recommended texts, St. Katherine's eventually possessed both Humbert of Romans's commentary on the Augustinian Rule and that of Pseudo-Hugh of St. Victor.[80] The table reading catalog specifies that these commentaries be read in alternating years.[81] That this was actually carried out is shown in a note in the records of St. Katherine's in St. Gallen. In 1485 the sisters in Nürnberg sent their manuscript of Humbert of Romans's commentary to St. Gallen to be copied, saying that they had just finished using it for their table reading and would not need it again for two years. Nevertheless, the accompanying letter begs the St. Gallen sisters to copy and return the book quickly, because the Nürnberg women are fond of reading in it on their own, as well.[82] Humbert's commentary on the Rule fostered devotion to the Dominican *forma vitae* both through its use as table readings and in the sisters' private perusal.

To take one example from Humbert of Romans's commentary on the Rule, he associates the seven canonical hours with important moments in the life of Christ. It is fitting, he concludes, to commemorate the actions and passions of Christ at the times of day during which important events occurred. In addition to events from Christ's life, Pentecost is also included in the list.

> Nocte enim natus est Salvator, circa primam horam diei surrexit, circa tertiam Spiritum Sanctum misit, circa sextam ascendit, circa nonam mortuus est in cruce, circa undecimam id est vespere corpus suum et sanguinem in sacramentum tradidit in coena, circa duodecimam sepultus est. Juste ergo horae istae deputatae sunt laudibus

divinis et orationibus sanctis plus quam aliae, in quibus non legitur aliquod factum hujusmodi contigisse.[83]

For our Savior was born at night, he rose around prime, he sent the Holy Spirit at terce, he ascended at sext, he died on the cross at none, at eleven (that is, vespers) his body and blood were transformed into a sacrament at the Last Supper, and he was interred at twelve. These hours are therefore justly assigned to divine praise and holy prayer more than others, in which it is not read that anything happened.

Humbert of Romans was not the first to make such associations, but his *Commentary* furnishes the source with which the Observant Dominican nuns would have been familiar. We have already seen the influence of such a spiritualization of the canonical hours in the sisterbooks. For example, Elisabeth of Weiler bled from the mouth every day at none in compassion with Christ's suffering.[84] Not only the prayers of the Divine Office, but even the fact that there are seven hours at these particular times, bears spiritual significance.

These explanatory table readings were not limited to commentaries on the Rule. I noted in Chapter 2 that librarian Kunigunde Niklas developed a program for reading Tauler's sermons at collations for their spiritual interpretations of the feasts within the liturgical calendar. Niklas also copied a full translation of William Durandus's *Rationale divinorum officiorum*, the sixth book of which contained explanations of the texts and procedures of Mass for specific feasts and was also extensively used for table readings.[85] For just a brief example of the contemplative material Durandus offers, he explains that Mass on Holy Saturday does not have an introit, which means head, because the head and beginning of the Church has been taken from us and lies buried.[86] The translator renders the entire epistle in German, interpreting the individual phrases along the way and commenting that the text (Colossians 3:1–4: "Seit ir erstanden mit Christo [if you be risen with Christ]") refers especially to those newly baptized.[87] He then ingeniously explains yet another common element of Mass that is absent from Holy Saturday: the gradual, a chant which was usually sung after the epistle during Mass.

Item man spricht das ALLELUIA an daz gradwall und maint daz unser hawp ruet. Wo rwe ist, do ist nicht rueren, wo daz rueren nicht ist, do ist chain auffganckch von aim staphen zw dem andern.

> Daz pedewt daz gradwal. Daz spricht man nicht, wann die getauften
> habent noch nicht fuer sich gegangen mit den werchen der tugent.[88]

> Item, one says the *Alleluia* without the gradual and contemplates
> how our head rests. Where there is rest, there is no movement;
> where there is no movement, there is no ascending from one step to
> the next. That is what "gradual" signifies. One does not say this,
> because the baptized have not yet gone forth with virtuous works.

Needless to say, the gradual does not in fact derive its name from anything
involving progress toward virtue.[89] Yet Durandus's translator not only man-
ages to convey a spiritual interpretation of the Latin term "gradual," he also
provides a symbolic reason for why it is not sung. Like the explanation of the
missing introit, this interpretation reads the structure of Mass in light of the
liturgical year, in this case as a series of new beginnings. Christ's crucifixion
and resurrection mark the beginning of the seventh world age, the new law,
and the birth of the Church, while the baptisms traditionally performed on
this day similarly represent shedding the "old Adam" for new life in Christ.
Lying between Good Friday and Easter, between the crucifixion and the
resurrection, Holy Saturday symbolizes a new beginning that has not quite
yet, gradually, started. While this reading of Mass on Holy Saturday is particularly striking, the Durandus translation provides similar interpretations of
the Mass texts and rituals for almost every feast throughout the year.

The communal table readings ensured that the Observant women of St.
Katherine's would be exposed to their Rule and Constitutions, as well as
allegorical or devotional interpretations of the Office and the liturgical year
in Humbert's commentary, Tauler's sermons, and the Durandus translation,
among other works. This literature rendered the specific texts of Mass, the
forms of the Office, and special processions or changes in liturgical routine
in German so that all would understand and be able to participate knowl-
edgeably in the liturgy. The need for legislative and liturgical texts in German
translation, however, calls into question the extent to which the Latin Office
texts were well enough understood to inspire devotional contemplation.

In fact, these sermons and commentaries constituted only one part of
the extensive program of German table readings intended to expand and
deepen Dominican women's appreciation of liturgical ceremony. Table readings also included German translations of the Mass, the epistles and the
gospel readings which were performed on and around a given reading's

appointed day.[90] As we have seen, the sixth book of Durandus's *Rationale* provides both a translation and an exposition of the liturgical Mass texts throughout the course of the year. As Antje Willing notes, "die nahezu täg- liche Lesung aus dem 'Rationale divinorum officiorum' begleitete erklärend die volkssprachliche liturgische Lesung und diente dazu, bei den Schwestern das Verständnis der täglichen lateinischen Liturgie zu vertiefen [the almost daily reading from the *Rationale divinorum officiorum* accompanied and clari- fied the vernacular liturgical reading and served to deepen the sisters' under- standing of the daily Latin liturgy]."[91] Although they continued to perform the liturgy in Latin, the nuns were exposed to German translations both of the texts they sang and of highly regarded commentaries and sermons on the ceremonies and feasts more broadly. The program of table readings in St. Katherine's was oriented entirely around providing the nuns with the means to understand the liturgy on two levels, both literally, through translations of liturgical texts, and spiritually, through translations of commentaries and sermons.

Kunigunde Niklas never designed a program of table readings for the German translation of Cassian's *Conferences*. Having been composed long before the liturgy as the Observant Dominicans knew it, these dialogues with desert fathers could not have been keyed to points of the liturgical year as easily as Tauler's sermons or Durandus's *Rationale*. Nevertheless, the way of life promoted by Cassian's Abbas conformed to the expectations placed on Observant Dominican nuns. The *Conferences* depict an ordered *forma vitae* as both the prerequisite and the path to spiritual perfection. Fasting, vigils, poverty, and above all, liturgical prayer prepare one for the divine insight that is the goal of religious life. In broad strokes, the *Conferences* supports the Observant program of respiritualizing the order and the Office.

The gift of a complete translation of the *Conferences* to St. Katherine's shortly after his transfer to Basel means that Nider's excision of mystical and liturgical material from the *Twenty-Four Golden Harps* cannot be interpreted as a statement about what he thought was appropriate for Dominican nuns. Rather, his heavy-handed redaction of the *Conferences* in the *Harps* had elimi- nated the liturgically oriented devotion that he and his fellow reformers were attempting to reawaken in friars and sisters alike, making the original a neces- sary supplement, but only for those within an order. Nider and the Obser- vant Dominican friars, at least in this instance, were not trying to quash mystical impulses in their second order but to channel them into a renewed liturgical spirituality. Cassian's Abbas insist on religious life and, above all, liturgical prayer as the source of spiritual perfection. Their vision conforms both to the ideals of the fourteenth-century sisterbooks and to the objectives of the Observant reform.

Subsequent generations of German Dominican reformers maintained and expanded the interests already emerging during Nider's time. The middle decades of the fifteenth century witnessed an exponential growth in translation of normative documents and devotional literature into the vernacular, accompanied by an increased reception of fourteenth-century German spiritual writing. Twenty years after Nider's death, another Basel friar launched what would become a lengthy career writing vernacular chronicles and practical literature for Observant Dominican women in Teutonia. Johannes Meyer assimilated the texts and traditions of two centuries of Dominican spirituality into a form of life oriented entirely around shaping communal space into an orderly garden of devotion.

CHAPTER 6

Liturgical Community and Observant Spirituality in the Work of Johannes Meyer

Ad omnes sorores nostras presentes et futuras [To all our sisters, present and future]

—Chronicle of the Inselkloster, Bern

Johannes Meyer (1422/23–1485) was born and entered the Dominican order in Zürich, but transferred to the Observant house in Basel in 1442. He never attended a *studium generale*, but remained in Basel until 1454, when he was appointed confessor to the Dominican nuns of the Inselkloster in Bern. Meyer continued mentoring Observant women and writing for their benefit until his death thirty years later at the convent of Adelhausen, where he also served as confessor.[1] Over his decades of service to the Observant reform and to women's communities, Meyer composed weighty chronicles in both German and Latin, translated Humbert of Romans's *Book of Duties*, collected and recorded visitation letters and other official documents written by Johannes Nider and other reformers, edited several sisterbooks, and excerpted Heinrich Seuse's *Vita* to write the life of Elsbeth Stagel. It seems that everywhere he went, Meyer combed the archive for histories, bulls, letters, ordinances, and deeds which he copied and incorporated into his own works.[2] In fact, we have Meyer to thank that some of the material I have examined survives at all. Through both his compilatory work and his original contributions, Meyer exercised an enormous influence on late medieval German Dominican normative literature for women.

Meyer understood his role as translator and chronicler to be an extension of his official assignment as confessor and spiritual mentor to Observant Dominican women. Namely, through making the historical trajectory and normative texts of their order available to the sisters, he would enable them to assume agency in shaping the order's future.[3] Meyer's goal was that "armed with knowledge about their order's past, reformed Dominican women would be able to live the life prescribed by Dominic as Meyer understood it."[4] Both his normative texts and his chronicles were meant to ground his sisters in the past while giving them the tools to live—and record—a vibrant, Observant future, as is testified in his repeated injunctions to leave blank pages at the ends of his works so that they may continue his task. This aspect of Meyer's work reflects the same purpose and priorities as the fourteenth-century sister-books. Meyer, too, depicts a community of the past that grounds the readers who construct their own future. Like the authors I treat in the previous chapters and whose works he redacted, Meyer conceived of the order and the Office as the foundation of Dominican spiritual life. Whereas Tauler and Seuse present the liturgy as a means of spiritual formation of the individual and the sisterbooks depict it as a catalyst for spiritual grace, Meyer represents liturgical rituals as formative of the community. Meyer chronicles the past in order to transform the community of the future, and he assigns the liturgy a central role in shaping more broadly defined communities that extend beyond the walls of the individual convent, as well.

In his chronicle of the Bern Inselkloster Meyer recorded a set of texts acquired by prioress Anna von Sissach on behalf of her reformed convent. As Claudia Engler points out, this list simultaneously presents a catalog of works owned by the Inselkloster as well as a set of desiderata for aspiring Observant convents.[5] Anna obtained:

> einen newen Collectarium vnd ander latinsche bücher, die dem chor fürderlichen worent; auch die nottel oder ruberick des ordens ze teutzsche; das amptbuch der swestern ze teutzsche; daz buch der swestern leben ze teutzsche; die regel, die Constitucio, die exposicio ze tutzsch vnd ander vil, die den swestern tröstlichen vnd hilflichen sind zu der behaltung der heiligen obseruancz.[6]

> a new Collectarium and other Latin books that were useful in the choir; also the Ordinary or rubrics of the order in German; the *Book of Duties* of the sisters in German; the sisterbooks in German; the

Rule, the Constitutions, and the Commentary in German, and
much else that is comforting and helpful to the sisters in keeping
holy observance.

Many of the items in this list are recognizable as Meyer's own contributions.
The *amptbuch* represents his *Book of Duties*, the *swesternleben* his edition of
the sisterbooks, and the Rule, Constitutions, and Commentary are contained
in Bern, Burgerbibliothek, Cod. A 53, whose constellation of German normative texts Engler attributes to Meyer himself. First and foremost, however,
stands liturgical material: Latin books for the choir and a German translation
of the Dominican Ordinary. Meyer presents observance of the Office as an
essential component of reformed Dominican life. It is tempting to imagine a
third volume that contained this German Ordinary as a complement to A 53
and the lost Bern copy of the *Book of Duties*. If such a codex existed, it either
has been lost or remains unidentified. Fortunately, it is possible to discern
Meyer's attitude toward liturgical observance from his other works.

This chapter focuses on two works, the *Book of Duties* and the *Book of
the Reformation*. In his first year as confessor at the Inselkloster in Bern,
Meyer translated and quite radically adapted Humbert of Romans's *Liber de
officiis ordinis*, a description of each of the posts a Dominican friar might
hold, from Master General to confessor to cellarer. Humbert's work was not
officially binding, but, stemming from the same pen as the Dominican Rite
and the women's Constitutions, it provided a well-respected normative
source.[7] In producing his *Amptbuch* (*Book of Duties*), Meyer did not adhere
slavishly to his source text, but altered it in order to suit the governmental
structure and particular needs of women's communities.[8] Sarah DeMaris and
Claudia Engler have suggested that precisely in altering his source so radically, Meyer may nevertheless have seen himself as Humbert's inheritor; just
as Humbert had adapted the Constitutions of the friars for Dominican
women, so Meyer adapted the *Liber de officiis* to serve them better.[9]

After serving for seven years as confessor at Schönensteinbach, the first
Observant women's house in Teutonia, Meyer completed the *Buch der
Reformacio Predigerordens* (*Book of the Reformation of the Order of Preachers*)
in 1468. This work draws on several genres, beginning as a sisterbook, continuing with something akin to a *Liber de viris illustribus*, and ending with a
lengthy chronicle, itself interspersed with *vitae* of exemplary women. The
first three books provide the foundation history, reform history, and lives of
the first sisters of the Observant convent Schönensteinbach. Book 4 lists the

names and accomplishments of important male reformers in Teutonia, and
the lengthy Book 5 chronologically recounts the reform history of each and
every Observant house in Teutonia, both male and female, including failed
attempts. Throughout the chronicle, Meyer explicitly states that the history
he recounts is intended to inspire future readers.

Like Nider's *Harps*, the Cassian translation, and commentaries on the
Rule, Meyer's *Book of the Reformation* and *Book of Duties* were disseminated
by St. Katherine's in Nürnberg as part of Observant reforming literature.[10]
Both works outline expectations and ideal conduct with regard to the Divine
Office, albeit by very different means. The *Book of Duties* describes practical
matters extensively, such that it sometimes seems as though the spirituality
gets lost in nit-picking detail. The *Book of the Reformation*, while less explicitly normative, is more obviously spiritually exemplary, with its lists of virtues
and graces granted to the mothers and fathers of Observant devotion. Both
works, however, present the Divine Office as a necessarily and inherently
communal act. According to Meyer, liturgical performances both found and
shape Observant communities; liturgical celebration requires the efforts of a
focused and trained team; and finally, devout longing to sing with the community can call down miracles. For Meyer, the Divine Office does not provide a locus for individual contemplation but draws the entire convent into
prayerful activity that is better because it is together. In addition, liturgical
rituals symbolically connect the convent community with the city surrounding it and, through the liturgical teachers Meyer praises, with future generations of Observant Dominican women.

Devotion to the Office in Meyer's *Book of the Reformation*

Johannes Meyer's *Book of the Reformation* belongs to the genre of the sisterbook, but differs markedly from the earlier works I treat in Chapter 3 in its
portrayal of liturgical devotion. Meyer directs attention away from individual
grace received either during the Office hours or at private prayer and instead
celebrates the transformational rituals that establish Observant communities.
The liturgical ceremonies that celebrate the enclosure of a convent replace
the devotion to calendrical feasts that characterizes the sisterbooks. Meyer was
intimately familiar with the fourteenth-century sisterbooks, four of which he
edited with varying degrees of intervention.[11] Meyer completed three of these

editions (Töss, St. Katharinental, and Oetenbach) while still at the Inselkloster in Bern, adding a chronicle of the Inselkloster to the collection, as well. The newly composed life of Margarete Stülinger of Oetenbach notes that the Inselkloster's prioress, Anna von Sissach, helped him compose the *vita* from notes sent by the Oetenbach sisters for this purpose.[12] He may have acquired the other sisterbooks through similar channels. However Meyer learned of the fourteenth-century works, he zealously contributed to the genre in his own writing; in addition to the chronicle of the Inselkloster and the *Book of the Reformation*, Meyer mentions having written a chronicle, now lost, of St. Agnes in Freiburg im Breisgau.[13] Throughout his life, he continued to rely on the help and information of Observant women in writing these works.[14]

The third part of the *Book of the Reformation* lingers over the lives and virtues of the early sisters of Schönensteinbach, the first Observant convent north of the Alps.[15] This section bears resemblance to the genre of sisterbooks both in its structure and in the manner by which Meyer acquired the material for it. He explains in his introduction that the information included in the book was gathered by a team of people recording oral history and perusing written records.

> Dise bücher sind mit arbait in söliche ordnung zů samen bracht und gemachet von semlichen personen, die mit sundrem fliss vil gelesen hand bullen und brieff und [ander] geschrift, die von der reformacio des ordens sagent, oder och als sie semlichs von erwirdigen personen gewarlich vernomen hand, ja och offt und vil sölchs selb befunden hand, und dar umbt vil erliten.[16]

> With hard work these books have been compiled, organized, and composed by several persons, who with special zeal have read many bulls and letters and other writings that deal with the reform of the order, or who have recorded it according to the witness of worthy persons. Many experienced such things firsthand and suffered much for it.

Meyer evidently had done much of this work while serving as Schönensteinbach's confessor, in which capacity he could not only interview the women under his spiritual care but also access their archive. In composing these *vitae*, Meyer fairly accurately reproduces the style of the sisterbooks compiled by

Dominican women in the previous century. By structuring the work according to a female-authored genre and drawing on the witness and records of Dominican women, Meyer both lent historical authenticity to the chronicle and strengthened the call for female imitation.

In his survey of the *Book of the Reformation*, Carl Pfaff found many of the same virtues as those praised in the fourteenth-century sisterbooks, such as strict silence, humble service to the community, generosity to the poor, devotion to the Eucharist and to Christ's passion, and dedication to enclosure.[17] Nevertheless, several aspects of fourteenth-century spirituality are either downplayed or outright missing. Aside from revelations, which Meyer discourages because they may come from the devil,[18] "von der klösterlichen Liturgie, der Feier der Tagzeiten und der täglichen Messe ist aus Meyers Viten wenig zu erfahren [Meyer's *vitae* reveal little about the convent liturgy, the celebration of the hours, and the daily Mass]."[19] Pfaff's observation seems initially surprising, since Meyer does mention liturgical reform as an important component of Observance.[20] Indeed, echoing the earlier sisterbooks, Meyer frequently praises sisters for zealous attendance at choir. Margreth Schlaffig was devoted to silence and "och zů den halge VII ziten [also to the holy seven hours]."[21] Margaretha von Klingental also "hat besunder fliss zů dem götlichen dienst [had particular zeal for the Divine Office]."[22] Katherina Langmantel easily understood Latin songs, which may be why "yr jubiliert yr hertz, so sy in dem cor sang [her heart was jubilant when she sang in the choir]."[23] Two biological sisters, Clara and Dorothea von Ostren, were both choir mistresses deeply devoted to the Office, and Clara's *vita* provides a remarkable example of liturgical devotion, to which I will return.[24] Prefacing the collection of lives, Meyer notes dedication to the Office as a trait of the community at large.

> Da waz grosse liebe zů got und zů sinem dienst, der hailgen messen und der VII ziten und des andren gemainen gebettes, also daz man den cor und die gewichtent hailgen stet selten un swöstren fand, besunder an den hailgen hochzitlichen tagen.[25]

> There was great love for God and for his Office, the holy Mass and the hours, and other common prayers, such that one seldom found the choir and other sacred spaces empty of sisters, especially on high holy days.

Such comments continue in the accounts of other reforms in Book 5. Agnes Vig, for instance, who had instigated the reform of her own convent of St. Nicolaus in undis in Strasbourg, inspired devotion in others through her great passion for the Office. Even when she passed seventy years of age, she had such a beautiful voice that one would have guessed her no older than thirty.[26] General expressions of devotion to the Office proliferate throughout the *Book of the Reformation*, making clear that liturgical piety is an important component of Observance.

What Pfaff identifies as missing are the visions inspired by a liturgical celebration or glossed with liturgical text that are so characteristic of the fourteenth-century sisterbooks. Thomas Lentes makes the same observation, but notes further that the difference is in quantity, not quality.[27] Only in one instance does Meyer reveal that the announcement of Christ's birth during the chapter meeting on Christmas Eve sends Margaretha von Kentzingen into ecstasy.[28] A sister in Westeroye "etwen [sometimes]" saw the Christ child circulating in the choir or refectory, but these visions are not associated with any particular feast. In most accounts, Meyer abstracts even further, removing the vision entirely but retaining the grace. He recounts of several sisters that "sy dick von yr selbs kam [she went frequently into ecstasy],"[29] but the very frequency he ascribes to these experiences decontextualizes them. These women's spiritual rewards thus seem oddly unmotivated, and, aside from the general expressions of pious attendance, liturgical devotion seems largely absent. However, Meyer does not suppress or condemn liturgical devotion per se. Rather, in a treatment that parallels his position on devotional images, he shifts the catalyst for spiritual experience from private devotion to communal event.

The arguments that Jeffrey Hamburger and Thomas Lentes have made with regard to visual piety in the *Book of the Reformation* illuminate Meyer's ideal liturgical piety, as well. Both Lentes and Hamburger read Meyer's treatment of devotional art as an attempt to disperse the power of individual sanctity by prioritizing worship in and with the community. Hamburger focuses on Meyer's representations of devotional objects, such as painted images of the crucifixion or small icons of Mary. He shows that Meyer is fundamentally ambivalent toward religious art, but not to the extent of being iconoclastic. Namely, "Meyer is less concerned about the presence of the image per se than how the nuns use (or abuse) it."[30] In particular, Meyer is motivated by the Observant militancy regarding personal poverty to remove devotional objects from the women's private possession and install them as sites for communal devotion. In the repeated accounts of confiscation, "it is not the images per se that are at fault, however, only that they are held in private."[31] Private visions inspired by privately owned images created the spiritual problems that Hamburger claims Meyer wished to avoid: the spiritual pride resulting from a sense of unique grace as well as legitimizing power over the confessor.[32] Thomas Lentes argues that Meyer tried to disempower both the women and the images themselves by emphasizing that devotional images are not sites of a saint's power and presence but merely aids for focusing contemplation.[33] Removing the object from personal possession to community ownership transferred the spiritual reward from the individual to the community, as well, and defused claims to individual sanctity.

Both Hamburger and Lentes read the single episode in which a devotional image is given to individual nuns as supporting rather than undermining the emphasis on community. As part of the ceremonial enclosure of the first sisters in Schönensteinbach, the Observant founder, Conrad of Prussia, gives each of them a small devotional image of Christ's passion. He would have liked them all to be the same, but they depicted different moments in the event. Christ himself miraculously resolves the issue. "Do verwandlet unser lieber her mit ainem grossen zachen die bildlin alle, also daz sy alle glich förmige crucifix wurdent, und Maria und Iohannes under dem crütz stůndent [So as a great sign, our dear Lord transformed all the images to be all identical crucifixes with Mary and John standing under the cross]."[34] As Hamburger aptly explains, "a miraculous transformation of images defines the transfiguration of persons embodied by the act of entering enclosure."[35] Just as their crucifixes all are identical, so too ought the Observant sisters to give up individuality and self-will. Lentes also emphasizes that the gift does not validate private experience, "vielmehr bleibt durch den gleichen Bildinhalt noch die private Bildandacht in die *vita communis* integriert [rather, through the uniformity of the depicted content, private contemplation remains integrated in the *vita communis*]."[36] In this context, it is significant that the transformed images themselves represent a small community. Rather than Christ being flogged or crowned with thorns by the angry mob, the miraculous image depicts him flanked by Mary and John, a small community of mourning and mutual support. Through the miraculous image, Christ himself approves the Observant emphasis on uniformity and encourages the sisters to devote themselves to their community.

This argument may be taken yet further. The miraculous transformation of these images takes place in the context of the ritual enclosure of the first

Observant women in Schönensteinbach, a ceremony which Meyer describes in detail. Four of the thirteen sisters who formed the original Schönenstein-bach community were new to the order. The other nine were drawn from the convents of St. Katharinental, Sylo, Unterlinden, and St. Katherine's in Colmar. All thirteen gathered together in the nearby city of Ensisheim while construction was being completed. On November 11, 1397, both secular priests and friars, with burning candles and devout song, led the women in a procession from Ensisheim to the restored cloister at Schönensteinbach. They were accompanied by a crowd of laypeople, who "fûrtent die selgen mûttren mit gesang und mit gebett in die kirchen [led the blessed mothers with song and prayer into the church]."[37] Conrad of Prussia himself said Mass, and "nach dem offertorium wurden die fier weltlichen personen an gelayt von dem selgen vatter Cûnrat mit des ordens clayd mit sölicher hochzitlicher wirdikait, also söliches von ordens recht gewonhait ist [after the Offertory, the four worldly persons received the habit of the order from the blessed father Conrad, with such ceremonial dignity as is the legal custom of the order]."[38] Conrad then publicly read all the bulls and letters confirming the new convent and appointed Claranna von Hohenburg prioress. Claranna then led her sisters in thanking their donor, Catherine of Burgundy, receiving the devotional images and retiring into their new home. The miraculous transformation of the images was therefore the culmination of an elaborate ritual of enclosure in which not only the future sisters and their superiors participated, but also their benefactress, members of the secular clergy, and a multitude of curious townsfolk. The liturgical ritual both constituted and created the community of women, rhetorically transforming each into a stone that laid "aller reformierten swöstren clöster prediger ordens in tüschen landen hailges fundament und gruntfest [the holy foundation and cornerstone of all reformed houses of Dominican sisters in German lands]."[39] A large assembly of the faithful watched in awe as the thirteen women were transformed into a single Observant community, just as the women's images were transformed into a single likeness.

Strict enclosure and reform of the liturgy were the two major elements of Observant practice. Although some women argued that liturgical reform was sufficient (like the prioresses of Oetenbach and Engelthal, whose resistance to enclosure I discussed in Chapter 4), the Observant friars do not seem to have shared this opinion and equally held enclosure as a *sine qua non*.[40] Strict physical enclosure was a prerequisite for the "inner enclosure" which the Observance set as their spiritual goal.[41] Johannes Meyer expressed this

idea most clearly in his *Buch der Ersetzung* (the *Supplement*, 1455), often transmitted with the *Book of Duties*.[42] The second chapter of this work presents
an extended meditation on enclosure, much of which details a *Herzklosteral-
legorie*, an allegory of the heart as a cloister, in which parts of the convent's
architecture and the personnel that staff it represent the virtues and habits
that a nun must cultivate in order to develop interior devotion.[43] Enclosure of
the cloister constituted both a return to the Constitutions and a fundamental
spiritual practice and was therefore a non-negotiable issue in reform. It was
also, however, the most contentious, since many Dominican women were
loath to stop seeing their families.[44] The enclosure ceremonies served an
important role in Observant propaganda. More than transforming the Dominican women into a single community with "one soul and one heart in
God,"[45] as the Augustinian Rule enjoins, the elaborate public processions also
rallied the laity and the secular clergy around the Observant convent. Drawing these other groups to participate in the ceremony would have reassured
the sisters and their families that they remained connected even if they could
not see each other. It was imperative for the Observants to cultivate this
attitude, since an enclosed convent was actually more dependent on the surrounding lay community.[46]

Public enclosure ceremonies accordingly seem to fascinate Meyer and
wholly displace the accounts of devotion to feasts in the liturgical calendar
that pepper the fourteenth-century sisterbooks. Over the course of Book 2 of
the *Book of the Reformation*, the Schönensteinbach community is forced by
regional unrest and violence to leave their cloister no less than five times. In
1445–46 and 1448, the Schönensteinbach sisters are forced into exile for
longer periods of time, and in 1445 are even separated and sent to various
other convents in the region. Once the crisis had been averted, the sisters
returned to Schönensteinbach from their various places of exile. Meyer
describes the Mass and public procession in which the sisters who had been
sent to Basel were ceremonially led to a ship that would take them home
down the Rhine.

> Also sy von Basel soltent schaden, do wurdent sy gar erlich von den
> edel frowen und burgerinn der statt Basel gefüret in crütz ganges
> wiss von dem huss, da sy ain iar und IV monet beschlossen warent
> gewesen, in der prediger kirchen und trůg der bichtiger ainer den
> swöstren daz crütz vor. Also non die swöstren in die kirchen koment,
> do sungen die brůder an erlich frü mess, und der prior dett den

swöstren ain schöne predig, und dar nach do fûrt man die swöstren
an den Rin, und sasent in daz schyf und fûrent in gottes namen
hyn.[47]

When it was time for them to leave Basel, they were led very honorably by the noble and patrician women of Basel in a line from the
house where they had been enclosed for a year and four months.
They led them into the Dominican church and one of the confessors
carried the cross before them. When the sisters came into the
church, the brothers honorably sang an early Mass and the prior
held a beautiful sermon for the sisters. Afterward, they were led to
the Rhine and sat in the ship and sailed away in God's name.

In the case of the Basel exiles, the departure ceremony as well as that of
reenclosure is described. The public procession of laywomen, the Mass and
sermon in the friars' church, and the farewell at the harbor on the Rhine
reaffirm the support of the various Basel communities for the exiled sisters
even after they leave. Indeed, Meyer tells us that when the women reached
the village where they exited the ship to continue their home journey over-
land, they were fed by villagers paid by the Basel convent of Klingental. The
public ritual binds the exiled sisters to the Basel communities in gratitude
even as they depart. Similar ceremonies are then repeated to resituate the
exiles within the lay and religious communities around Schönensteinbach.
The Basel exiles as well as the other dispersed groups return, each accompanied by a public procession of laity, secular clergy, and Dominican friars and
received back to their home convent with *Te Deum laudamus*.[48] A similar
ritual celebrates their homecoming after another exile in 1448.[49] Each reenclosure requires a new ceremony to reaffirm the convent's identity, to bind the
sisters back together and to recreate ties with the lay communities of the
region.

Schönensteinbach is not the only community for which Meyer describes
such rituals. Narratives of enclosure ceremonies stand at important points in
his work. Meyer opens Book 5, which chronicles the spread of the Dominican
Observance in German territories, with a brief account of the enclosure ritual
at the first convent reformed with the help of Schönensteinbach sisters, Wijk-
bij-Duurstede in the diocese of Utrecht. Upon the arrival of the party from
Schönensteinbach, there was a public ceremony in which new novices
received the Dominican habit before the cloister was locked in the name of

God, the Holy Trinity, the Virgin Mary, Saint Dominic, and Mary Magdalene, the patron of the convent.[50] This account is one of the most brief, likely due to lack of information, but it is symbolically important for Meyer to include, standing as it does at the opening of the final book and the beginning of the reform histories. The enclosure of Wijk-bij-Duurstede symbolically opens the gates of the Observant community, broadly conceived, which grows continually larger with each new enclosure.

Meyer is able to provide extensive descriptions of the enclosure ceremonies of the three convents in Freiburg im Breisgau, at which he personally presided. In Freiburg, as well, large groups of laypeople accompanied the parties of reforming sisters to public ceremonies held in the churches of the three convents.[51] Six sisters from St. Katherine's in Colmar were sent to reform Adelhausen, five from the Steinenkloster in Basel were sent to St. Agnes, and three from Schönensteinbach reformed the Penitents of Mary Magdalene. The sisters from St. Katherine's and the Steinenkloster were both initially led by an entourage of twenty honorable laywomen to the convent of Adelhausen. After the ceremony there and a short break, the laywomen led the Basel sisters from Adelhausen to St. Agnes, where they were received by local nobility, mayor Thüring von Hailwil, and the city council. The sisters from Schönensteinbach arrived separately in a covered wagon, which they left for a procession through the city on foot, led by banners and crosses and welcomed by the clangor of their new convent's bells. The extensive involvement of the lay townsfolk and secular government in these ceremonies seems to fly in the face of the Observant ideals of withdrawal and strict enclosure. Meyer provides numerous descriptions of the lengths taken to rig wagons and boats so that reforming sisters will not be seen while in transit, yet the Schönensteinbach sisters are removed from their wagon and publicly paraded through the whole city. However, even though the sisters themselves disappeared behind spiked grates, each convent remained embedded in and dependent upon the city's spiritual life and civil economy.

The Observant reformers relied heavily on the support of the regional nobles and civil authorities to support and fund local reforms, and, once enclosed, the Observant women relied on the continued support of the lay community.[52] In Freiburg, the secular authorities (especially Thüring von Hailwil) rendered more than financial assistance, petitioning the religious authorities for approval and helping Meyer talk the Adelhausen sisters into accepting the Observance through frequent exhortation.[53] By including the laity in the ceremonies of enclosure, Meyer and his fellow Observants acknowledged dependence on and promised continued involvement in the surrounding lay community. The inclusion of these ceremonies in the chronicle for the edification of future Dominican sisters reminded them of their indebtedness to the laity that surrounded and (ideally) protected them.

Meyer's accounts include more than the public processions and describe portions of the liturgical ritual, as well. Although there seems to have been a "Rite of Reform" that was sung in all convents, each ceremony is somewhat personalized, as well.[54] Adelhausen, the first of the three, provides a baseline on which the two following descriptions build. Upon arriving in the church in the company of the laity, the six reforming sisters from Colmar knelt before the main altar and sang the Marian antiphon *Sub tuum praesidium.* They were then led into the choir where they sang *Veni creator,* versicles, and prayers, and other things "als man denn pfligt zů tůn, so man an closter reformieren ist [that one does when one is reforming a convent]."[55] The sisters from Basel were received first in Adelhausen, where they knelt in the choir together with the Adelhausen community and the Colmar reformers to sing the *Salve regina.* The twenty laywomen then led them to St. Agnes, where *Veni creator* again was sung, "und ander ding, die da zů sölichen grossen sachen gehortent, ordentlich volbracht warent [and other things that belong to such great affairs were duly accomplished]."[56] Meyer describes the ceremony for the Penitents in the greatest detail. Once the procession with crosses and banners arrived at the convent, the Freiburg sisters received those from Schönensteinbach in the outer church and then

> fůrtent sy do in den cor singent den ymnus "Veni creator"; dar nach die frümden swöstren růfftent unser lieben frowen an und sungent "sub tuum," und dar nach die brůder und priester sungent der wirdigen sant Maria Magtdalena, der matron des selben closters, die antiphon "Intercede" und die collecten sang der andechtig gaistlich vatter Iohannes Meger, die dar zů gehortent, und dar uf ward gepredigt, won och vil gemaines volkt da engegenwürtig waz; zů dem letzten hielt capitel der vor genamt gaistlich vatter und macht swöster Katherina Karthuserin priorin diser observantz.[57]

led them into the choir, singing the hymn *Veni creator.* The foreign sisters then called upon Our Dear Lady and sang *Sub tuum.* In honor of the worthy saint Mary Magdalene, matron of this convent, the friars and priests then sang the antiphon *Intercede,* and the

devout father Johannes Meyer sang the appropriate collects. There
followed a sermon, since many common folk were also present.
Finally, the aforesaid devout father held chapter and appointed
Sister Katherina Kartäuser prioress of this Observance.

Certain liturgical elements remain the same for each ceremony, while others
shift. The ritual in each of the three convents begins with the hymn *Veni
creator*, which may have been considered appropriate since it also opened the
ceremony for receiving the habit.[58] Submitting to Observant reform may
have been seen as a reaffirmation of commitment to the order and therefore
was appropriately marked by liturgical elements from that rite. The invoca-
tion of Mary is also a constant with *Sub tuum*, an antiphon for the Assumption of the Virgin, and the *Salve regina*.[59] The ceremony for the Penitents is
personalized with a lauds antiphon for the feast of their matron saint, Mary
Magdalene.[60] None of the events involved a Mass, as the enclosure of Schönensteinbach had, nor does Meyer distribute gifts to the sisters. The readership
is expected to have a basic understanding of the ritual, as is revealed by
Meyer's *ander ding* (other things). The rite itself seems always to start with
the *Veni creator* and conclude with a chapter where the overseeing friar
appoints the new prioress from among the reforming party.[61] What comes in
the middle may be tailored to the occasion, as at the reform of the Penitents,
where they sing an antiphon particularly to honor the convent's patron (or
matron) saint, and Meyer delivers a sermon for the benefit of the assembled
laity. These enclosure ceremonies were orchestrated and narrated in order to
construct a communal identity that was distinct, but embedded within both
civil social networks and the Dominican order.

The importance of enclosure ceremonies for the formation of new convent identities is supported by two other accounts in Meyer's works that
describe enclosure rituals not associated with the Observant reform. In a late
and unfinished chronicle compiled for Adelhausen, Meyer briefly describes
the reception of St. Agnes into the Dominican order, on Septuagesima Sunday in 1284. Four sisters from Adelhausen were transferred there to teach
them the order's *forma vitae*.

Do die swestern von Adelhusen kamen zů Sant Agnesen, do gieng
die priorin mit iren swestern vs dem closter vnd waren dz closter
den komenden swestern mit ir zůgehörd vf geben. Also giengen die
von Adelhusen vor in, vnd die andern swestern, die vor im closter

gewesen waren, volgten in nach in den chor. Vnd ward da gesungen dz Responsorium *Qui sunt isti qui ut nubes* etc vnd *O lumen ecclesie.* Vnd hie bÿ worent vil brüder vnd anders volkes.[62]

When the sisters from Adelhausen came to St. Agnes, the prioress with her sisters went out of the convent and turned the cloister and all its possessions over to the arriving sisters. Then the sisters from Adelhausen went in first and the others, who had been in the convent before, followed them into the choir. There they sang the responsory *Qui sunt isti qui ut nubes* and *O lumen ecclesiae.* Many friars and other people were also in attendance.

Many of the elements of the Observant enclosure rituals appear here, as well: the sisters process from outside the convent into the choir, Dominican friars and laypeople participate, and the new community sings symbolically significant chants. *Qui sunt isti* is a responsory for the Common of Apostles, and *O lumen ecclesiae* an antiphon for the feast of St. Dominic.[63] With these chants, the new Adelhausen sisters welcome the convent of St. Agnes into the apostolic life of the Dominican order. Like the Observant enclosure ceremony for the Penitents of Mary Magdalene, this ceremony is also tailored with liturgical material that reflects and even shapes the new community's identity and its place within the larger community of the order.

Such narratives are also at work in the chronicle of the Bern Inselkloster. Meyer delivers a lengthy account of their 1439 enclosure, which was accomplished prior to their acceptance of the Observance.[64] Here, thousands of people gathered for Mass in the newly dedicated church. The sisters took communion, and after the Mass the Friars Preachers and secular priests, bearing crosses and candles, led the entire gathering in a procession through the convent grounds, singing *Veni creator spiritus* and calling upon the Virgin. The procession exited the main gate, which was then firmly locked, the presiding friar, Conrad Rosenbach, opened the choir door, and the assembled laity tearfully looked on as the sisters filed in and locked that door behind them, as well. Since no reforming party had yet arrived, no chapter was held to select a new prioress, but the other common elements are all present: the entire city turns out for the event, Mass is celebrated, the *Veni creator* is sung, and the Virgin is invoked. Here, too, the enclosure of the sisters is a public event in which laity, religious, and secular clergy all participate. The ritual that formally cuts the sisters off from the outside world also symbolically binds them back to it by representing enclosure as a civil project.

These enclosure ceremonies thus constitute Meyer's version of the liturgical visions of the sisterbooks. The fourteenth-century works used liturgical citations in order to create and explore multiple levels of spiritual meaning that drew not only on the texts of the chants they quoted but on the liturgical context, as well. Meyer uses liturgical material but also ceremonial choreography to form, reform, distinguish, and connect the various interlocking communities on which Observant Dominican women depended. Antiphons for patron saints, invocations of the Virgin and the Holy Spirit, and lively processions through cloister grounds and city streets drew the outlines of the new communities and the networks of protection, both worldly and divine, that would allow them to thrive. Nevertheless, these events were singular occasions, unlike the yearly feasts that inspire the fourteenth-century sisters or the daily cycle of the hours to which Meyer's exemplary sisters are devoted. The chronicles give little insight into the daily liturgical piety Meyer expected from Observant sisters. For this, we must turn to the *Book of Duties*.

The Divine Office in Meyer's *Book of Duties*

Meyer's *Book of Duties* makes the Divine Office a communal endeavor on two levels. In a practical sense, successful performance of the liturgy requires an entire convent to cooperate in preparing and observing it. The choir mistress and sacristan serve as the central organizers, who direct large teams in a wide variety of important duties, from experienced hebdomadarian to novice candle-bearer. Observance of the Office depends upon the entire community's dedication and effort. Despite the pragmatic tone of the *Book of Duties*, Meyer makes clear that the times of togetherness and the ceremony of the Office should foster each sister's personal devotion through her role in communal worship.

Meyer's *Book of Duties* is primarily practical in orientation and purpose. Ekkehard Borries has noted that the work's emphasis on effectiveness and practicality outweighs devotional edification to the point of eclipsing it. He remarks that "Überlegungen zur spirituellen Anleitung und Erziehung der Schwestern fehlen nahezu vollständig [consideration of spiritual guidance and instruction of the sisters is almost completely absent]."[65] As Meyer explains in the epilogue, he has written it, "dz die swestren, denen da etwan empter befolhen werden vnd aber nit wol nach dar jnn gevbt vnd getriben sind, dz si hier zu ir zu flucht nemen [so that sisters who are appointed to offices for which they do not have sufficient experience may have recourse to it]."[66] The *Book of Duties* lacks many of the characteristic elements of late medieval devotional literature and of Meyer's chronicles, such as exemplary anecdotes or advice concerning the discernment of spirits. Nevertheless, the ultimate goal of the *Book of Duties* was indeed to foster the spiritual lives of the women who used it, not by providing contemplative material for readers but by helping officers to create a space in which their sisters could develop their piety.

Whether or not Meyer's suggestions were considered compulsory, they were certainly considered useful. Meyer gathered the *Book of Duties* and its companion, the *Supplement*, in a single codex with German translations of the Constitutions for laybrothers, laysisters, and Dominican Tertiaries. More-over, this codex itself was likely originally designed as a companion volume to Bern, Burgerbibliothek, Cod. A 53, which contains German translations of the Augustinian Rule, the Constitutions for Dominican sisters, and the Pseudo-Hugonian commentary on the Augustinian Rule.[67] The association of the *Book of Duties* with official normative texts lent it an aura of author-ity.[68] The *Book of Duties* came to St. Katherine's in Nürnberg from the Bern Inselkloster in 1458, quite soon after its 1454 composition.[69] The Nürnberg sisters produced an imaginatively illuminated copy of the *Book of Duties* as well as of its companion piece, also sent from the Inselkloster: namely, Mey-er's edition of the sisterbooks of Töss, St. Katharinental, Oetenbach, and the Inselkloster.[70] In their efforts to help other convents institute reform, the Nürnberg sisters loaned the *Book of Duties* further to both St. Katherine's in St. Gallen and Medlingen for copying, and these communities disseminated it to others in turn.[71] Every single surviving manuscript of the *Book of Duties* also contains at least one other German-language regulatory document.[72] Meyer's translation formed an important part of the normative material to instruct and govern Observant communities.

Several of the chapters in the *Book of Duties* include a note at the outset about where binding descriptions of the duties may be found. The sacristan, for instance, is required to know "alle die ding, die jn dem selben buch der nottel von irem ampt geschriben sint [all the things that are written about her office in the Ordinary],"[73] and the choir mistress likewise must perform her office "als denn söllichs geschriben ist an mengem end der nottel vnd sust an andren bucheren [as laid down in many parts of the Ordinarium and in other books]."[74] The instructions contained in the *Book of Duties* supplement such regulations with advice regarding the banal day-to-day activities that need to happen behind the curtains, such as maintaining the church and cloister grounds, overseeing the community's finances, purchasing food and materials, and correcting the books as the Divine Office is updated. The elements foreign to Humbert's *Liber de officiis* are drawn, Meyer explains, from the Constitutions, the Ordinary, specific ordinances, or even "vs des ordens güten bewerten gewonheitten, als ich den bei vil clöstren, besunder vnsers prediger orden, das gesehen, gemerckt oder gelesen hab [from what I have seen or read of the accepted customs of religious orders in many houses, especially those of our own order]."[75] The product is a compendium of both official regulations and best practices geared toward facilitating the effective running of a community. Devotional life recedes behind the day-to-day worries of administrators.

Nevertheless, as I have argued throughout the previous chapters, life under the order was itself considered a devotional or ascetic exercise. Through their labors the office-holders sustained the other sisters so that they might devote themselves more fully to contemplation and praise. As many narratives from both the sisterbooks and Meyer's chronicles show, these duties were considered an obstacle to a sister's individual devotion but could become a source of grace through the virtue of obedience. In the *Book of Duties,* the ideal role of officers in fostering the community's spiritual life appears yet more clearly. Devotion, even in private prayer, appears not as an individual accomplishment but as the product of a great collaborative effort. The highest purpose of all the requirements and regulations for Dominican women was to create a nurturing spiritual environment. This goal could be accomplished in strict observance, but only through the collaborative participation of the entire community. Whereas the enclosure rites of Meyer's chronicles delineate the broader communities of the faithful on which the convent relies, the *Book of Duties* explains how the internal community sustains and nurtures its members, physically and spiritually.

The convent life that Meyer depicts in the *Book of Duties* provides two main places where spiritual edification or devotional meditation might take place, namely table reading and the Divine Office. As I have noted in previous chapters, in St. Katherine's the table reading itself was largely geared toward promoting devotional understanding of the Office and Mass. Two officers, the reader and the correctrix mensae, are immediately responsible for the reading itself, with the support and input of the subprioress and choir mistress. Meyer's advice for the reader primarily addresses issues that affect her comprehensibility, such as placement in the refectory, her speed and volume, and how to announce the topic of the reading.[76] She is assisted by a correctrix, whose task is to watch over her shoulder in order to provide help with difficult passages and correct mistakes.[77] The task of selecting spiritually beneficial texts falls primarily to the subprioress, although the correctrix and the choir mistress both advise her. Together, these sisters are to design a program of readings that instructs the community in the order and Office while fostering their devotion.

Meyer's recommendations for the content of table readings are dispersed and repeated through several chapters. In the chapter on the subprioress, for instance, Meyer recommends Cassian's *Conferences* and the *Lives of the Desert Fathers* as devotional aids, a suggestion which he repeats in the chapter on the correctrix but expands to include the *Dialogues* of Gregory the Great.[78] However, the table reading was intended not only to provide private meditative material but also to support and inform observance of the order's *forma vitae*. First and foremost, "die regel sol man lesen an dem ersten tag nach dem sunentag [the Rule should be read on the first day after Sunday]."[79] In addition to the weekly reading of the Rule, the subprioress is urged to schedule

> die constitucion, ordinacion, die send prieff des meisters des ordens oder der andren öberen, dar an denn sunder vermanung an stand, vnd auch ettliche stück auß der nottel oder ruberick von dem göttlichen ampt, der küntschafft denn die swestren aller meist bedürffent, also das die swestren die ding merkent vnd lerent vnd dez ordens gewonheit nit vergessent, besunder das sie dar jnnen zu nement.[80]

> the constitutions and ordinations, and letters from the master of the order or other superiors containing special admonitions, . . . and also the sections of the Ordinarium which the sisters most need to know, so that they will note these things and learn them and not forget the order's usages but become more proficient in them.[81]

The chapter on the correctrix mensae repeats this list item for item.[82] The assembly of the entire community at collation provided an opportunity to facilitate observance of the order by reminding the sisters of their vows and obligations. The Rule, the Constitutions, and Humbert's Rite were all considered binding legislation. Reading them at the communal meal removed the possibility for a sister to excuse an infraction by arguing ignorance.

This purpose, however, was not the only motivation to read normative documents before the convent. The table reading could be used to prepare sisters for upcoming feasts, especially during the seasons when the liturgy changed or special observances were introduced. Meyer writes that the choir mistress must advise concerning the selection of readings from the Ordinary in order to ensure that unusual celebrations run smoothly.

> Dar vmb sol si die priorin vil manen, dz si lasse in dem reuental
> lesen die ruberick vs der nottel, die sunder nott ze wissen sint von
> dem götlichen ampt, vnd öch die ding, jn den die swestren nit als
> wol getriben sint, also do ist dz ampt der letzsten wüchen in der
> fasten vnd öch etliche ander zit.[83]

> She should frequently urge the prioress to have the reader in the
> refectory read from the Ordinarium the liturgical rubrics which
> most need to be known, and also the things in which the sisters are
> less practiced such as the liturgy of Holy Week and some other
> seasons.[84]

The periods immediately preceding and following such feasts as Christmas and Easter marked this important time in the liturgical year with special ceremonies, extra Masses, and unique processions. At the time around Easter, as we saw Tauler mention in Chapter 2 and Durandus in Chapter 5, liturgical obligations were radically altered. In order to prevent the sisters from singing out of habit something not part of the Eastertide liturgy, the pertinent sections of the Ordinary were to be read in advance at refectory. On a basic level, this measure certainly was intended to remind sisters of the unusual rituals in order to avoid confusion and disruption. These very rituals, however, bore symbolic meaning that reflected the theological significance of the feast, something the Nürnberg sisters also would be reminded of in table readings from Tauler's sermons or Durandus's *Rationale*. Reading the Ordinary in advance gave the sisters the opportunity to reflect on the spiritual meaning of the altered liturgy while preparing to perform it.

Meyer does not specifically advise that sisters read commentaries on the Rule or William Durandus's *Rationale divinorum officiorum*, which St. Katherine's in Nürnberg used to elucidate the spiritual meaning of the liturgy during their collations. Nevertheless, he does write that such works should be available, and assigns the sacristan the task of ensuring that they are. The sacristan "sol öch wol mit flisse dz bestellen durch die oberen, dz man habe etwz bewerter gütter bucher der lereren, die da sagen von dem gotlichen dienst vnd von dem gotlichen ampt vnd des gelichen [through her superiors she should arrange for there to be some good, reputable books by theologians who write about liturgy and the worship of God and so on]."[85] Encouraging the purchase of certain kinds of theological works seems an odd duty for the woman responsible for items within the choir and the church. The sacristan, however, was responsible for decorating the church and laying out the vestments for the priests celebrating Mass. Meyer notes specifically that she must choose the appropriate items "nach gelegenheit der hochtzitlichen tagen, vnd je als sich denn dz zit vnd die sachen ergebent [in accordance with the rank of the feast, or as the season or other circumstances dictate]."[86] Not only the liturgy but also the vestments and altar cloths changed with the season and had special symbolic meaning. Just as the choir mistress was responsible for the performance of the Office throughout the changes of the liturgical year, the sacristan had to understand the significance of the various feasts in order to decorate the church appropriately and meaningfully. There were indeed treatises that dealt with the meanings of church decorations and vestments, such as, for example, the first book of Durandus's *Rationale*. Although the St. Katherine's table readings catalog only schedules the sixth book on Mass ceremonies, this first book explaining decorations and vestments was also available to that community and their sacristans.

The sacristan and choir mistress collaborated in preparing the community for the Divine Office in other ways, as well. Both are required to maintain boards hung in the choir or some other communal space which remind the other sisters of their liturgical obligations and inform them of any special duties. The sacristan's board was to contain an overview drawn from the Constitution and the Ordinary, so that if sisters were unsure what the daily Office entailed they might check it there.[87] The choir mistress was responsible for assigning particular liturgical tasks, such as reading the lessons or intoning antiphons, and posting this "duty-roster" on the board.[88] Both the sacristan and the choir mistress ought furthermore to know the Office and the Ordinary inside out and to be available to help other sisters prepare for it. The choir mistress was especially responsible for helping both individuals and the whole community rehearse the chants and practice difficult passages "also dz es den swestren wol kund würde [until they have thoroughly learned it]."[89]

The sacristan and the choir mistress thus worked together to ensure that the entire community was certain of their role and could perform the Divine Office with assurance and accuracy.

Several other office-holders also helped draw the community together in devout liturgical prayer, the monitors doing so quite literally. Their job was to circulate through the convent (Meyer calls them *cirkarin*) and watch for infractions against the order.[90] In addition to noting whether any sisters broke silence, the monitors checked attendance at the hours and made particular note of those who stayed in bed at matins. Meyer requires the sisters to recite the Little Office of the Virgin in between the first and second bells for choir, as the friars did.[91] The monitors report to the prioress if any fail to participate. The prioress herself was indirectly involved in encouraging devotion to the liturgy. At the very beginning of the chapter on her duties, Meyer writes that the prioress should provide a role model for her community by faithful attendance. "Sie sol sich auch nit geren enzihen von dem göttlichen ampt, besunder von der conplet [She should not willingly absent herself from the divine office, especially compline],"[92] unless she is ill or must attend to a matter of great importance. Even then, she should devoutly recite the hours privately. These similar duties show that, although the sacristan and choir mistress were most directly responsible for ensuring correct and devout obser-vance of the Office, many others played important ancillary roles. The table reader and her correctrix, the monitors, and the prioress, all contributed to the communal project of the liturgy.

Numerous sisters were involved in organizing, instructing, and ensuring attendance at the Divine Office. Nevertheless, the sister to whom Meyer ascribed the most important role in preparing the community to perform the liturgy both correctly and devoutly was the novice mistress. Her primary objective was to teach the novices and young sisters to live according to the order. To this end, he advised that a "school" be provided where she may teach them "von der regel, von der constitucio, von dem gotlichen ampt, von dem orden, vnd wz anders si denn ze vnder wisen sint [about the rule, the constitutions, the divine office, the order's observance, and anything else that calls for instruction]."[93] Meyer's description of the novice mistress constitutes the work's most complete summary of the Dominican *forma vitae*. In survey-ing the information she must impart, he explains the regulations concerning the habit, behavior during the meal and in the chapter of faults, as well as permissible conversation at the speaking grille. In each instance, the novice mistress should communicate not only the statutes but also less explicit expectations for behavior and self-regulation. This instruction includes comportment both during the Office and in paraliturgical prayer. The novice mistress teaches her charges to participate in the life of the community through correct observance, assumption of responsibilities, and spiritual dedication.

First and foremost, in addition to behavioral requirements, the novice mistress must prepare the young sisters to assume the roles and responsibilities they will eventually have to take on themselves, something they learn by doing. In the school, the novice mistress should have the young sisters rehearse the hours and other prayers that they will be required to know.

Do selbs mag man inen vber singen vnd lesen oder si über hören,
wz si denn ze singen vnd ze lesen hand in dem conuente, vnd öch
dz si da lerent die ding, die si vs wendig sond leren, als das ampt der
totten, die zit von unser lieben frawen, die teglichen vesper psalmen,
vnd der gemeinen zitten vnd des gelich.[94]

Whatever they are to sing or read should be rehearsed there, and
there they should be tested to make sure they learn everything they
ought to know by heart such as the office of the dead, the office of
Our Lady, the psalms for each day's vespers, and those used in the
unvarying hours.[95]

In addition to attending the communal Office with the older sisters, the young ones practice in their school until they have memorized all that is required. Meyer makes this quite explicit with regard to the Little Office of the Virgin, which was not obligatory during certain high feasts. Even if the community was not required by the Ordinary to say it, the novice mistress would recite the Little Office with the young sisters in the school.[96] In addition to rehearsing texts and chants, the novice mistress taught them "wie si sich halten sond nach geistlichen sitten vnd wisen, vnd besunder die ding, die in der nottel geschriben sind [how to conduct themselves according to spiritual habits and practices, especially regarding the things contained in the Ordinary]."[97] The novice mistress thus also instructed them in the rituals and proper methods of standing, kneeling, and prostration. Through constant practice and repetition, the young sisters would learn the Office to which they were obligated.

The novice mistress would also train the young sisters in particular duties and responsibilities. For example, the chapter on the novice mistress includes a discussion in miniature of the office of the sacristan. The schoolroom, namely, should have its own altar, and the novice mistress should appoint a young sister to care for and decorate it just as the sacristan maintains and decorates the rest of the convent's devotional sites.[98] Similarly, the young sisters would learn to assume the more important rotating liturgical duties, such as hebdomadarian, through frequent practice in the smaller roles, such as calendarian, versicularian, or candle-bearer. Meyer writes that when young sisters are assigned roles by the choir mistress, the novice mistress "sol inen denn sagen, wz in der nottel oder in dem ampt buch von einem sollichen ampt oder dienst geschriben ist, vnd sol si baß vnd volkommenlicher vnder wisen denn si es geschriben finde [should tell them what it says in the rubrics or in the *Book of Duties* about whatever the task or service may be, and she should explain it better and more fully than the book does]."[99] While he thus makes allowance for the transmission of local practice, Meyer also expands on these kinds of roles himself. Similar to the mini-treatise on the school sacristan, Meyer includes a brief description of the duties of each of the three liturgical posts mentioned, "dz man die jüngen swestren dester bas möge vnd könne vnder wisen in söllichen empteren [so that young sisters can be better instructed about such jobs]."[100] Meyer translates these duties from the Ordinary to provide the novice mistress with concise summaries which she could use in instructing the young in their duties. By assigning smaller tasks or duties limited to the space of the schoolroom, the novice mistress facilitates the young sisters practicing for the more important duties they will eventually assume.

The novice mistress is also responsible for teaching the young sisters how to conduct themselves in the time allotted for private contemplation, in particular after matins and after compline. Officially, sisters were allowed to return to bed after matins but might choose to stay in the choir and pray. All sisters were required to spend time after compline in contemplation, and in the chapter on the sacristan Meyer describes precisely how much time she is to give them before ringing the bell for bed: "das man do zwischen gepeten möcht mit rwe sittenlich die siben psalmen mit der lettanie [long enough for the penitential psalms and the litany to be recited calmly and without rushing]."[101] Although this sounds prescriptive and may indeed betray an unspoken expectation for the older sisters, Meyer outlines an elaborate paraliturgical prayer practice for the novice mistress and her charges. After the conclusion of compline, they all kneel before the high altar and silently recite several hymns, *Kyrie eleison*, the *Pater noster*, and *Ave Maria*. When the novice mistress signals, they file out toward the schoolroom, saying the *De profundis* if the path leads past the cemetery. Once in the school, they recite several more versicles and prayers before the novice mistress dismisses them for bed.[102] After matins also the young are expected to kneel before the high altar and pray a prescribed set of prayers silently, and before the community hears a sermon, the young assemble in the school and say a set of prayers together before the school altar. The older sisters are allowed free time for self-directed contemplation and prayer, but the young sisters are not trusted to govern themselves yet. The novice mistress prepares them communally in spiritual direction and contemplative prayer.

These paraliturgical exercises and extra prayers fulfill two purposes in the education of the young. On the one hand, they provide yet another opportunity to practice prayers and hymns which were devotionally significant but appear infrequently in the Office or only at special times of the liturgical year. This would be the case for the hymn *Veni creator spiritus*, which was only sung around Pentecost, at the reception of a new novice, at the election of officials or, as we have seen, for a reform and reenclosure.[103] More importantly, these practices were intended to instill in the impressionable youth habits of prayer and meditation which they would maintain throughout their lives. At the end of the chapter, Meyer insists that, even though he included all of these requirements in the chapter on the novice mistress, age does not exempt one from them.

> Die jungen swestren, die man hie von lerenen sol, sond sich nit allein in ir jugend nach dißer ler reygieren, by sunder si sond dis obgenanten heilsamen gutte gewonheit vnd ler vnd alles anders, dz zu dem heilligen prediger orden hört vnd zu geistlichem tugenrichem leben, in ir jugend also in sich fassen vnd es niemer me gelassen.[104]

> Young sisters, whose training it is meant to serve, should not only guide themselves by this teaching in their youth. These salutary practices and this teaching and everything relating to the holy Order of Preachers and to a religious, virtuous life should be absorbed while they are young and never abandoned.[105]

The duty of the novice mistress is not only to instruct the young sisters in their obligations under the statutes, but also to inculcate the devotional habits that will sustain a woman through a lifetime of piety. The specific prayers that Meyer requires of the young sisters for the time after compline and matins are not themselves obligatory. An attitude of devotion and prayerfulness, however, is expected, and the prayers recited under the guidance of the novice mistress provide a variety of options among which the mature nun may choose. More importantly, obligating the youth to such a practice inculcates a virtuous habit that they will, hopefully, feel compelled to continue after the obligation is lifted.

Finally, the novice mistress was supposed to impart to the novices and young sisters the appropriate attitude or spirit with which to approach prayer. Citing the Augustinian Rule, Meyer admonishes that young sisters "sond och fliß dar zu tun, wz si mit dem mund in den wortten betten sind, dz och da by sige dz hertz vnd gemütte [should take care that what they pray in words with their mouths is also in their hearts and minds]."[106] Echoing Tauler, he urges them to focus on developing a state of inner devotion and grace, rather than saying as many prayers as possible.[107] Above all, in a statement that directly confirms the conclusions of Hamburger and Lentes, Meyer urges that the young sisters be taught to prize communal prayer over private contemplation.

> Jtem si sond me hoffnung vnd getrüwen haben in dz gemein gebet denn in ir sundrig eigen gebet, vnd sond och lieber by dem selben gebet sin, es sige in den siben zitten oder in den vigilien oder wie es sich ergibet, dz der conuent mit ein andren betten ist, oder och nach conplete vnd nach mettin, vnd dz si dz selb mit andacht betten sigen, sond si grossen fliß tun.[108]

> They should place more confidence and trust in common prayer than in their own private prayer, and they should give preference to being present at it in the divine office or the office of the dead or on other occasions when the community prays together, as in the period after compline and matins, and they should take great care to say these prayers devoutly.[109]

Meyer thus makes utterly explicit that he expects complete dedication to the community's worship practices. He permits sisters to pray by themselves before the various devotional images erected around the convent if they have nothing better to do, but the times in which the community customarily prays together are imperative. Moreover, while the Divine Office stands foremost, Meyer includes those times that are not officially compulsory but simply customary, such as after matins and compline. The spiritual devotion of an Observant Dominican woman ought primarily to be practiced in and fostered by her whole community of sisters.

In the *Book of Duties*, Meyer constructs the liturgy as the source for spiritual life and spiritual life as a communal affair on a variety of levels and in a variety of ways. The main spaces for devotional contemplation are the community events of table reading and the Divine Office. Even the free time after matins and compline ought to be spent with the community rather than in private. Moreover, the table reading and the liturgy are complex affairs that require the collaboration of a team to prepare for the rest of the convent. Sisters must work together in order to create a space in which spiritual life flourishes. Aside from devout attentiveness and concentration at times when the community is assembled, Meyer is somewhat short on examples of what such communally focused devotion would entail. In the *Book of the Reformation*, however, he does provide one crowning example in the life of the Schönensteinbach choir mistress, Clara von Ostren.

Clara's Office

In Meyer's portrayal of her life, Clara von Ostren exemplifies the ideal dedication to spiritual life within the community in two ways. Initially excluded from it, she longs to be part of communal worship, and, with this desire miraculously granted, she becomes an inspired teacher who draws the young sisters into the community of the Observance. Clara came from St. Katherine's in Colmar as one of the original thirteen women to found the first Observant female cloister at Schönensteinbach. Although Clara eventually became choir mistress, her first office was marginal to convent life: she served as the *Raderin* or turnkeeper, who was responsible for communication with the world outside the convent walls. Even in strict enclosure, there were of necessity several types of openings in a cloister wall. The speaking grilles allowed the nuns to speak with friends and family outside, give confession to priests, and hear sermons, all without being seen. The largest opening was the turn or wheel, a wooden rotating device with at least three "spokes" by which food and goods might be pushed into the convent without visual contact.[110] Although the turnkeeper's primary task was to oversee the use of this device, Meyer recommends absorbing any other offices that might deal with the turn or grille into this office as well, in order to minimize the number of sisters in contact with the outside world. The turnkeeper would distribute alms, talk to the people who came to the convent on business, and chaperone the conversations other sisters had with visitors.[111] This officer served not only as the community's mediator but also as their lifeline to the world outside. All communications and materials of any kind were passed through her or in her presence.

Unfortunately, the important duty of community mediator relegated the turnkeeper to a literally liminal position within the convent. In the *Book of Duties* Meyer asserts that, unless the prioress allows otherwise, someone must be present at the turn or grille at all times, even during meals, liturgical celebrations, and the mid-afternoon rest. To this end, the turnkeeper should be provided with a little house (*hüslin*) by the turn where she could perform some useful labor for the community when nothing required her attention.[112] Meyer does not expect the turnkeeper to be with the other sisters in the workroom nor in the refectory, since she should eat her meals separately when someone is able temporarily to relieve her. Importantly for Clara's *vita*, the turnkeeper could also be permitted or even expected to miss the Office and Mass.

> [Die raderin vnd fensterin mögent] von etlichen zitten des chors sin mit der priorin vrlöb, also doch dz si des conuenten mess nit versüment, noch kein predige, vnd dar vmb so mögent die raderin vnd fensterin die seil der glöklein von jnnen vff ziehen, oder man mag besliessen von vssen die türen, die dar zu gand, zu den zitten der predige, mess vnd non schlaffe vnd vff den tag so die swestren dz heillig sacrament enpfangen hand, vs genomen villicht dz groß rad, vff dz dz man dester minre vnnützes vberlöffs haben, oder zu dem minsten, dz si doch ein lesende messe sigen teglichen hören, vnd da zwischen etliche si verwesen, die messe gehört hand oder hören werden darnach.[113]

> [Turnkeepers and fenestrarians may,] with the prioress's permission, absent themselves from some of the hours in choir, but they should not miss the community mass or any sermon, and to this end they

may pull the bell-ropes up from inside during sermons and mass, and also at the time of siesta and on days when the sisters have received holy communion; or doors leading to turns or grilles may be locked from outside, except perhaps at the main turn, to reduce the amount of unnecessary traffic. At the very least they should be able to attend a [low] mass every day while others who have already attended mass, or will do so later, take their place.[114]

Meyer begins this passage urging the sisters to close up shop during the hours and Mass so that no one, not even the turnkeeper, will have to miss the times of communal devotion. Yet by the end of the sentence (and it is one sentence in the German) he has relented so far that the minimal expectation is a low Mass daily. Should such a situation come to pass, the turnkeeper may be present only at matins and otherwise participate in none of the liturgical celebrations of the community. In this context, an omission from Humbert's *Liber de officiis* takes on significance. Humbert had allowed that a prior might give the porter permission to miss matins so that he could stay awake at the gate during the none rest.[115] Meyer omits this phrase from his translation, requiring the turnkeeper to attend matins and the superiors to find another solution for her lack of sleep. Nevertheless, absent from refectory, absent from the workroom, absent from the diurnal Office, absent even from the community's Mass, the turnkeeper would suffer such severe isolation that it is no wonder Meyer suggests that the duties be split between sisters working on a weekly or biweekly rotation, in order to ameliorate any one nun's marginalization from the community.

This context clarifies both the reasons for Clara's appointment as fenestrarian and her dissatisfaction with the post. In the *Book of the Reformation* Meyer writes that Clara had been assigned turnkeeper for two reasons; first, she was spiritual and holy and improved others with her devout words, and second, "won sy nit stym zů singen hatt [because she could not sing]."[116] This inability was a critical failing; Dominican nuns could be denied entrance to the order or accepted only as laysisters if they proved to be unable to contribute gracefully to the Divine Office.[117] From the perspective of her superiors, Clara's virtuous demeanor and poor singing voice must have been well placed at the wheel. If a sister is to be absent from the hours, it might as well be one who cannot participate fully even when there.

Although Clara humbly assumed her office, she had such devotion to the choir that being at the wheel was hard and disagreeable for her. She accordingly prays to the Virgin Mary for relief in a way that exemplifies dedication to the community. "Aber do ir dis ampt so swer was und ir begird so gross zů dem cor, zů den hailgen VII ziten zů singen, do kam sy sin mit grossem ernst ain unser lieben frowen mit andechtigen gebett [But since this office was so hard for her and her desire for the choir, to sing the holy hours, so great, she earnestly appealed to Our Dear Lady with devout prayers]."[118] Clara reminds (*ermanet*) Mary of three important voices in her life: of her own election as mother of God, of Gabriel's annunciation, and of Christ's appearance after his resurrection. Clara's prayer is so pleasing to Mary that the holy Virgin answers with one of the few miracles Meyer recounts. Clara receives such a good voice, "das sy obrysengerin gemachet ward . . . und also kam sy des amptes ab by dem rayd [that she was appointed choir mistress . . . and so she was relieved of her duty at the wheel]."[119] With the miraculous gift of a singing voice, Clara is able to leap from the marginal and excluded position of turnkeeper to the office at the very center of convent life. She becomes the person who organizes the Office. Clara's approach to rectifying her situation models devotion to the community in two ways. On the one hand, Clara's very desire to worship together with the rest of the convent promotes this ideal. Yet in her case this desire conflicts with the call to obedient service to the community as an office-holder. Clara's prayer to Mary reconciles these forms of dedication to the community, as she prays, not to be relieved of her post, but rather to have a good voice so that she might participate in the communal liturgy if permitted by her superiors.

The rest of the chapter describes Clara's virtues and devoted service to the community as choir mistress. Meyer specifically mentions that she zealously monitored "daz alle bůcher wol und gerechtiklich wurdent corrigiert [that all the books were well and rightly corrected]."[120] Her greatest passion, however, and the activity over which Meyer lingers, is teaching the young sisters to sing the Office.

> Sy hatt sunderlich ernstlichen, grossen fliss, daz die jungen swöstren wol lernentent singen und alles, daz zů dem götlichen dienst not ist, zů wissen und zů konent, dar umm daz sy dem cor nütz wurdint und got den heren ordenlich loben und eren möchtent als billich ist. Zu den vigilien in dem werck huss und zů dem gemaynen gebett und zů dem gebett, daz an priorin uf setzet, hatt sy gar grossen fliss und mit allen tugenden zoch sy die iungen swöstren gar mynsamklich dar zu.[121]

> She was especially and very seriously diligent that the young sisters learned to sing, know, and be able to do everything that is needed for the Divine Office, so that they would be useful in the choir and be able to praise and honor the Lord God in an orderly way as is just. She had great zeal for the vigils in the workroom, for the common prayer, and for prayers imposed by the prioress, and in all virtue she lovingly instructed the young sisters herein.

According to Meyer, Clara is devoted less to the Office itself than to her office as choir mistress. Meyer does not describe her as one of the sisters who goes into ecstasy in the choir. Nor does she experience liturgical visions, display especial devotion to high feasts, or model devotional interpretation of liturgical text. Instead, Clara's past choral uselessness inspires her to become a great educator, devoted not to the Office as such but rather to training a community capable of ordered and correct performance. This zeal extends beyond the Mass and hours to include instruction in all the forms of communal prayer in which young sisters and novices ought to be instructed. Prayers in the workroom, the times of communal contemplation after matins and compline, and even the memorial services imposed by the prioress are all important components of the community's life of prayer, in which it is imperative that all Observant sisters participate. Clara's devotion to the Office expresses itself in dedicated instruction of the community that performs it.

Meyer composes one of the longest *vitae* in the entire *Book of the Reformation* for Clara, dedicating an unusual amount of space to extolling her virtues and describing her devotions. Throughout the eight chapters of her *vita*, Meyer continually emphasizes her role as teacher. She convinces her biological sister to give up her dancing lessons and join the order,[122] she allegorizes the various parts of the Dominican habit with episodes from Christ's passion,[123] and she associates each note of the musical scale with a virtue and moment in Christ's life at which he displayed that virtue.[124] Although in her capacity as choir mistress, the Office and musical education represent a particular focus, Clara offers spiritual interpretations of such banal things as what the nuns wear and how many windows are in the dormitory, seeking to infuse every aspect of the convent's life with devotional significance. Furthermore, the devotional exercises she teaches to the young sisters are so effective and memorable, Meyer writes, "daz die selben swöstren, dy sy gelert hatt, mir noch gar wol kundent sagen mer den XVII jar nach irem tod [that the same sisters whom she had taught could still easily tell me about it more than seventeen years after her death]."[125] Clara's devotion to the Dominican order and Office finds expression in her passion for teaching.

As the choir mistress of the first Observant women's house in Teutonia, Clara von Ostren occupies an important position of exemplarity in Meyer's *Book of the Reformation*. He has recorded the lives of these first Observant sisters, he explains, "won sy nit allain des wirdigen closters Stainbach, sunder aller reformierten swöstren clöster prediger ordens in tüschen landen hailges fundament und gruntfest und kosper, edel, lebidig stayn gewessen sind [because they are the holy ground, foundation, and priceless, noble, living stone not only of the worthy convent in Steinbach but also of all the reformed houses of the sisters of the Order of Preachers in German lands]."[126] Recording the way Clara educated young sisters in the Office and shaped their devotional lives places her at the origin and center of a much larger and ever-growing community. Meyer appoints Clara choir mistress over all reformed Observant sisters, present and future.

In both the *Book of the Reformation* and the *Book of Duties*, Meyer presents community as the most important factor in Observant life and spirituality and liturgical ceremony as the framework that defines, structures, and holds the Observant community together. In the *Book of the Reformation*, Meyer provides a short list of eight pieces of general advice for Observant communities. Meyer admonishes superiors to be responsible in their duties and to practice mercy in punishing their charges. He urges his readers to avoid strife and discord, since a kingdom divided against itself shall fall (Matthew 12:25), and finally, "daz der götlich dienst flissklich volbracht werd, nit gemynret noch verkürtzet [that the Divine Office be zealously accomplished, neither lessened nor abbreviated]."[127] For Meyer, liturgical celebration does not present a distraction from the true contemplative goal of the order nor an opportunity for private spirituality or contemplation. As Hamburger notes, "Meyer, in contrast, offered his female readers a countervailing model of unimpassioned communitarian cult practice in conformity with the rule."[128] For Meyer, as for the authors I examined in previous chapters, the spiritual lives of Dominican sisters take root in the order's *forma vitae* and grow with the nourishment of the Divine Office.

The immediate community of enclosed sisters overseeing and participating in the Office constitutes only the most important and intimate of a series of concentric circles. The elaborate rituals of enclosure which Meyer recounts in his chronicles demonstrate the continuing importance of the surrounding laity to the enclosed Observant women through their paradoxical separation from and dependence upon them. For Meyer, the Office engages the whole community in a collaborative performance that strengthens and defines their communal identity within their cloister, within their city, and within the Dominican order. Following Meyer's recommendations in the *Book of Duties* and the exemplary lives from his chronicles, an Observant Dominican sister would join a community constituted by ordered practice, rooted in the past, and committed to building the order's future. Through observing the Office according to the Rule, Constitutions, and ordinances, inspired by the exemplary lives of fourteenth-century sisters and directed by the sermons and treatises heard at table reading, an Observant sister pursued a spiritual self-formation that Meyer believed could reform the Dominican order.

Conclusion

From the early decades of the Dominican order, the Divine Office had been considered a fundamental part of regular observance. Since Dominican nuns did not preach, the liturgical regulations in their Constitutions were altered from those of the friars to reflect its greater importance in their lives and spiritual devotion. Yet the perceived loss of Latin fluency among the fourteenth-century sisters meant that, in the eyes of the Observant reformers, the women were robbed of the focus of their piety. Within the Observant movement, both friars and nuns were enjoined to follow the Dominican Office without embellishment or exception, but the women required special effort. Works such as the Cassian translation sought to reanimate cloistered life by spiritualizing its practices and reorienting religious practice around liturgical prayer.

The avid transmission of fourteenth-century German-language Dominican spiritual literature played in important role in this project, as well. In the eyes of Teutonia's reformers, German fourteenth-century spiritual literature both witnessed to an original fervor and inspired readers to its imitation. Seuse's *Vita* and the sisterbooks provided narrative models for liturgical piety, while Tauler's sermons explicated the significance of the cycle of feasts. The Observant reformers additionally worked to inspire renewed devotion among the women by expanding their educational basis, translating liturgical and regular texts into the vernacular, and thereby imbuing the practice of liturgical performance itself with new spiritual meaning. For the Observance, strict

adherence to legislation was not an end in itself but should reignite a devotional ardor that they believed had animated the order's founders. Fifteenth-
century reformers, such as Johannes Meyer and St. Katherine's librarian Kunigunde Niklas, recruited fourteenth-century Dominican literature that shared
their vision of the order's *forma vitae*, its legislation, and its liturgy, as a
wellspring of spiritual devotion.

NOTES

INTRODUCTION

Note to epigraph: Vetter, ed., *Töß*, 33.

1. Ebner, *Engelthal*, 6–7.

2. Bynum, *Fragmentation and Redemption*, 181–238.

3. I will address the fraught issue of Latinity below, but for a directly relevant example, see Ehrenschwendtner, "Puellae Litteratae."

4. Ochsenbein, "Latein und Deutsch," 48.

5. Lindgren, *Sensual Encounters*, 99.

6. Hindsley, *The Mystics of Engelthal*, xvii–xx.

7. Williams-Krapp, "Henry Suso's 'Vita'."

8. Winston-Allen, *Convent Chronicles*; Uffmann, *Wie in einem Rosengarten*. See also Hirbodian and Kurz, eds., *Die Chronik der Magdalena Kremerin*; Woodford, *Nuns as Historians*.

9. von Loe, *Teutonia*, 3, 6. For an extended discussion, see Tugwell, "The First Dominican Provinces."

10. Hinnebusch, *The History of the Dominican Order*, 1:377. There is no fully satisfactory explanation why the Dominican life appealed to the women of this region so much more than elsewhere in Europe, but the *locus classicus* is Grundmann, *Religious Movements*, 89–137.

11. von Loe, *Teutonia*, 7; Heimann, "Der Umfang," esp. 236–37. The division of the provinces of Saxony and Teutonia was evidently conducted with an eye to splitting the men's houses evenly but without regard for the location and number of the women's houses. In 1303 Saxony encompassed 45 men's houses—about equal to Teutonia's 47—but only 9 convents of women. See von Loe, *Saxonia*, 11–12; Hinnebusch, *The History of the Dominican Order*, 1:377.

12. Colmar, in Alsace, was reformed in 1389. Barthelmé, *La réforme*, 28; Wittmer, "Berceau."

13. Raymond of Capua, the former confessor of Catherine of Siena and Master General of the order, died in Nürnberg in 1399 and was buried there before the altar of the Dominican church. Bock, "Nürnberger Predigerkloster," 154.

14. Roest, "Observant Reform," 450; Winston-Allen, *Convent Chronicles*, 81–96; Löhr, *Teutonia*, 17–18.

15. Winston-Allen, "Making Manuscripts."

16. Willing, *Bibliothek*, esp. LXXI–CXIV. For their reform, see Steinke, *Paradiesgarten*. For descriptions of the characteristics of manuscripts produced by the Nürnberg sisters, see Carroll, "Subversive Obedience," 716–17; Sauer, "Zwischen Kloster und Welt."

17. Willing, *Bibliothek*, XII.

18. Willing, *Konventsbuch*, 169.

19. For broad, international interventions in the area of religious women's literacies, see the three volumes edited by Blanton et al., *Nuns' Literacies in Medieval Europe*. These volumes include multiple essays on religious women in both Northern and Southern German regions.

20. Mengis, *Schreibende Frauen*; Willing, *Bibliothek*; Thali, *Beten, Schreiben, Lesen*, 243–85; Rüther, "Schreibbetrieb, Bücheraustausch und Briefwechsel"; Schromm, *Kirchheim am Ries*; Fechter, *Deutsche Handschriften*; Lentes, "Gebetbuch und Gebärde"; Rüther and Schiewer, "Predigthandschriften."

21. Ehrenschwendtner, *Bildung*, 86–87. For more, see also Ehrenschwendtner, "Bildungswesen" and Ehrenschwendtner, "Puellae Litteratae."

22. "Es ist och gewon wenn sy ain nouitzen in wend nemen, so lasend sy sy vor etwz ain wenig lernen latin lesen an dem psalter, oder etwz singen als die hand, oder soluasiern darnach. Vnd aini zit hant, aber vrsach der lernung halb lassend sy kaini da vssen, so lang das sy aller ding vsgelerni, sunder sy lerend sy selb innen im closter singen vnd lesen. Aber kain swöster lasend sy by inen lernen exponiern im closter. [It is also their custom when they want to accept a novice that they first have her learn a little Latin reading from the psalter or singing something by the hand or solmizing from it. They have some time, but for the sake of the instruction, they do not leave any outside for so long that she would learn everything. Instead, they teach them singing and reading inside the convent themselves. But they do not let any sister learn exposition in the convent.]" Willing, *Konventsbuch*, 650. I have lightly altered her transcription, since I read the manuscript differently. The sisters continue their liturgical education within the convent but do not learn "exponiern" or exposition, which I take to entail grammatical analysis. It is also interesting to note that new entrants must read musical notation or sing "by the hand." On the Guidonian hand and its uses in musical education, see Berger, "The Guidonian Hand."

23. Mengis, *Schreibende Frauen*, 67–69; Schlotheuber, "Bücher und Bildung," 248. Clarissan choir nuns were also expected to be literate upon entrance. Roest, "Education and Religious Formation," 52; Roest, *Order and Disorder*, 288. For the city schools, see Kammeier-Nebel, "Frauenbildung im Kaufmannsmilieu"; Endres, "Das Schulwesen in Franken."

24. Ehrenschwendtner, *Bildung*, 92–99.

25. Mengis, *Schreibende Frauen*, 69–75.

26. Willing, *Bibliothek*, XLI.

27. Mengis, *Schreibende Frauen*, 72; Ehrenschwendtner, *Bildung*, 313.

28. Translations were undertaken very early in Alsace. Sack, "Bruchstücke von Regel und Konstitutionen." This older translation rendered a different version of the Augustinian Rule, not the one that was binding for Dominican women. The correct version was translated for St. Katherine's in Nürnberg in 1431 (shortly after their 1428 reform). Engler, *Regelbuch*, 143–45.

29. "Eine Hebung der lateinischen Sprachkenntnisse (v. a. in den Frauenklöstern) war kein Ziel der Ordensreform; vielmehr passte man sich der Situation in den Frauenklöstern an, die durch nachlassende Lateinkenntnisse der Schwestern gekennzeichnet war [Elevation of the Latin language abilities (above all in women's convents) was not a goal of the reform; instead they adapted to the situation in the women's convents, which was characterized by decreasing Latin literacy]." Mengis, *Schreibende Frauen*, 70.

30. Schlotheuber, "Bücher und Bildung," 249. She cites Grundmann, "Litteratusillitteratus." See also Briggs, "Literacy, Reading and Writing"; Bäuml, "Varieties and Consequences."

31. Schlotheuber, "Bücher und Bildung," 257–61.

32. Hamburger and Schlotheuber, "Books in Women's Hands"; Hamburger et al., *Liturgical Life and Latin Learning*.

33. Brandis, ed., *Weltbild und Lebenswirklichkeit*; Mecham, *Sacred Communities*; Hascher-Burger et al., *Liturgie und Reform*; Kruse, ed., *Rosenkränze und Seelengärten*; Koldau, ed., *Passion und Ostern*; Kruppa and Wilke, eds., *Kloster und Bildung*; Schlotheuber, *Klostereintritt und Bildung*; Signori, ed., *Lesen, Schreiben, Sticken und Erinnern*. Cynthia Cyrus provides a sweeping overview of scribal culture in German women's communities in *The Scribes for Women's Convents*. Alison Beach's work on women, writing, and reform provides a good source for comparison but focuses on a period prior to the foundation of the Dominican order and therefore is not directly applicable. Still, see Beach, *Women as Scribes* and the studies collected in Beach, ed., *Manuscripts and Monastic Culture*.

34. Mengis, *Schreibende Frauen*, 73–74; Ehrenschwendtner, *Bildung*, 127, 147–48. Eva Schlotheuber remarks that the Latin ability of a community could only be as good as their *magistra*, and in the absence of a good teacher a convent's literacy could suffer dramatically. Schlotheuber, "Sprachkompetenz und Lateinvermittlung," 68–69.

35. Bell, *What Nuns Read*, 60.

36. Zieman, "Reading, Singing and Understanding," 105–6.

37. Yardley, "The Musical Education of Young Girls," 51–52.

38. Nürnberg Stadtbibliothek Cod. Cent. VII, 82, fol. 1r–1v. Schneider, *Handschriften*, 398–99.

39. A statement to the same effect is found among the writings of the reformed Benedictine nuns in Ebstorf: "Magnum tedium est, stare in choro, legere, cantare, et non intelligere [It is very boring to stand in choir, read, sing, and not understand]." Cited in Lähnemann, "Per organa," 401.

40. Jones, "Rekindling the Light."

CHAPTER 1. THE OFFICE IN DOMINICAN LEGISLATION, 1216–1303

Note to epigraph: *Année Dominicaine*, 888.

1. "De florido orto ecclesie, rose quedam in Alemania prodiere, que sicut specie sua et pulchritudine alliciunt prope positos, ita etiam suavissimo odore suo attrahunt in remotis partibus constitutos. Sane rosas istas esse dicimus sorores quasdam ordinis Sti Augustini quas olim in preclaro rosario roseo videlicet ordine vestro, felix ille plantaverat ortulanus pie recordationis dominus Innocentius papa quartus. . . . Verum licet predicte sorores priusquam tempus putationis veniret, a prefato rosario fuerint amputate per quamdam litteram ejusdem domini Innocentii priores suas litteras revocantem. [From the flowery garden of the church, certain roses blossomed forth in Germany, which by their splendor and beauty attract those near, just as they draw by their sweet odor those placed remotely. Truly we say these roses are the sisters of the Order of St. Augustine who once were in the illustrious ruddy rose garden that is your order. That happy gardener of blessed memory, the lord Pope Innocent IV, planted them. . . . Nevertheless, before the time of their harvest had come, the aforesaid sisters were ripped from this rose garden by a certain letter of this same Lord Innocent, which revoked his earlier letters.]" *Année Dominicaine*, 888.

2. Galbraith, *Constitution*, 181–83.

3. Decker, *Stellung des Predigerordens*.

4. Tanner, ed., *Decrees of the Ecumenical Councils*, 1:242.

5. Smith, "Prouille, Madrid, Rome," 347.

6. "Oportuit ergo talem eligere regulam quae non haberet aliqua quae contrariarentur hujusmodi statuendis, sed talis esset cui hujusmodi convenienter superadderentur et aptarentur: talis autem est regula beati Augustini. Cum enim pauca contineat, nisi spiritualia quaedam et quae ratio dictat mandata, quod non invenitur in aliis regulis, convenienter possunt ei apponi statuta omnia pertinentia ad statum praedicationis [It was therefore right to choose such a rule that would not have anything contradictory to that which was to be established but rather one to which these things could easily be added and applied: such a one is the Rule of St. Augustine. Since it contains little (except certain spiritual matters and those things which reason mandates) that is not found in other rules, all statutes pertaining to the situation of preaching may easily be added to it]." Humbert of Romans, *Opera de vita regulari*, I:51. John Van Engen sees the order's flexible legal culture as one of its innovations and strengths. Van Engen, "From Canons to Preachers."

7. On communal life according to the Augustinian Rule, see Schreiner, "Communio"; Schreiner, "Ein Herz und eine Seele."

8. Lappin, "From Osma to Bologna"; Hinnebusch, *The History of the Dominican Order*, 1:145–68.

9. Verheijen, *La règle de Saint Augustin*, 420–21.

10. This was an ancient and persistent concern among religious communities. Fulton, "Praying with Anselm at Admont"; Constable, "The Concern for Sincerity."

11. Whereas the propositions of General Chapters required ratification by two subsequent General Chapters, the decisions of a Most General Chapter (*capitulum generalissimum*) went immediately into effect. The Constitutions adopted by the Most General Chapter of 1228 are edited by Thomas, *De oudste constituties*, 309–69.

12. Simon Tugwell treats the development of the procedure for approving changes to Dominican legislation in Tugwell, "The Early Development of the Second Distinction of the Constitutions."

13. Galbraith, *Constitution*, 181–84.

14. It is not certain what the order was using before this time. They were constitutionally permitted to use the Rite of the region in which they happened to find themselves singing Office publicly, but it seems they must have had a special Rite, as well. For an overview of theories regarding the early Rite of the order, see Gleeson, "The Pre-Humbertian Liturgical Sources Revisited."

15. Bonniwell, *History*, 77–79, 82.

16. Ibid., 83–84. For a series of studies on Humbert's exemplar or prototype, see Boyle and Gy, eds., *Aux origines de la liturgie dominicaine*.

17. Creytens, "L'ordinaire," 128–30.

18. Grundmann, *Religious Movements*, 102–4; Sack, "Bruchstücke"; Hinnebusch, *The History of the Dominican Order*, I:380–81; Barth, "Die Rolle des Dominikanerinnenklosters St. Marx." Although these statutes have a place in the history of Dominican legislation, I agree with Tugwell that imposing the statutes and entrusting the communities to the care of Dominican friars "did not turn the Magdalens into Dominicans," not by Humbert's encyclical in 1259 and not by Cardinal Giovanni Boccamazza's letter in 1287. Tugwell, "Were the Magdalen nuns," here 58.

19. Creytens, "Les constitutions primitives des soeurs."

20. *Litterae encyclicae magistrorum generalium*, 51; Hinnebusch, *The History of the Dominican Order*, I:381.

21. Boyle, "A Material Consideration," 41–42; *Bullarium* 1:481, 486. Klaus Schreiner discusses Humbert's reliance on textual precision in establishing uniformity within the order in "Verschriftlichung," 40–42.

22. There was, however, some room for tailoring it. There were different versions of the Augustinian Rule in circulation, and, as Claudia Engler has shown on the basis of Observant manuscripts, the female branch of the Dominican Order used a different redaction from that of the friars. The differences do not affect the liturgical stipulations. Engler, *Regelbuch*, 133–39.

23. "Liber Constitutionum (1256)," 36–37.

24. The 1242 General Chapter forbade any kind of "discantus," and the 1250 General Chapter prohibited friars from singing "in octava." *Acta Capitulorum* I:23, 53; Hinnebusch, *The History of the Dominican Order*, 1:352.

25. Smith, "Apostolic Vocation," 16–18, 21; Smith, "Literate Practices," 86–87.

26. "Liber Constitutionum Sororum," 346.

27. Ibid., 339.

28. Anne Bagnall Yardley considers a similar injunction from Syon Abbey, in which the choir mistress is instructed to intone and direct the liturgical song in a way that neither strains nor bores her singers. Yardley, "Musical Education," 55.

29. "Liber Constitutionum (1256)," 36.

30. *Acta Capitulorum*, 1:150.

31. "Liber Constitutionum Sororum," 339.

32. "Praeterea quamvis habeat constitutio, quod horas de beata virgine in choro debeant dicere, ratam tamen habens ordinationem magistri in contrarium, hoc attente requiro, quod audito primo signo ad matutinas omnes in communi dormitorio quiescentes surgant et binae ac binae vel tres simul stando dicant matutinas de beata virgine distincte et aperte [Although there is a constitution that says they should say the hours of the Blessed Virgin in the choir, there being nevertheless an authoritative order of the master to the contrary, I thoughtfully require that upon hearing the first call to matins, all who are resting in the common dormitory get up and standing two by two or three together say the matins of the blessed virgin clearly and openly]." Ritzinger and Scheeben, "Beiträge," 27.

33. "Liber Constitutionum Sororum," 339.

34. Johannes Meyer points this out in the *Buch der Ersetzung* (*The Supplement*, written in 1455). "Wöl so ist wor, dz die swester clöster nit bedörffen haben in sunderheit die zwey bücher, die do heissent Ewangeliarium vnd Epistolarium vnd ist gnůg, dz sÿ haben in dem meß bůch, do der priester meß jnnen singet, die Ewangelien, die Epistlen, prophetigen, Jte missa est, vnd Benedicamus geschriben, wie man sÿ singen sol, won doch gemeinlichen bÿ den swestren clöstren der priester dis alles selber singen můß [It is true that the women's convents do not need, in particular, the two books called evangeliary and epistolary. It is enough that the missal from which the priest sings Mass should have the gospels, the epistles, the prophets, ite missa est and benedicamus, and how one should sing these, since in the women's houses it is usually the priest who must do this all himself]." Freiburg im Breisgau, Stadtsarchiv, B₁ H 108, f. 185v. (HMML 43443) Normally, deacons and subdeacons would have used the evangeliary and epistolary to perform their part of Mass. In a women's convent, the priest would have had to perform all these roles himself and required a special format of missal that included the parts usually delegated. I thank Fr. Innocent Smith, OP for this point. The missals from which the priest sang Mass would nevertheless have been considered the property of the convent. St. Katherine's in Nürnberg owned five, as well as a presumably superfluous epistolary. Willing, *Bibliothek*, XV–XVI. See also Naughton, "Friars and Their Books," 92; Naughton, "Manuscripts from the Dominican Monastery of Saint-Louis de Poissy," 182.

35. "Liber Constitutionum Sororum," 347.

36. Creytens, "L'ordinaire," 117.

37. This situation persisted for many communities with fraught relationships to their male branch. The Northern German Cistercian convents of Medingen, Wienhausen, and

Derneburg only adopted the Cistercian Rite upon their reform in the late fifteenth century, up until which point they had been using the Rite of the secular priests who ministered to them. Hascher-Burger, Lähnemann, and Braun-Niehr, *Liturgie und Reform*, 91. See also Uffmann, *Wie in einem Rosengarten*, 198–202.

38. The only document that perhaps could be interpreted as constraining the sisters to use Humbert's Office is Clement's bull, which commands that "ordinatio huiusmodi per uniuersas partes ipsius ordinis debeat obseruari [an order like this should be observed throughout all parts of this same order]." Although the wording clearly is intended to apply geographically to all Dominican provinces, one could perhaps argue for applying it to both branches. Boyle, "Material Consideration," 42.

39. Ritzinger and Scheeben, "Beiträge," 27. I thank Fr. Innocent Smith, OP for his observations on the foregoing. He takes the absence of a specification in the sisters' Constitutions to imply use of Humbert's Rite, in which case these Teutonic ordinances would codify something that was already implicitly expected.

40. In her survey of thirteenth- and fourteenth-century liturgical manuscripts from Southern German Dominican convents, Erika Lauren Lindgren found that the vast majority conformed to Humbert's exemplar. Lindgren, *Sensual Encounters*, 134–42. Despite admonitions that individual nuns and convents were not to express partiality toward particular saints, regional devotions and variations were common. Joan Naughton writes that the Dominican nuns of Poissy celebrated their founder Louis IX at the rank of totum duplex, the highest possible liturgical honor, even though the order had instituted the feast as simplex. Naughton, "Books for a Dominican Nuns' Choir," 72; Bonniwell, *History*, 201. For a Northern German example that departs from the exemplar, see Fassler and Hamburger, "The Desert in Paradise."

41. "The religious women's competence in languages and their literary scope can thus not be deduced only from the normative sources, but also have to be critically assessed and worked up concretely from historical tradition," Hamburger and Schlotheuber, "Books in Women's Hands," 134.

42. Marie-Luise Ehrenschwendtner and Simone Mengis follow Claudia Opitz in citing the San Sisto Rule for the Magdalenes beside the 1259 Constitutions. Opitz, "Erziehung und Bildung," 74; Ehrenschwendtner, *Bildung*, 125; Mengis, *Schreibende Frauen*, 63–64.

43. Schlotheuber, "Bücher und Bildung," 243; Hamburger and Schlotheuber, "Books in Women's Hands," 133–34.

44. Unlike Humbert's *De tribus votis* (On the Three Vows), *De eruditione* was not translated and disseminated for reading. Whether any of the statements from it were actually repeated in orally delivered sermons is unknowable. Kaeppeli, *Scriptores*, II:287–88.

45. Smith, "Literate Practices."

46. "Liber Constitutionum Sororum," 343.

47. "Dicant autem in profestis diebus pro matutinis viginti octo pater noster. In festis autem nouem leccionum, quadraginta. Pro uesperis, quatuordecim. Loco preciosa, tria. Pro benediccione mense, unum. Post mensam pro graciis, tria [However, on ferial days they should say twenty-eight *pater nosters*. On feasts of nine lections, forty. At vespers, fourteen. Instead of the preciosa, three. For the table blessing, one. After table, for grace, three]." "Liber Constitutionum Sororum," 343.

48. The clause is found in the chapter on novices in the friars' Constitutions but restricts application to novices: "Item nouitii infra tempus probationis sue in psalmodia et officio diuino studeant diligenter." "Liber Constitutionum (1256)," 55. The men's Constitutions also required continuing education even for those who did not go on to regional *studia* or the university, but do not link this to "study" of the Office. Mulchahey, *First the Bow*, 133.

49. "Liber Constitutionum Sororum," 340.

50. "Si qua designatum sibi legendi uel cantandi officium, non attente compleuerit: uel responsorium, uel antiphonam, uel aliud inceptura chorum turbauerit. Si qua male legendo, uel cantando offendens: non statim se coram omnibus humiliauerit. Si liber in quo legendum est in collacione, uel in capitulo, uel in ecclesia cuiusquam neglectu defuerit. [If any does not attentively perform the office she has been assigned to read or sing and disrupts the choir in intoning the responsory, antiphon, or other chant. If any offends by reading or singing badly, she is not to be humiliated immediately in front of everyone. If the book to be read from in collation, in chapter, or in church is missing because of her neglect.]" Ibid., 344. Compare, for example, with Syon, where the offending sister was expected to acknowledge her own mistake and humble herself immediately. Yardley, "Musical Education," 61–62.

51. Smith, "Literate Practices," 89.

52. "Liber Constitutionum Sororum," 348.

53. Creytens, "Montargis," 75.

54. Ibid., 80.

55. Simon, "Statuts de Marie-Madeleine," 165. Julie Ann Smith notes that the two German translations consulted by the editor reverse the prohibition and encourage learning grammar. Smith, "Literate Practices," 87. These translations, however, are from the eighteenth century and thus have no bearing on this discussion. Simon, "Statuts de Marie-Madeleine," 154.

56. "Liber Constitutionum (1256)," 172.

57. Ibid., 51; Mulchahey, *First the Bow*, 81–85.

58. Ehrenschwendtner, *Bildung*, 125.

59. Ritzinger and Scheeben, "Beiträge," 33.

60. "Poterit tamen quandoque aliquid legi in laborerio vel exponi de interpretatione regulae, de admonitionibus magistrorum et provincialium." Ibid., 37.

61. Ibid.

62. Historical evidence of this practice survives. See, for example, Marti, "Schwester Elisabeth."

CHAPTER 2. DETACHMENT, ORDER, AND OBSERVANCE IN JOHANNES
TAULER AND HEINRICH SEUSE

Note to epigraph: Sermon Vetter 63, *PT*, 342.

1. For the use of vernacular sermons as devotional reading material, see Schiewer, "Sermons for Nuns"; Rüther and Schiewer, "Predigthandschriften." Debra Stoudt argues that sermons were received more frequently and intensively as written texts and that oral preaching was less important in the women's spiritual lives. Stoudt, "The Influence of Preaching."

2. Whether or not Tauler also preached to the laity, the sermons that survive were directed to male and female religious. All of the sermons I refer to in this chapter were used as table readings at St. Katherine's in Nürnberg, so I will consider them as if addressed to women, regardless of the original audience. Gnädinger, *Johannes Tauler*, 117. For more thorough studies of reception and transmission, see Blumrich, "Überlieferung"; Mayer, *"Vulgata"-Fassung*.

3. Sauer, "Zwischen Kloster und Welt," 114–15.

4. *MBK* III/3:615. St. Katherine's also owned at least four more copies of the *Little Book of Eternal Wisdom* and several manuscripts with Seuse's liturgical prayer cycle, the Cursus of Eternal Wisdom.

5. Willing, *Bibliothek*, LXVI.

6. Williams-Krapp, "Henry Suso's 'Vita,'" 47.

7. "In contrast to traditional scholarship, recent feminist studies, on the other hand, frequently recast women's literary 'simplicity' more positively as an example of 'body-centered' spirituality. . . . Whereas 'simplicity' connotes inferiority for pre-feminist scholars, 'embodiedness' now becomes the marker of medieval female autonomy. . . . The hermeneutic battle has been straightforward: One interpretive model tries to prove the superiority of male authorship, the other that of female authorship." Wiethaus, "Thieves and Carnivals," 211.

8. Charlotte Radler provides a concise description of the differences between the three friars. Radler, "Meister Eckhart, Johannes Tauler, and Henry Suso."

9. As the disciple learns in the Little Book of Truth, "Ich heisse den grund den usqual und den ursprung, us dem die usflüsse entspringent [I call the ground the font and the source from which the outpourings spring]." *DS*, 330. For translations of the *Exemplar*, I have consulted Frank Tobin's edition (*The Exemplar, with Two German Sermons*) but have generally preferred to do my own in order to stay closer to the wording of the German.

10. Bibliothèque Nationale et Universitaire de Strasbourg, Ms. 2929, f. 82r, https://w1.bnu.fr/Bibliotheque%20Virtuelle/MS/cgi-bin/include/showimage.asp?image=/msrhenane_image/MS.2929/2929_169.jpg, accessed February 10, 2017. See Hamburger, *Visual and Visionary*, 200–202; McGinn, "Theologians as Trinitarian Iconographers," 200–201.

11. McGinn, *Harvest*, 232.

12. Ibid., 257–58.

13. Wyser, "Taulers Terminologie vom Seelengrund," 344.

14. McGinn, *Harvest*, 255–56. For a systematic appraisal of Tauler's use of *gemuete*, see also Gnädinger, *Johannes Tauler*, 241–48.

15. Hollywood, *Soul as Virgin Wife*, 169.

16. Hollywood describes Eckhart's theory of action from the ground as an "apophatic ethics." Ibid., 193–94.

17. Susanne Bernhardt points out that even within these works discussions of *Gelassenheit* fall overwhelmingly into certain chapters only. Bernhardt, "Implizite Pragmatik."

18. *Vita*, prologue, *DS*, 7.

19. The debate about whether or not each anecdote of the *Vita* represents a historical event is moot, since medieval people had an attitude toward history and self-narrative different from ours. For a summary of the debate about the "reality" of the *Vita*, see McGinn, *Harvest*, 202–3. For an excellent problematization of selfhood and narrative in the Middle Ages, see the first chapters of Schmitt, *The Conversion of Herman the Jew*.

20. Indeed, Seuse's *Vita* provides the attribution of the Töss sisterbook to Stagel. *Vita*, ch. 33, *DS*, 97.

21. Walter Blank provides a table outlining the structure of the *Vita* in Blank, "Seuses Vita," 289. Jeffrey Hamburger confirms that this division was perceived as such by medieval readers, since historiated initials fall at these points in the manuscript. Hamburger, *Visual and Visionary*, 272–76.

22. Bernhardt, "Implizite Pragmatik," 115.

23. *Vita*, ch. 16, *DS*, 43. Several scholars have commented on the unusually high degree of similarity between Seuse's practices of mortification and those of Elsbeth von Oye. It is usually taken to be an explicit correction of Elsbeth von Oye's persistence in physical castigation. See, for exaample, Williams-Krapp, "Nucleus totius perfectionis," 417–19.

24. "Das Defizitäre an diesen äußeren Bußübungen besteht allerdings darin, daß noch immer der Eigenwille vorherrscht, wogegen das Ziel eigentlich die Einswerdung des menschlichen Willens mit dem göttlichen sein soll [The deficiency of these external penitentiary practices is that self-will still predominates, whereas the goal should actually be the union of human with divine will]." Ulrich, "Zur Bedeutung des Leidens," 127.

25. *Vita*, ch. 6, *DS*, 23.

26. Kieckhefer, *Unquiet Souls*, 50–88, esp. 60–62.

27. For example, *Vita*, ch. 29, *DS*, 85–86.

28. The incident occupies the entirety of chapter 38, but the lament is to be found on 127.

29. Bernhardt, "Implizite Pragmatik," 127–28.

30. Ibid., 124.

31. Büchlein der ewigen Weisheit, ch. 9, *DS*, 232.

32. The allegorical figures of Wisdom and Truth are represented as female, according to their grammatical gender, but are associated with Christ. For the instability of gender paradigms in Seuse's writings, see Newman, *God and the Goddesses*, 206–22; Newman, "Henry Suso and the Medieval Devotion to Christ the Goddess."

33. Buch der Wahrheit, prologue, *DS*, 326.

34. For a more thorough exposition of this chapter, see Haas, *Kunst rechter Gelassen-heit*, 263–65.

35. McGinn, *Harvest*, 120–22.

36. Barbara Newman elegantly outlines the shifts in spiritual meaning of the term *annihilatio*, showing that even this term did not always entail mystical self-abnegation, but was also deployed in contexts of Eucharistic union or humility as an *imitatio Christi*. Newman, "Annihilation and Authorship."

37. Buch der Wahrheit, ch. 4, *DS*, 334–35.

38. This scheme had been adopted by Aquinas, who is more likely Seuse's source. Kretzmann, "Philosophy of Mind."

39. Buch der Wahrheit, ch. 4, *DS*, 336.

40. Ibid., 335.

41. Früh, "Zeichen und Kontext," 154–58.

42. Haas, *Gottleiden, Gottlieben*, 145. Richard Kieckhefer also draws the conclusion that Tauler exploits "the double sense of *leiden*, which corresponds to that of the Latin *pati*. These verbs can refer either to the endurance of pain, physical or mental, or to a state of passivity in which one accepts whatever befalls one, whether it is painful or plea-surable." Kieckhefer, "The Notion of Passivity," 208.

43. Früh, "Zeichen und Kontext," 166.

44. Enders, "Selbsterfahrung als Gotteserfahrung," 657.

45. Sermon Vetter 1, *PT*, 9–10.

46. Eckhart uses metaphors of sight and cognition much more frequently and more elaborately than Tauler does. For a recent study of this metaphor in Eckhart's sermons, see Gottschall, "Dô gedâhte ich ein glîchnisse."

47. Sermon Vetter 1, *PT*, 10. See also "das ist wol ein notrede das man dem worte ze hörende nút bas enkan gedienen denne mit stillin und mit losende, mit swigende; sol Got sprechen, alle ding müssen swigen [it must be repeated that, in order to hear the word, one cannot serve better than with silence and with letting-go, by being silent; if God should speak, all things must be silent]." Sermon Vetter 43, *PT*, 181–82.

48. McGinn, *Harvest*, 269.

49. *Ordinarium*, 151. The Introit in its entirety is: *Dum medium silentium tenerent omnia, et nox in suo cursu medium iter haberet, omnipotens sermo tuus, Domine de coelis a regalibus sedibus venit.*

50. Cabaniss, "Wisdom 18:14f."

51. Sermon Vetter 1, *PT*, 11–12.

52. Theisen, *Predigt und Gottesdienst.*

53. Theisen, "Tauler und die Liturgie," 415.

54. Ibid., 417.

55. The other major sermon cycle used for table readings there, the voluminous collection of sermons by the secular priest Albrecht Fleischmann, shares Tauler's emphasis on the liturgical cycle over the "microcontext" of a given Mass. "In den Prothemen seiner

Predigten spricht Fleischmann auch über die Bedeutung des Kirchenjahrs für die Gläubigen. Er macht immer wieder deutlich, daß jeder Sonntag eine besondere Funktion hat, der die von der Kirche sorgfältig ausgewählten Perikopen entsprechen. [In the prologues of his sermons, Fleischman also speaks of the meaning of the liturgical year for believers. He repeatedly emphasizes that every Sunday has a special function, which is reflected in the pericopes carefully selected by the Church.]" Wrigge and Eisermann, "Albrecht Fleischmann," 210.

56. See, exemplarily, the two chapters on Seuse in Hamburger, *Visual and Visionary*, but also van Aelst, "Visualizing the Spiritual"; Rozenski, "Von Aller Bilden Bildelosekeit"; Hamburger, "Visible, Yet Secret."

57. Rozenski, "The Visual, the Textual, and the Auditory," 36.

58. *Ordinarium*, 199.

59. *Vita*, ch. 38, *DS*, 117–18.

60. Roth, "Aufzeichnungen," 131–32; *Ordinarium*, 110, 113.

61. For an examination of this principle particularly with regard to the Observance, see Herzig, "Female Mysticism, Heterodoxy, and Reform."

62. Angenendt, "Die Liturgie bei Heinrich Seuse," 897.

63. Briefbüchlein, letter 8, *DS*, 385–86. *Lux fulgebit* is the Introit for the dawn Mass on Christmas. Tauler also mentions it in Vetter 1, discussed above. *Ordinarium*, 151.

64. *Vita*, ch. 5, *DS*, 18.

65. Sandra Fenten has demonstrated in this context that, for Seuse, the heart represents the interface between body and soul and is therefore the physical organ in which experiential overflow occurs. "Durch das Herz als physisches Organ werden innere Emotionen und Erfahrungen auf den Körper übertragen und dadurch äußerlich wahrnehmbar. Die mit dem Herzen gegebene Schnittstelle von Leib und Seele läßt aber auch den Schluß auf den umgekehrten Weg zu, daß also eine vom Körper ausgehende Bewegung über das Herz das Innere des Menschen beeinflußt. [Through the heart as a physical organ, inner emotions and experiences are transferred to the body and thereby made externally visible. The intersection of body and soul, represented by the heart, nevertheless also permits the inverse conclusion, namely, that a movement beginning in the body may influence a person's interior through the heart.]" Fenten, *Mystik und Körperlichkeit*, 100.

66. Sermon Vetter 39, *PT*, 160.

67. Both Tauler and Seuse do use the terms *jubilacio* and *jubilieren* to describe the involuntary expression of divine joy. For overviews of this phenomenon in Christian mystical literature, see Fuhrmann, *Herz und Stimme*, 112–17, 286–317; Grundmann, "Jubel"; Wiora, "Jubilare sine verbis."

68. *Vita*, ch. 50, *DS*, 174.

69. Sermon Vetter 39, *PT*, 159.

70. Früh, "Zeichen und Kontext," 151–52; Bernhardt, "Implizite Pragmatik," 119.

71. For the most influential German-language treatise on discernment, see Hohmann, trans., *Heinrichs von Langenstein "Unterscheidung der Geister."* For general treatments, see Anderson, *The Discernment of Spirits*; Sluhovsky, *Believe Not Every Spirit*; Caciola, *Discerning Spirits*; Voaden, *God's Words, Women's Voices*.

72. "Nu sprach min herre S. Paulus: 'der geist wúrket und git underscheit der geiste.' [Now, my lord Saint Paul said: 'the Spirit works and gives discernment of spirits.']" *PT*, 180.

73. *DS*, 3.

74. *Vita*, ch. 35, *DS*, 108.

75. Ibid.

76. Ibid., 107.

77. Tinsley, *Scourge and Cross*, 139–44.

78. *Vita*, ch. 50, *DS*, 171.

79. *Vita*, ch. 53, *DS*, 194.

80. Köbele, "Emphasis, überswanc, underscheit," 992.

81. Sturlese, "Einleitung," LV–LXI.

82. Köbele, "Emphasis, überswanc, underscheit," 994. Uta Störmer-Caysa also provides a slightly fuller summary of the argument with regard to the correct understanding of differentiation, even if one does not accept her overarching argument that *wilde* should be read as *bilde*. Störmer-Caysa, "Das Gespräch mit dem Wilden."

83. Buch der Wahrheit, ch. 6, *DS*, 352.

84. Ibid., *DS*, 354–55.

85. Ibid., *DS*, 353.

86. Ibid.

87. Although I agree with Stefan Zekorn that *Bescheidenheit* is a fundamental characteristic of Tauler's spirituality, I prefer to emphasize its relation to the themes of order and regulation. Zekorn describes *Bescheidenheit* as moderation and writes at length of its role in maintaining the middle path between giving oneself to God and continuing to live in the world. Zekorn, *Gelassenheit und Einkehr*, 227–33.

88. Sermon Vetter 24, *PT*, 97. See also sermon Vetter 15: "also der mensche mit sante Johanse geruffet wurt von der welte, daz ist das der mensche alle sine innersten kreften regniere und ordene usser der obersten bescheidenheit [thus with St. John man was called from the world, which is to say that man rules and orders all his inner faculties out of the highest, which is prudence]." *PT*, 70.

89. "Wissent, wel werg ir wúrckent das die bescheidenheit nút meistert, das ist nút gůt, wanne es ist Gotte nút geneme [know that whatever work you might perform, if you have not mastered discernment, it is not good, for it is not pleasing to God]." *PT*, 323.

90. Sermon Vetter 74, *PT*, 401.

91. "und also man liset: dum medium silencium, in dem mittele des swigendes, do alle ding uf das höhste usgeswigen worent, und in dem tieffesten der naht, herre, do kam din almehtige rede obenan hernider von dem kúniglichen stůle. Zů diser edeler stillen súllent alle wisen, alle werg dienen und nút irren, sunder sú súllent stercken. [and so one reads: *dum medium silencium*, in the middle of the silence, when all things were silent in the highest, and in the deep of the night, Lord, your almighty Word came from on high down from the royal seat. To this noble silence should all ways, all works serve and not err, rather they should strengthen it.]" Ibid.

92. Sermon Vetter 42, *PT*, 179.

93. Ibid., 178.

94. "Kinder, alsus sol man leren sich üben in tugenden. Wan du mûst dich üben, solt du kúnnen. Nút enwarte das dir Got die tugende in stúrze sunder din arbeit [Children, thus one should learn to practice virtue, for you must practice, if you want to be able to do. Do not wait for God to pour virtues into you without your effort]." Ibid., 179.

95. "Der vijent ist durch si gevarn und si wider durch in, und ist marg und bein durch geübet. Und dise lúte bekennent underscheit der geiste [The devil has passed through them and they back through him and their bone and marrow have been tried. And these people recognize discernment of spirits]." Ibid., 180.

96. Sermon Vetter 12, *PT*, 57.

97. "Insgesamt kann Tauler aber dem Stundengebet keine besondere Bedeutung abgewinnen. Es ist für ihn eine Vorschrift, die es möglichst sinnvoll, und das heißt innerlich, zu verrichten gilt. [In sum, Tauler cannot glean any special significance from the prayer of the Hours. For him, it is a regulation that should be fulfilled as meaningfully, i.e., as contemplatively, as possible.]" Zekorn, *Gelassenheit und Einkehr*, 114.

98. Großes Briefbuch, letter 11. *DS*, 438.

99. "Liber Constitutionum Sororum," 341–42; "Liber Constitutionum (1256)," 50–51.

100. Chapter 14 is entitled "Von der núzzen tugende, dú da heisset swigen." *DS*, 37.

101. Sermon Vetter 51, *PT*, 233.

102. "Der mensche werde angetan mit den tugenden unsers herren Jhesu Christi, als ist: demütkeit, senftmütikeit, gehorsamkeit, luterkeit, gedultikeit, barmherzikeit, swigen und gemeine minne [The person puts on the virtues of Our Lord Jesus Christ, which are: humility, meekness, obedience, purity, mercy, silence, and common love]." Sermon Vetter 60f, *PT*, 311. In sermon Vetter 23, silence shows up among a list of natural virtues ordered by *Bescheidenheit*: "demütikeit, senftmütekeit, miltekeit, barmhertzikeit, stillekeit, und diser glich [humility, meekness, mildness, mercy, silence, and such things]." *PT*, 93.

103. "Gebet ist nút anders wanne ein ufgang des gemütes in Gotte." Sermon Vetter 3, *PT*, 20. McGinn, *Harvest*, 260.

104. Sermon Vetter 3, *PT*, 20. Zekorn draws together a number of different sermons in which Tauler uses the term "prayer of the mouth." Zekorn, *Gelassenheit und Einkehr*, 102–4.

105. "dise richen lúte kummet an úch und gent armen verzerten krancken kinder vier haller oder sehsse, und heissent sú úch enweis wie vil venien machen und lihte hundert pater noster sprechen [These rich people come to you and give poor, exhausted, sick children four hallers or six, and they command you to do I don't know how many prostrations and say maybe a hundred *pater nosters*]." Sermon Vetter 15, *PT*, 67. In sermon Vetter 43, he also attacks priests and nuns who fulfill their liturgical obligations in order to earn blessedness and not out of love for God. *PT*, 182. Here Tauler is drawing on a typology of different motivations for pursuing virtue that Lydia Wegener describes in *Der "Frankfurter,"* 286–93. The second of four groups comprises people seeking to earn their salvation. These are called "Lohner," or wage-workers. Wegener writes, "insbesondere in den

Predigten Johannes Taulers sind die Angehörigen der zweiten Gruppe als Vertreter eines pharisäischen Gebotszwanges omnipräsent [especially in the sermons of Johannes Tauler, the members of the second group, as representatives of a pharisean legal compulsion, are omnipresent]." Wegener, Der "Frankfurter," 289–90.

106. Sermon Vetter 39, PT, 155.

107. Sermon Vetter 62, PT, 338. Throughout the Dominican Ordinary the phrase "nisi in Tempore Paschali [except during Eastertide]" punctuates almost every directive.

108. Ibid.

109. Sermon Vetter 60a, PT, 284.

110. Büchlein der ewigen Weisheit, ch. 24, DS, 308–9.

111. Observant reformers avidly read and received Seuse's Vita and the Latin treatise Horologium sapientiae, but there is no evidence of a direct influence of this letter on the way reformers framed their concerns.

112. Großes Briefbuch, letter 2, DS, 413–14.

113. Sermon Vetter 47, PT, 211.

114. Vita, ch. 9, DS, 27.

115. See my introduction and Ebner, Engelthal, 6–7.

116. Sermon Vetter 63, PT, 342.

117. Although Martina Wehrli-Johns's theses about the authorship of the Exemplar should be taken with a strong helping of salt, she provides a good overview of the respect for Seuse among Observants. Wehrli-Johns, "Das Exemplar." For Tauler's continued influence, see Gieraths, "Johannes Tauler und die Frömmigkeitshaltung des 15. Jahrhunderts."

CHAPTER 3. LITURGICAL DEVOTION AND VISIONARY ORDER IN THE FOURTEENTH-CENTURY SISTERBOOKS

Note to epigraph: Vetter, ed., Töß, 16.

1. For introductions to the genre, see Van Engen, "Communal Life"; Garber, Feminine Figurae, 9–32; Lewis, By Women.

2. These attributions of authorship have often been quite fraught. See Tinsley, "Gender, Paleography, and the Question of Authorship." For the individual authors, see "Stagel, Elsbeth (Staglin) OP," DLL II:189–92; Classen, "From Nonnenbuch to Epistolarity"; Grubmüller, "Viten"; "Katharina von Gebersweiler," DLL, I:982–984; "Anna von Munzingen," DLL, II:136–37; "Elisabeth von Kirchberg," DLL, II:140–41; Jansen, "Kirchberg," 111–15; "Ebner, Christine," DLL, II:143–46; Thali, Beten, Schreiben, Lesen, 211–12.

3. For a summary of the nineteenth and early twentieth century's negative evaluations of the sisterbooks, see Langer, Mystische Erfahrung, 47–54; Lewis, By Women, 67–74. John Van Engen's survey of scholarship includes more recent contributions. Van Engen, "The Sister-Books," 106–8. A lengthy history of scholarship particularly with regard to the Engelthal sisterbook may be found in Thali, Beten, Schreiben, Lesen, 46–95.

4. Siegfried Ringler was particularly influential in promoting the idea that the sister-books contained "eine Lehre von der praktischen Mystik, vermittelt . . . in den Formen der Legende [instruction in practical mysticism, mediated . . . in the forms of the legend]." Ringler, *Viten- und Offenbarungsliteratur*, 14.

5. See, for example, Lindgren, *Sensual Encounters*; Ochsenbein, "Latein und Deutsch im Alltag"; Dinzelbacher, "Zur Interpretation."

6. In addition to Ringler's foundational work, the classic studies are Peters, *Religiöse Erfahrung*; Bürkle, *Literatur im Kloster*. Frank Tobin summarizes the argument and pleads for a middle path in Tobin, "Suso and Stagel," 125–28. For Anglophone contributions that are indirectly relevant, see Newman, "What Did It Mean"; Justice, "Miracles."

7. Wegener, "Eckhart and Women's Spirituality," 417.

8. "Explosion" is his word. Williams-Krapp, "Ordensreform"; Williams-Krapp, "Dise ding"; Williams-Krapp, "Frauenmystik"; Williams-Krapp, "Observanzbeweg-ungen"; Williams-Krapp, "Bedeutung."

9. Uwe Neddermeyer corroborates Williams-Krapp's association of reform and increased literary production, although he is more cautious about ascribing causal signifi-cance. Neddermeyer, *Von der Handschrift zum gedruckten Buch*, 224–55.

10. A great deal of scholarship has addressed the ways in which visions, prophetic talent, or feats of asceticism arrogated power to women who otherwise had none, as well as privileging the men who became their mediators. See Griffiths and Hotchin, eds., *Partners in Spirit*; Coakley, *Women, Men, and Spiritual Power*; Bilinkoff, *Related Lives*; Benedict, *Empowering Collaborations*; Morgan, "Spiritual Autobiographies"; Hollywood, "Inside Out."

11. Williams-Krapp, "Frauenmystik," 312.

12. Hamburger, *Visual and Visionary*, 386.

13. Ibid., 443–44, 449–51.

14. Vetter, ed., *Töß*, XVI–XVII.

15. Carroll, "Subversive Obedience," 710.

16. "These aspects of the *vitae* [promoting communal piety] may have been of such paramount importance that Meyer could turn a blind eye to the mystical visions and terrestrial/celestial interactions peppering the three texts." Ibid., 720.

17. For a thorough overview of the scholarly discussion and a refutation of Williams-Krapp's thesis, see Jansen, "Kirchberg," 133–41.

18. Ibid., 140.

19. Willing, *Bibliothek*, XXII; Willing, *Literatur und Ordensreform*, 33. See also Gott-schall, "Meister Eckhart-Rezeption in Nürnberg."

20. Nemes, "Re-Skript und Re-Text," 92.

21. Winston-Allen, *Convent Chronicles*, 204.

22. Williams-Krapp and Williams, "Eberhard Mardach"; Williams-Krapp and Wil-liams, "Eine Warnung."

23. Anne Winston-Allen calls it a "register" and "alphabetical catalogue." Winston-Allen, "Rewriting Women's History," 145.

24. König, "Chronik," 217.

25. Thali, "Gehorsam," 213.

26. He notes that some editor reorganized Elsbeth's writing by grouping visions and anecdotes thematically, but ascribes this role to a mediator rather than to Meyer himself. Schneider-Lastin, "Leben der Elsbeth von Oye," 396–97.

27. "Zu fragen bleibt schließlich auch, ob man den Texten—indem man sie, wie Williams-Krapp, als potentiell kontraproduktiv im Sinne der Reform einstuft—nicht ein geradezu heterodoxes Potential unterstellt, das ihnen gar nicht zukommt. Denn dafür sind eigentlich jene Themen, die den vorbildlichen monastischen Lebensvollzug betreffen, wie etwa das Tugendleben der einzelnen Schwestern, zu präsent und zentral [It remains for us to ask whether—by classifying these texts as potentially counterproductive to the reform, as does Williams-Krapp—we do not presume a downright heterodox potential that does not belong to them at all. Indeed, precisely those themes which pertain to the ideal monastic life, such as the virtues of individual sisters, are too present and central to support this]." Jansen, "Kirchberg," 140. More practically and less polemically, Amiri Ayanna reads the St. Katharinental sisterbook as betraying an internal chronological development, in which the more severe didacticism and asceticism of later *vitae* more closely reflect Observant concerns. Her argument is not incompatible with my claim that even the earliest *vitae* in the sisterbooks support Observant concerns. Ayanna, "Bodies of Crystal," 37–42.

28. Kieckhefer, *Unquiet Souls*, 4.

29. For the specialties of particular convents, see Jansen, "Kirchberg," 84–85; Thali, *Beten, Schreiben, Lesen*, 221–33; Garber, *Feminine Figurae*, 64–65.

30. Lewis, *By Women*, 247; Hindsley, *Mystics of Engelthal*, 6.

31. Garber's inaccurate characterization of Dominican regular documents does not invalidate her point. Garber, *Feminine Figurae*, 64.

32. Schneider-Lastin, "Von der Begine zur Chorschwester," 534.

33. "Gehorsam definiert sich als die persönliche Annäherung an Gott, da er die völlige Unterwerfung des Religiosen unter den Willen Gottes bedeute [Obedience is defined as personal intimacy with God, since it signifies the complete submission of the religious to the will of God]." Melville, "Gehorsam," 182–83. Melville notes that Humbert of Romans holds that disobedience to a superior is permitted when a command conflicts with the order to which one has vowed obedience.

34. Meyer, *St. Katharinental*, 102.

35. Ayanna interprets this vision similarly, noting that, "walls and bodies made of glass must be monitored for breakage." Ayanna, "Bodies of Crystal," 51.

36. Bihlmeyer, "Mystisches Leben," 73–74.

37. Schneider-Lastin, "Leben der Elsbeth von Oye," 426.

38. Meyer, *St. Katharinental*, 101.

39. Ibid., 104.

40. Ibid., 97–98.

41. Ibid., 109.

42. Ayanna, "Bodies of Crystal," 36.

43. Langer, *Mystische Erfahrung*, 99–100.

44. Hindsley, *Mystics of Engelthal*, 3.

45. For an overview of the representation of the liturgy in the sisterbooks, see Lewis, *By Women*, 227–33; Wilms, *Das Beten der Mystikerinnen*, 24–49.

46. Vetter, ed., *Töß*, 92.

47. Ibid., 17–18.

48. Creytens, "L'ordinaire," 126–28.

49. Ritzinger and Scheeben, "Beiträge," 27.

50. Zeller-Werdmüller and Bächtold, *Stiftung*, 251.

51. Bihlmeyer, "Mystisches Leben," 84.

52. "Ez kom zu eim mal daz sie die vers in baiden choren las. Da sprach die priolin zu ir: "Du tust sam ein gans: sing in dinem chör und laz einen chor sten." Da fledert sie mit den armen und wont, sie wer ein gans, biz die priolin sprach: "Du bist kein gans." Da liez sie aller erst von der ungeperde. [Once it happened that she read the verses of both choirs. The prioress said to her: "You are acting like a goose. Sing in your choir and leave the other choir alone." Then she flapped her arms and thought she was a goose until the prioress said: "You are not a goose." Only then did she leave off her wild gestures.]" Ebner, *Engelthal*, 14. This anecdote could also be read as an example of radical obedience; Alheit behaves as what her prioress tells her she is.

53. Lindgren, *Sensual Encounters*, 98.

54. Langer, *Mystische Erfahrung*, 108. For his reading of liturgical prayer as an inspiration to subjective, private experience, see ibid., 110–15.

55. Ebner, *Engelthal*, 21.

56. Ochsenbein, "Latein und Deutsch im Alltag," 47.

57. Ebner, *Engelthal*, 22.

58. Verheijen, *La règle de Saint Augustin*, 421.

59. "Liber Constitutionum Sororum," 343.

60. Ebner, *Engelthal*, 20.

61. Ibid., 30.

62. "Es studiret, und vestet, das es gelernet hete." Roth, "Aufzeichnungen," 141.

63. Ibid., 143.

64. Meyer, *St. Katharinental*, 132; *Ordinarium*, 179.

65. "Ein mensch begert zu wissenne, waz des heiligen geistes gehörde were, als unser herr Jesus Christus sprach zu seinen jungern: 'Alles, das er gehöret von meinem vater, das wirt er euch kundende.'" This is John 16:13 and is used both for Ascension and for Pentecost. "Ich gedachte des wortes, als Christus sprach zu seinen jungern 'Ich lasse euch mein frid, ich gibe euch meinen frid': 'Herr, welches ist der frid, den du gibst?'" This is John 14:27, which is also read during the week after Pentecost. Schneider-Lastin, "Leben der Elsbeth von Oye," 437; *Ordinarium*, 54, 56, 184.

66. Vetter, ed., *Töß*, 86.

67. Ochsenbein, "Latein und Deutsch im Alltag," 46.

68. "Dicant autem in profestis diebus pro matutinis viginti octo pater noster. In festis autem nouem leccionum, quadraginta. Pro uesperis, quatuordecim. Loco preciosa, tria. Pro benediccione mense, unum. Post mensam pro graciis, tria. In ieiuniis et uigiliis et aliis, que earum statui competunt, se aliis conformabunt. [However, on ferial days they should say twenty-eight pater nosters. On feasts of nine lections, forty. At vespers, fourteen. Instead of the preciosa, three. For the table blessing, one. After table, for grace, three. In fasting and vigils and other things that are relevant to their station, they should conform to the others.]" "Liber Constitutionum Sororum," 343.

69. Lindgren, *Sensual Encounters*, 127.

70. "Vulneraverat caritas Christi cor meum." Vetter, ed., *Töß*, 65; *Ordinarium*, 100.

71. Lindgren, *Sensual Encounters*, 130.

72. "Bonum certamen certavi, cursum consumavi, fidem servavi." Bihlmeyer, "Mystisches Leben," 70; *Ordinarium*, 94.

73. For ways in which sisters would be familiar with scriptures, see Hindsley, *Mystics of Engelthal*, 113–24; Boynton, "The Bible and the Liturgy." Many of the essays in this same volume provide excellent introductions to the various contexts in which Biblical texts would have been encountered by religious.

74. See, for example, Hilpisch, "Chorgebet und Frömmigkeit." Such visions are a feature of Elisabeth of Schönau's revelations, as well as those of the Helfta mystics, especially Mechthild von Hackeborn. Both Elisabeth's and Mechthild's revelations were disseminated widely in excerpts intended for devotional reading and, although they were not Dominican, almost certainly influenced the devotional forms found in the sisterbooks. For more on the liturgical piety of Elisabeth of Schönau, see Dinzelbacher, "Offenbarungen"; Heinzer, "Imaginierte Passion"; Clark, "Elisabeth of Schönau." For Mechthild von Hackeborn, see especially Barbara Newman's new translation, Mechthild of Hackeborn and the Nuns of Helfta, *The Book of Special Grace*. Also Voaden, "Mechthild of Hackeborn." I thank Barbara Newman for this point and for drawing my attention to her translation.

75. *Ordinarium*, 115.

76. Bihlmeyer, "Mystisches Leben," 78.

77. *Ordinarium*, 7.

78. Meyer, *St. Katharinental*, 106–7.

79. "Mit den in diesen Chroniken erzählten Kurzgeschichten, in denen die Aneinanderreihung von Begriffsstutzigkeiten ersetzt ist durch den Nonnen vertraute, szenische Bildfolgen, wird bei den Schwestern nicht auf die Indoktrinierung theologischer Formeln, sondern vielmehr auf deren persönliche Betroffenheit abgezielt [With the anecdotes narrated in these chronicles, which replace perplexing concepts with scenic imagery familiar to the nuns, the sisterbooks do not aim for indoctrination of theological formulae but rather lessons of personal import]." Acklin Zimmermann, "Die Nonnenviten," 580; Acklin Zimmermann, *Gott im Denken berühren*, 168.

80. Holsinger, *Music, Body, and Desire*, 242. Citing Holsinger, Harrison writes that "liturgical observance offered individual nuns the opportunity for intellectual productivity, perhaps paralleling, supplementing, or fueling the work a contemporary monastic reader might associate with the scriptorium." Harrison, "I Am Wholly Your Own," 562.

81. Jansen, "Kirchberg," 167.

82. *Ordinarium*, 98.

83. Jansen, "Kirchberg," 172.

84. *Ordinarium*, 108.

85. Meyer, *St. Katharinental*, 109.

86. *Ordinarium*, 85.

87. Bihlmeyer, "Mystisches Leben," 70.

88. Julie Ann Smith argues that the women were conceptually included in the order's apostolic mission. Smith, "Apostolic Vocation."

89. Roth, "Aufzeichnungen," 131–32.

90. The first citation appears in both Matthew 16:24 and Luke 9:23. The second is John 12:26.

91. *Ordinarium*, 110 and 113.

92. This story bears remarkable resemblance to an instance in Heinrich Seuse's *Vita* where he employs liturgical citation to a similar purpose. Visionary singers intone an antiphon for the Office of martyrs and he asks why they are singing this when it is not a martyr's feast day. The vision goes on to relate the antiphon to Seuse's own suffering. *Vtia*, ch. 38, *DS*, 117–18.

93. See the introduction for a discussion of levels of literacy.

94. For an extraordinary example of this kind of composition, which draws on many of the texts I include in this study, see Brückner, *Dorothea von Hof.*

95. Carroll, "Subversive Obedience," 721.

96. Vetter, ed., *Töß*, 61–62.

97. Carroll, "Subversive Obedience," 721.

98. Hamburger, *Visual and Visionary*, 460–64.

99. Vetter, ed., *Töß*, 64.

100. Ibid., 65.

101. *Ordinarium*, 100.

102. Newman, "Love's Arrows," esp. 269.

103. Newman's essay treats such reception extensively. See also Hamburger, *The Rothschild Canticles*, 76–77, fig. 137; Hamburger, *Nuns as Artists*, 118–19.

104. For a broad-ranging meditation that argues for creative freedom within the "spiritual claustration" of the liturgy, see Heinzer, "Claustrum non manufactum." Although he begins with a reference to St. Katherine's in Nürnberg, he does not consider any examples from Observant houses.

105. Poor, "Transmission and Impact."

CHAPTER 4. THE OFFICE IN DOMINICAN LEGISLATION, 1388–1475

Note to epigraph: *Acta Capitulorum*, III:94.

1. Bonniwell, *History*, v–vi.

2. Ibid., 233–35.

3. This grand narrative was maintained by historians internal to the Dominican Order well into the twentieth century, with the works of William A. Hinnebusch, O.P. as a late representative with *The Dominicans: A Short History*, as well as *The History of the Dominican Order*. On Dominican historiography, see Vargas, *Taming a Brood of Vipers*, 39–47; Huijbers, "Zealots for Souls," esp. 183–218.

4. Kaminsky, "From Lateness to Waning to Crisis"; Huijbers, "Observance as Paradigm."

5. Vargas, "Weak Obedience."

6. Mixson, *Poverty's Proprietors*.

7. On the bifurcation of the Dominican Order into an Avignonese obedience and a Roman obedience, see Hinnebusch, *Dominicans*, 62–63 and 79. On the Schism more broadly, see the essays collected in Rollo-Koster and Izbicki, eds., *A Companion to the Great Western Schism (1378–1417)*.

8. Zarri, "Ecclesiastial Institutions"; Hlaváček and Patschovsky, eds., *Reform von Kirche und Reich*; Elm, ed., *Reformbemühungen*.

9. *Acta Capitulorum*, II:394.

10. Most of this translation is drawn from Bonniwell's version with some alterations. Bonniwell, *History*, 234–35.

11. "Singularis vite, qui regularia servat, ab irregularibus reputetur [He who upholds the regulations is considered by the unruly to have a singular lifestyle]." *Litterae encyclicae magistrorum generalium*, 312.

12. *Acta Capitulorum*, II:430, 442. See Creytens, "L'ordinaire," 132.

13. Bonniwell, *History*, 217–26.

14. Nimmo, "The Franciscan Regular Observance," 194.

15. *BdRP*, IV–V:8; Huijbers, "Zealots for Souls," 211–13.

16. *Beati Raymundi Capuani Opuscula*, 117–19; Barthelmé, *Réforme*, 28–29, 34; Hillenbrand, "Observantenbewegung," 227.

17. Hillenbrand, "Observantenbewegung," 221; *Bullarium*, II:315–16.

18. Neidiger, "Selbstverständnis," 79–83; Bock, "Nürnberger Predigerkloster," 153–55.

19. Fries, "Kirche und Kloster," 20–21; Steinke, *Paradiesgarten*, 19–21.

20. Tschacher, *Der Formicarius*, 51–52. On the time leading up to Texery's election, see also Huijbers, "Zealots for Souls," 189–91.

21. Roest, "Observant Reform," 450.

22. Roest, *Franciscan Learning*, 132–86; Mixson, *Poverty's Proprietors*; Roest, *Franciscan Education*, 153–71; Neidiger, "Selbstverständnis"; Neidiger, "Armutsbegriff."

23. Mixson, "Conceptual Frameworks," 77–78.

24. "Auch für die Reformen unter Ordensgeneral Bartholomäus Texerius stellten die Augustinusregel und die Ordenskonstitutionen die verbindliche Richtschnur dar [Also for the reforms under Master General Bartholomew Texery, the Augustinian Rule and the Constitutions of the order provided the binding precepts]." Neidiger, "Selbstverständnis,"

86. Yet the Brill *Companion to Observant Reform*, Mixson and Roest, eds., does not even include an entry for "liturgy" or "Divine Office" in the subject index.

25. The acts of the General Chapters of the Roman Obedience prior to 1397, as well as some intermediate years, do not survive.

26. *Acta Capitulorum*, III:94.

27. "Fratres, qui divinum officium dicere neglexerint, illud coram conventu sedentes ad terram sub eadem pena dicere compellantur." Ibid., III:104. The discussion of the various duties pertaining to the liturgy in Chapter 6 helps clarify why a certain minimum number of participants would be necessary.

28. Ibid., III:115–16, 128. Heightened concern for the textual accuracy of regular documents was not unique to the Dominican order. Schreiner, "Verschriftlichung," 52–54, 72.

29. Ibid., III:137–38.

30. Ibid., III:356, 377.

31. Ibid., III:149, 183, 202, 209, 227, 242, 245, 252, 259, 269–70, 292–93, 302, 321, 332, 338, 356, 377, 395, 416–17, 424.

32. The acts of the 1474 chapter in Rome, for example, refer to a decision made at the previous General Chapter in Basel, whose fragmentary acts no longer contain this clause. Ibid., III:332.

33. Ibid., III:220.

34. Bonniwell, *History*, 231–32, 237.

35. Creytens, "L'ordinaire," 138–39. The assignment of Nider and Flamochetti was not the first time an Observant had undertaken to revise the Office. An anonymous friar in Nürnberg produced a correction in 1421 which had no traction. Ibid., 135–37.

36. "Imprimis a divino cultu exordium faciens, volo et ordino quod officium diurnum pariter et nocturnum devote, distincte, cum pausis in medio versus et nota Ordinis ab omnibus fratribus simul in choro convenientibus, nisi judicio presidentis aliquo merito essent excusandi, suo tempore semper dicatur sine discantu in acutis vel in octavis vel quomodolibet aliter quam Ordinis nota contineat [To begin with the liturgy, I want and order that the diurnal as the nocturnal office always be said devoutly, distinctly, with pauses in the middle of the verses, and according to the rubrics of the order by all brothers at the same time gathered together in the choir (unless excused by some reasonable decision of the head of the community), at the right time and without a descant either at higher notes or on the octave, or indeed in any way other than what is contained in the notation of the order]." Löhr, *Teutonia*, 54. It may be worth noting that *distincte* is a citation not from the men's Constitutions but from the women's.

37. Von Kern, "Reformation des Katharinenklosters," 17.

38. Muschiol, "Geistliche Migrantinnen"; Muschiol, "Migrating Nuns"; Willing, *Bibliothek*, LXXV–LXXXI.

39. Löhr, *Teutonia*, 68.

40. Halter, *Geschichte*, 118.

41. Thali, *Beten, Schreiben, Lesen*, 274.

42. As Susan Marti remarks, the Dominican convent of Paradies bei Soest neither was enclosed nor prohibited private property, yet this decadence did not preclude a vibrant spiritual life and the production of lavish liturgical manuscripts. Marti, "Sisters in the Margins," 21.

43. Nürnberg Stadtbibliothek Cod. Cent. VII, 82. Schneider, *Handschriften*, 398–99.

44. A statement to the same effect is found among the writings of the reformed Benedictine nuns in Ebstorf: "Magnum tedium est, stare in choro, legere, cantare, et non intelligere [It is very boring to stand in choir, read, sing, and not understand]." Cited in Lähnemann, "Per organa," 401.

45. Von Kern, "Reformation des Katharinenklosters," 20. It seems Texery could have stood to reread the Constitutions himself, since the prologue explicitly states that infractions out of ignorance do not incur guilt but simply merit a penalty. See "Liber Constitutionum Sororum," 338; Van Engen, "From Canons to Preachers," 293.

46. Von Kern, "Reformation des Katharinenklosters," 19.

47. "Die volkssprachliche liturgische Lesung konnte insbesondere denjenigen Schwestern den Sinn und die Bedeutung der gesprochenen und gesungenen lateinischen Texte erschließen, die nur über solche Lateinkenntnisse verfügten, die ihnen gerade eben eine aktive Teilnahme an der lateinischen Liturgie ermöglichten [The vernacular liturgical reading made the meaning and significance of the spoken and sung Latin texts available in particular to those sisters who only had just enough of a command of Latin to take active part in the Latin liturgy]." Willing, *Bibliothek*, XLVII. See also Hasebrink, "Tischlesung"; Mengis, *Schreibende Frauen*, 177–92.

48. Wallach-Faller, *Ein alemannischer Psalter*, 59–61.

49. Jones, "Rekindling the Light."

CHAPTER 5. CONTEMPLATIVE VISUALIZATION VERSUS
LITURGICAL PIETY IN JOHANNES NIDER

Note to epigraph: Prague National Museum Cod. XIII C 20, fol. 99va.

1. Abel, *Harfen*, 8; Bailey, *Battling Demons*, 15; Tschacher, *Der Formicarius*, 32–35. For biographical details of Nider's life, I rely on these recent studies. The only extended biography of Nider remains, however, Schieler, *Magister Johannes Nider*. For the house in Colmar as the "cradle" of the reform, see Wittmer, "Berceau." Nider may have known Conrad of Prussia himself, but he was definitely a young protegé of the prominent reformer Johannes Mulberg, calling himself in the *Formicarius* Mulberg's *socius itineris*. See von Heusinger, *Johannes Mulberg*, 5; Bailey, *Battling Demons*, 15.

2. Tschacher, *Der Formicarius*, 49–52.

3. Brett, *Humbert of Romans*, 140, 147; Humbert of Romans, *Opera de vita regulari*, II:230, 300.

4. Van Engen, "Nyder on Laypeople."

5. Abel, *Harfen*, 117–18.

6. Ibid., 113. A number of studies have been conducted on the sermons in manuscripts from St. Katherine's Nürnberg, many of which manuscripts were produced by the sisters themselves. See the list of studies gathered by Steinke in *Paradiesgarten*, 10, n. 42., and most prominently Willing, *Nürnberger Eucharistiepredigten.*

7. Dahmus, "Preaching to the Laity," 58–61.

8. The manuscript has three owner's inscriptions. The first designates the owner as "Swester Kungund Clos Schryberin," while the others indicate that the book had gone over into possession of the convent's library. Schneider, *Handschriften*, 12. The convent library catalog, drawn up in 1455/57 by Kunigunde Niklas, confirms this with the note, "Das puch procht swester Küngunt Schreiberin herein." *MBK*, III/3:615.

9. Schneider, "Bibliothek," 76; Willing, *Bibliothek*, XXVIII. Willing gives the number sixteen, but, without comment, cites the same passage of Schneider's essay where she lists nineteen manuscripts with their modern or medieval shelf marks.

10. Neidiger, "Selbstverständnis," 79–80.

11. *BdRP*, IV-V:66–67.

12. For accounts of the reform of St. Katherine's, see Steinke, *Paradiesgarten*, 19–28; Willing, *Literatur und Ordensreform*, 19–25; Fries, "Kirche und Kloster," 22–26; von Kern, "Reformation des Katharinenklosters."

13. Karin Schneider speculates that Kunigunde Schreiber knew Nider personally. Schneider, "Bibliothek," 77.

14. Ibid., 73–75. For her own visions, see Williams and Williams-Krapp, eds., *Die "Offenbarungen" der Katharina Tucher.*

15. Van Engen, "Nyder on Laypeople," 583.

16. It is unclear whether Nider commissioned the translation itself or merely a copy of an existing translation. The surviving manuscript from St. Katherine's represents the earliest witness of this translation tradition, but Abel refrains from concluding that Nider commissioned the translation. Abel, *Harfen*, 166.

17. *MBK*, III/3:615.

18. For Niklas's central role in the book culture at St. Katherine's, first producing manuscripts as a scribe and then commissioning them in her capacity as librarian, see Sauer, "Zwischen Kloster und Welt," 114–18; Schneider, *Handschriften*, XIII, XVI.

19. *MBK*, III/3:612–13.

20. A number of incomplete copies also survive, one of which (Strasbourg, Bibliothèque nationale et universitaire, Ms. 2742) represents the second half of an originally complete copy in two volumes. Abel, *Harfen*, 163 n. 143.

21. "Item dz puch ist aus geschriben worden an des heiligen Byschoffs vnd marters tag Sant lamperti, do man czalt nach vnsers lieben herren gepurt M cccc vnd in dem lxxvj jar, vnd hat geschriben Schwester Magdalena Toppleryn zu nucz dem Closter ze Medingen prediger ordens. Orate pro me [The book was finished on the feast day of the holy bishop and martyr St. Lambert in the year of our Lord 1476. Sister Magdalena Topplerin wrote it for the use of the Dominican convent of Medingen. Pray for me]" (206vb). Abel, *Harfen*, 167–68; Willing, *Bibliothek*, LXXXVI; Fries, "Kirche und Kloster," 31.

22. Willing, *Bibliothek*, LXXXVIII–XC.

23. Brand, *Studien*, 108.

24. Abel, *Harfen*, 170. These two women produced a number of manuscripts containing German translations of theological and philosophical texts. Frank, *Söflingen*, 109–10.

25. Frank, *Söflingen*, 94; Johannes Kist, "Das Klarissenkloster in Nürnberg," 62. See also Miller, "Der Streit um die Reform."

26. Willing, *Bibliothek*, LXXXVI. For examples of similar exchanges between Dominican nuns and women of other orders, see Winston-Allen, "Artistic Production and Exchange"; Winston-Allen, "Networking in Medieval Strasbourg"; Fechter, *Deutsche Handschriften aus Inzigkofen*, 173–88; Mengis, *Schreibende Frauen*, esp. 218–31 and 234–36.

27. Brand, *Studien*, 109; Abel, *Harfen*, 72–78, 127–33.

28. Brand, *Studien*, 110–11.

29. Abel, *Harfen*, 78–86; Brand, *Studien*, 113–14.

30. Abel, *Harfen*, 60–63; Brand, *Studien*, 90–93; Brückner, *Dorothea von Hof*.

31. "Niders gezielte Auswahl von Abschnitten der CP [*Collationes patrum*], die dann in freier Bearbeitung in die GH [*goldenen Harfen*] eingehen sollten, orientierte sich an der Leitfrage nach dem geistlichen Nutzen und der Relevanz für die alltägliche Glaubens- und Frömmigkeitspraxis. Gleichzeitig berücksichtigte er dabei die geistigen Voraussetzungen des intendierten Adressatenkreises von *simplices* inner- und außerhalb des Klosters [Nider's targeted selection of excerpts from the *Conferences*, which entered the *Harps* in a loose treatment, was oriented by the principle of spiritual usefulness and relevance for everyday belief and pious practice. He simultaneously kept in mind the intellectual capacities of the intended audience of *simplices* both within and outside of the convent]." Abel, *Harfen*, 154.

32. Williams, "Schul der weisheit," 402.

33. "Das schließt die laikalen Adressaten und Schwestern ausdrücklich von der Schriftauslegung aus." Steinmetz, "Schule der heiligen Katharina," 354, n. 68.

34. Willing, *Bibliothek*, XXIV, n. 21.

35. Ibid., XIX.

36. Klaus Schreiner argued that precisely this kind of broader access to spiritual literature on the part of male laypeople and *conversi*, facilitated by growing vernacular literacy, posed a problem for the Latin-literate religious and clerical hierarchy. Although he does not specifically address the question of female vernacular literacy, his arguments are relevant. Schreiner, "Gebildete Analphabeten?"; Schreiner, "Laienbildung."

37. Abel, *Harfen*, 162.

38. See, for example, Bailey, *Battling Demons*, 112–13; Elliott, *Proving Woman*, 197–200. For Nider's misogyny more generally, see Tschacher, *Der Formicarius*, 188–99; Abel, *Harfen*, 21–26; Elliott, *The Bride of Christ*, 257–63; Klaniczay, "The Process of Trance."

39. Abel admits that he cannot account for the uncensored translation. "Es erstaunt sehr, dass gerade solche 'Tabu-Themen' in die oberdeutsche CP-Übersetzung eingegangen sind [It is quite astounding that precisely such 'taboo topics' ended up in the High German *Conferences* translation]." Abel, *Harfen*, 160.

40. The "monasticization of the laity" provides the entire departure point for John Dahmus's essay "Preaching to the Laity." Bailey also places a great deal of emphasis on this principle: "Nider's conception of religious reform was guided by his deeply held conviction that the cenobitic status, when properly observed, provided the most perfect model of life available to humanity on earth." *Battling Demons*, 82. Klaus Schreiner treats this tendency as a broader movement in late medieval spirituality that was particularly strong in the mendicant orders but also found expression in wider contexts. Schreiner, "Laienfrömmigkeit," 30.

41. Williams-Krapp, "Praxis pietatis," 150; Williams-Krapp, "Observanzbewegungen," 15; Tschacher, *Der Formicarius*, 179–88; Abel, *Harfen*, 130–31.

42. Studer, *Exempla im Kontext*, 52–76; Williams, *Die alemannischen Vitaspatrum*; Williams-Krapp, "Nucleus."

43. In this, southern Germany differed from other areas of Northern Europe, where Books of Hours became popular lay prayerbooks much earlier. Hamburger, "Book of Hours in Germany."

44. Abel conducts a thorough comparison of the *Harps* with the translation in *Harfen*, 163–77. My description of the differences between Nider's and the translator's treatments of the *Conferences* corresponds with his, although the conclusion I draw diverges.

45. I use the Prague manuscript for all citations because of its easy availability in digitized format at http://www.manuscriptorium.com/apps/index.php?direct=record& pid =KNM___-NMP___XIII_C_20___24U1WL1-en (Accessed February 10, 2017). Aside from spelling, the Prague text only differs from the Nürnberg manuscript in that it silently accepts corrections and marginal annotations found in the earlier copy. It also maintains the *nota bene* and *caue* annotations found in the Nürnberg exemplar.

46. I thank Barbara Newman for this observation. For a discussion of taste as a mystical sense, see Fulton, "Taste and See."

47. Eckhart's well-known Sermon 52 on *Beati pauperes spiritu* explains, "daz ist ein arm mensche, der niht enwil und niht enweiz und niht enhât [a poor person is one who wants nothing and knows nothing and has nothing]." Meister Eckhart, *Werke*, I:550.

48. Lentes, "Bild, Reform und *cura monialium*."

49. Lentes notes that the northern German reformer Johannes Busch was more extreme in this regard than the southern German Dominican Observants. Ibid., 181. For Busch's attempts to control devotional images and the response of at least one women's community, see Bynum, "Crowned with Many Crowns."

50. Lentes, "Bild, Reform und *cura monialium*," 188.

51. Abel both discusses the *Harps'* relation to Cassian (149–62) and compares the treatise to the translation (163–77). See also Williams, "Schul der weisheit"; Dahmus, "Fifth-Century Monastic Wine."

52. Abel, *Harfen*, 153. See also Williams, "Schul der weisheit," 395.

53. *Harfen*, 186. See also "Wann niht ein yetliche gute meinung maht ein werck gut. Aber ein yetliche pöse meinung maht ein werck pöß, wie wol es doch einen guten schein het [For not every good intention makes a work good. But every bad intention makes a work bad, no matter how good it appears]." Ibid., 188.

54. Abel also notes Nider's excision of this important point, calling it part of Nider's program to replace vague theoretical pronouncements with practical, hands-on advice. Abel, *Harfen*, 157.

55. "Des ist not vnd aller meist am suntag vnd an feiertagen. Vnd so du pist am suntag pey der meß, so pistu schuldig, dein hertz mit fleiß zü got zu keren [This is above all required on Sundays and feast days. When you are at Mass on Sunday, you are obliged to turn your heart zealously toward God]." Ibid., 186.

56. Ibid., 185.

57. Ibid., 188.

58. Williams, "Schul der weisheit"; Steinmetz, "Schule der heiligen Katharina."

59. Nider also removes the sections about the multiplicity of possible meanings in scripture from Conference VIII, sections 3–4. Abel, *Harfen*, 155.

60. For Seuse's vision, see Seuse, *Horologium Sapientiae*, 519–26.

61. Steinmetz, "Schule der heiligen Katharina," 351–52; Williams, "Schul der weisheit," 397–98.

62. *Harfen*, 269–70.

63. Although surgery was not generally respected as an art, instruction in anatomy was both taught and respected at the University of Vienna. Wolf, *Hof-Universität-Laien*, 58–59. Heinrich von Langenstein also includes both practical and theoretical medicine as separate disciplines in his sermon on Catherine of Alexandria. Steinmetz, "Schule der heiligen Katharina," 341.

64. *Harfen*, 279.

65. Steinmetz argues that Nider was explicitly forbidding both nuns and laypeople from engaging in scriptural reading. Steinmetz, "Schule der heiligen Katharina," 354.

66. *Harfen*, 241.

67. "Hye ynnen mag man wol mercken, das nyemant vmb die vngelertheyt der puchstaben wirt aus geslossen von der volkumenheyt des herczen [Herein one may well note that no one is excluded from perfection of heart by being unlearned in letters]" (101vb–102ra).

68. Bailey, *Battling Demons*, 85.

69. *BdRP*, IV–V:61.

70. Willing, *Bibliothek*, LXXII–LXXV.

71. Ibid., LXXIII, LXXXVI–XCI.

72. Ibid., LXXV–LXXX; Muschiol, "Migrating Nuns."

73. Sauer, "Zwischen Kloster und Welt," 122.

74. Schneider, "Beziehungen," 213; Freckmann, *Katalog*, 27–30.

75. Ehrenschwendtner, *Bildung*, 164.

76. "A. d. 1436 ultima julii ego fr. Johannes Nider reperi defectus infra notatos et ordinaciones memoriales notavi infrascriptas in monasterio in Subtilia." Löhr, *Teutonia*, 68. Löhr unhelpfully does not transcribe precisely what these corrections are, because he is uninterested in them, but he does note that they comprise a solid two-thirds of the letter.

77. "quod cantrices in aliis officiis non occupentur." Ibid.

78. Von Kern, "Reformation des Katharinenklosters," 17. In the Dominican convents there were only seven *horae canonicae*, because lauds was sung immediately after matins and not considered a separate hour. Bonniwell, *History*, 140. Humbert of Romans, who oversaw the codification of the order's liturgical practices, justifies this reduction on the grounds that seven is a holier number than eight (*sacratior numerus*). Humbert of Romans, *Opera de vita regulari*, I:157.

79. Von Kern, "Reformation des Katharinenklosters," 20. Willing notes only two major divergences in the table reading catalogs from St. Katherine's with regard to Texery's specifications, namely, that all table readings were in German, and texts pertaining to the Rule and Constitution were only read during Lent. Willing, *Bibliothek*, XLI.

80. The manuscript from St. Katherine's in Nürnberg (StB Cod. Cent. VI, 46e) is, in fact, the oldest surviving full translation of Humbert's commentary. Schneider, *Handschriften*, 151–52; Tanneberger, *Normative Basistexte*, 311–12. Tanneberger provides a thorough overview of German translations of regular literature, but his interest in translations of Humbert's commentary on the Rule lies in a Melk reception. For Dominican reception, see Kramp, *Deutsche Übersetzungen*; Kramp, *Renovamini spiritu*; Kramp, "Rezeption."

81. Willing, *Bibliothek*, XLI-XLII.

82. Ibid., CVII; Willing, *Konventsbuch*, 503.

83. Humbert of Romans, *Opera de vita regulari*, I:157–58.

84. Bihlmeyer, "Mystisches Leben," 68–69.

85. Willing, *Bibliothek*, 470–88. The work was contained in three volumes, all of which survive (Nürnberg Stdb Cod. Cent. IV, 80; III, 85; V, 29). It has been edited by G. H. Buijssen.

86. Buijssen, *Durandus' Rationale*, IV:45.

87. Ibid., IV:46. It was traditional to perform baptisms at Eastertide.

88. Ibid., IV:47.

89. It derived its name from being said on a step. James W. McKinnon, "Gradual (i)," *Grove Music Online; Oxford Music Online*, accessed February 10, 2017, http://www.oxfordmusiconline.com/subscriber/article/grove/music/11576.

90. Willing, *Bibliothek*, XLVII.

91. Ibid., LX.

CHAPTER 6. LITURGICAL COMMUNITY AND OBSERVANT
SPIRITUALITY IN THE WORK OF JOHANNES MEYER

Note to epigraph: Wroclaw University Library, Cod. IV F 194a, fol. 82ra, http://dk.bu.uni.wroc.pl/cymelia/displayDocumentFotos.htm?docId=5002000253, accessed February 10, 2017.

1. Sarah Glenn DeMaris provides an excellent and thorough overview of Meyer's career. DeMaris, "Introduction," 1–37. See also "Meyer, Johannes OP," *DLL*, III:754–62.

2. DeMaris suggests that he had already been engaged in this kind of activity in Basel before his assignment to the Bern Inselkloster. In the 1455 *Buch der Ersetzung* (the *Supplement*) he mentions having written "a summary of the most important ordinations passed by the general chapters." DeMaris, "Introduction," 33. For an overview of Meyer's works and an examination of his authorial project, see Seebald, "Schreiben für die Reform." Anne Huijbers refers frequently to Johannes Meyer's works in discussing the compilatory method of Observant historiography in "Zealots for Souls," 39–63.

3. I make this argument on the basis of his last works, the Chronicles of 1481 and 1484, in Jones, "Writing History to Make History." See also Winston-Allen, "Rewriting Women's History."

4. DeMaris, "Introduction," 12.

5. Engler, *Regelbuch*, 27.

6. Engler, *Regelbuch*, 27; Wroclaw, Cod. IV F 194a, fol. 131ra. I have made my own direct transcription from the manuscript, rather than following Engler's somewhat regularized version.

7. For an explanation of the various degrees to which different kinds of normative texts were considered obligatory, see Melville, "Regeln, Consuetudines-Texte, Statuten." For Humbert's work, see Brett, *Humbert of Romans*, 134–50; Humbert of Romans, *Opera de vita regulari*, II:179–371; Kaeppeli, *Scriptores*, II:290–91.

8. For a description of Meyer's alterations, see DeMaris, "Introduction," 33–37.

9. Engler, *Regelbuch*, 37–38; DeMaris, "Introduction," 37.

10. Sarah DeMaris and Christian Seebald both show how the *Book of Duties* followed the networks of Observant reform. DeMaris, "Introduction," 84–92; Seebald, "Handschriftenverhältnisse." Werner Fechter explains the relationships between the four surviving manuscripts of the *Book of the Reformation* in Fechter, "Nürnberger Handschrift."

11. See Chapter 3 for background on the fourteenth-century sisterbooks and a discussion of Meyer's reception. Johannes Meyer edited the sisterbooks from Töss, Diessenhofen, Ötenbach, and Adelhausen and was likely involved in the composition of Anna von Sissach's *Liber vitae* for the Inselkloster in Bern. Meyer, *St. Katharinental*, 66–68.

12. "Anna von Sissach OP," *DLL*, II:1052.

13. DeMaris, "Introduction," 32.

14. Winston-Allen, *Convent Chronicles*, 115–17.

15. Only the women's houses of San Domenico in Pisa and Corpus Christi in Venice had been reformed earlier. For the diffusion of the reform from these centers, see Duval, *Comme des anges sur terre*, 216–29.

16. *BdRP*, I-III:2. Emendations to this edition are from Strasbourg, Bibliothèque nationale et universitaire, Ms. 2.934, http://gallica.bnf.fr/ark:/12148/btv1b102247968, accessed February 10, 2017.

17. Pfaff, "Bild und Exempel."

18. Over the course of the fifteenth century, it became increasingly likely that extraordinary asceticism and ecstatic spirituality would be interpreted as a sign of demonic possession rather than a mark of grace. Although it has increasingly come under criticism, the classic study remains Dinzelbacher, *Heilige oder Hexen*. See also Herzig, "Female Mysticism"; Klaniczay, "Process of Trance"; Newman, "Possessed by the Spirit"; Kieckhefer, "The Holy and the Unholy."

19. Pfaff, "Bild und Exempel," 230.

20. Twice Meyer mentions that a community was taught "lesen und singen" in preparation for the arrival of the reforming party and formal enclosure. *BdRP*, IV–V:46–47, 61. One of Meyer's greatest failures as a reformer was in the convent of Gnadenzell near Offenhausen. They had already successfully resisted one reform attempt, when he was assigned as confessor in order to teach them to sing the Office according to the Observance. The women booby-trapped their convent and avoided learning anything. Winston-Allen, *Convent Chronicles*, 103; Crusius, *Schwäbische Chronik*, II:109.

21. *BdRP*, I-III:81.

22. Ibid., 91.

23. Ibid., 89.

24. Clara had "gar grossen fliss zů dem götlichen dienst des cores [great diligence in the Divine Office of the choir]," and Dorothea "übet sich besunder geträwlich in dem cor zů den hailgen VII ziten [exercised particular faithfulness in the choir for the holy hours]." *BdRP*, I-III:69, 83.

25. Ibid., 56.

26. *BdRP*, IV-V:93.

27. "Während die Schwesternbücher voller Berichte über Visionen sind, die gerade beim Gebet vor Bildern und Altären geschahen, sind bei Meyer solche Gnadenerfahrungen äußerst sparlich gesät. Die von ihm überlieferten Bildwunder halten einem quantitativen Vergleich mit den Schwesternbüchern keineswegs stand [While the sisterbooks are full of accounts of visions which take place during prayer before images and altars, in Meyer's work such experiences of grace are few and far between. The image miracles he recounts do not stand up in a quantitative comparison with the sisterbooks]." Lentes, "Bild, Reform und *cura monialium*," 184.

28. *BdRP*, IV-V:59–60; *Ordinarium*, 10.

29. *BdRP*, I-III:80, 82, 89.

30. Hamburger, *Visual and Visionary*, 445.

31. Ibid., 447. Meyer was unusually zealous regarding the issue of property in other contexts, as well. Neidiger, "Armutsbegriff," 156–58. The "Freiburger Chronist" of whom Neidiger writes is also Johannes Meyer.

32. Meri Heinonen presents a happier picture of collaboration between friars and sisters in the *Book of the Reformation* in "Between Friars and Nuns."

33. Lentes, "Bild, Reform und *cura monialium*," 185.

34. *BdRP*, I-III:35.

35. Hamburger, *Visual and Visionary*, 428.

36. Lentes, "Bild, Reform und *cura monialium*," 181.

37. *BdRP*, I-III:34.

38. Ibid.

39. Ibid., 33.

40. I say equally, because a convent could be enclosed, but not reformed, as the discussion of the Bern Inselkloster below makes clear, as well as the situation of St. Katherine's in Augsburg, which was enclosed but never Observant. See Ehrenschwendtner, "Virtual Pilgrimages." The most recent and thorough discussion of the Observant Dominican insistence on enclosure is Duval, *Comme des anges*, 53–85, 107–23. For studies that focus on enclosure in the German context, see Jäggi, *Frauenklöster im Spätmittelalter*, esp. 185–91; Winston-Allen, *Convent Chronicles*, 152–67; Uffmann, "Inside and Outside."

41. Ehrenschwendtner, "Creating the Sacred Space Within"; Steinke, *Paradiesgarten*, 45–54.

42. Seebald, "Handschriftenverhältnisse."

43. DeMaris, "Introduction," 57–62.

44. Ehrenschwendtner suggests that the Dominican women of St. Katherine's in Augsburg would routinely leave the cloister to visit their relatives, with the prioress's knowledge and permission. Ehrenschwendtner, "Virtual Pilgrimages," 50–51.

45. "Anima una et cor unum in deum." Verheijen, *La règle de Saint Augustin*, 417.

46. In his chronicle of the Bern Inselkloster, Meyer recounts a frightening episode in which the enclosed sisters almost starved because no one on the outside was looking after them. Wroclaw, Cod. IV F 194a, fol. 115v.

47. *BdRP*, I-III:47–48.

48. Ibid., 48–49.

49. Ibid., 51–52.

50. *BdRP*, IV-V:47.

51. The following derives from Meyer's extensive accounts in ibid., 114–21.

52. Sylvie Duval examines the patronage of Schönensteinbach by Catherine of Burgundy, but focuses on the Italian convents for continued relationships with the nuns' biological families. Duval, *Comme des anges*, 241–48. For examples of city-convent relationships in Teutonia, see Hirbodian, "Dominikanerinnenreform und Familienpolitik"; Steinke, *Paradiesgarten*, 24–28, 64–69; Neidiger, "Standesgemäßes Leben"; Armgart, "Klosterreform und Wirtschaft."

53. *BdRP*, IV-V:116–17.

54. To my knowledge, there are no studies of surviving liturgical material that outline precisely what such a Rite of Reform involved, or even whether there was such a fixed Rite or whether other Rites were adapted for the occasion.

55. *BdRP*, IV-V:118.

56. Ibid., 119.

57. Ibid., 120.

58. *Ordinarium*, 123.

59. The Dominican order had long celebrated the *Salve regina* procession every day after compline, and it formed an important component of the order's Marian devotion.

Fassler, "Music and the Miraculous"; Bonniwell, *History*, 148–67. Johannes Meyer notes in the *Supplement* that some convents sing *Sub tuum* at the end of Mass or after every Hour. See the footnote at Willing, *Konventsbuch*, 555, n. 23.

60. *Ordinarium*, 95.

61. Instructions for elections are found in both the Constitutions and the Ordinary. "Liber Constitutionum Sororum," 346; *Ordinarium*, 123–25.

62. Freiburg im Breisgau, Stadtarchiv, B1 (H) 107, 263v. (HMML 43442)

63. *Ordinarium*, 109, 97.

64. Wrocław, Cod. IV F 194a, fol. 114v–115v.

65. Borries, *Schwesternspiegel*, 421.

66. Meyer, *Das Amptbuch*, 349, 520.

67. Seebald, "Handschriftenverhältnisse," 420; Engler, *Regelbuch*, 9–14.

68. Seebald, "Handschriftenverhältnisse," 398. DeMaris and Seebald independently came to the conclusion that this co-transmission was Meyer's intention. DeMaris, "Introduction," 39–44, 91; Seebald, "Handschriftenverhältnisse," 400.

69. DeMaris, "Introduction," 124–25; Seebald, "Handschriftenverhältnisse," 398. For a description of the manuscript, see De Hamel, *Gilding the Lilly*, 148–49.

70. DeMaris discusses and reproduces the illuminations. DeMaris, "Introduction," 92–120.

71. For a stemma, see Seebald, "Handschriftenverhältnisse," 419.

72. DeMaris, "Introduction," xxxii.

73. Meyer, *Das Amptbuch*, 204.

74. Ibid., 206, 400.

75. Ibid., 157, 354.

76. Ibid., 329–31, 503–5.

77. Ibid., 333–34, 507.

78. These works should "sigen gutter anreissung zu jnnikeit vnd andacht [foster inwardness and devotion]." Ibid., 333, 506.

79. Ibid., 331, 504.

80. Ibid., 176–77.

81. Ibid., 373.

82. Ibid., 332, 506.

83. Ibid., 207–8.

84. Ibid., 402.

85. Ibid., 204, 399.

86. Ibid., 202, 397.

87. Ibid., 204, 399.

88. Ibid., 209, 404. St. Katherine's in Nürnberg sent to St. Gallen a summary of their duty-roster. Willing, *Konventsbuch*, 546–53.

89. Meyer, *Das Amptbuch*, 209, 404.

90. Ibid., 182–83, 378–79.

91. Meyer speaks of this at greater length in the chapter on the sacristan, who is responsible for ringing the bells. Ibid., 196, 391. This practice represents a departure from

the women's Constitutions, which stipulate that the Little Office should be said communally in the choir. However, the late thirteenth-century ordinances from an anonymous provincial of Teutonia already allow that the women follow the friars in saying the Little Office together in the dormitory before going to the choir for matins. Ritzinger and Scheeben, "Beiträge," 27.

92. Meyer, *Das Amptbuch*, 161, 359.

93. Ibid., 257, 443.

94. Ibid., 257.

95. Ibid., 443.

96. Ibid., 282, 465.

97. Ibid., 263. My translation.

98. Ibid., 279–80, 462. In both cases, these sites include not only altars but also devotional images.

99. Ibid., 272, 456.

100. Ibid., 273, 456.

101. Ibid., 196, 391.

102. Ibid., 281, 463–64. In the footnotes to her translation, DeMaris provides the liturgical context for each of the versicles and prayers Meyer recommends.

103. *Ordinarium*, 25, 55, 124.

104. Meyer, *Das Amptbuch*, 290.

105. Ibid., 471.

106. Ibid., 286, 469. The Rule enjoins that "psalmis et hymnis cum oratis deum, hoc uersetur in corde quod profertur in uoce [when praying to God in psalms and hymns, you turn over in your heart what you offer in your voice]." Verheijen, *La règle de Saint Augustin*, 421.

107. "Jtem si sond me achten, dz si in irem gebett sigen erfolgen vnd enpfahen jnnikeit vnd andacht vnd genad, denn dz si vil mit gebett wort sigent vs sprechen [They should pay more attention to achieving inwardness and devotion and receiving grace when they pray than to saying a lot of vocal prayers]." Meyer, *Das Amptbuch*, 285, 468.

108. Ibid., 286.

109. Ibid., 468.

110. An extraordinarily precise description of the turn in St. Katherine's in Nürnberg survives in the letters they sent to St. Gallen. Willing, *Konventsbuch*, 629–30. See also Lindgren, *Sensual Encounters*, 30; Uffmann, "Inside and Outside," 94.

111. See in particular chapters 4, 8, and 10 on the turnkeeper. Meyer, *Das Amptbuch*, 218, 224–27, 411–12, 417–19.

112. Ibid., 214, 409.

113. Ibid., 215.

114. Ibid., 409–10.

115. Ibid., 409 n. 96. "In hoc quoque loco, cum socium non habuerit, poterit tempore dormitionis diurnae remanere propter advenientes, vel vigilare, vel paululum dormitare, et in nocte a matutinis remanere [When he does not have a companion, at the time

of the day rest he may remain in that place in case of visitors and stay up or take a nap, and then at night remain away from matins]." Humbert of Romans, *Opera de vita regulari*, II:275.

116. *BdRP*, I-III:69.

117. Ehrenschwendtner, *Bildung*, 99.

118. *BdRP*, I-III:69.

119. Ibid.

120. Ibid.

121. Ibid.

122. Ibid., 72.

123. For example, the belt represents the ropes that bound Christ when he was whipped, and the veil represents the stone before his tomb. Ibid., 73.

124. "Ut," the lowest note, signifies humility and represents Christ's birth. "Re" signifies the obedience that Christ observed toward Mary and Joseph in childhood, as well as his father in heaven, etc. Ibid., 70.

125. Ibid., 69.

126. Ibid., 33.

127. Ibid., 53.

128. Hamburger, *Visual and Visionary*, 449.

BIBLIOGRAPHY

PRIMARY SOURCES

Acta Capitulorum Generalium Ordinis Praedicatorum. Ed. Benedict Maria Reichert. 9 vols. Rome: In domo generalitia, 1898–1904.

Année Dominicaine: ou vies des saints, des bienheureux, des martyres et des autres personnes illustres ou recommendables par leur piété de l'un et de l'autre sexe de l'Ordre des Frères-Prêcheurs distribuées suivant les jours de l'année. Vol. III/March. Lyon: X. Jevain, 1886.

Beati Raymundi Capuani XXIII Magistri Generalis Ordinis Praedicatorum Opuscula et Litterae. Ed. Hyacinthe-Marie Cormier. Rome: Ex Typographia Polyglotta, 1899.

Bihlmeyer, Karl. "Mystisches Leben in dem Dominikanerinnenkloster Weiler bei Eßlingen im 13. und 14. Jahrhundert." *Württembergische Vierteljahrshefte für Landesgeschichte* 25 (1916): 61–93.

Buijssen, G. H., ed. *Durandus' Rationale in spätmittelhochdeutscher Übersetzung nach der Hs. CVP 2765.* 4 vols. Assen: Van Gorcum, 1966–1983.

Bullarium Ordinis FF. Praedicatorum. 8 vols. Rome: Ex Typographia Hieronymi Mainardi, 1724–1740.

Creytens, Raymond. "Les constitutions primitives des soeurs dominicaines de Montargis (1250)." *Archivum Fratrum Praedicatorum* 17 (1947): 41–66.

Ebner, Christina. *Der Nonne von Engelthal Büchlein von der Genaden Uberlast.* Ed. Karl Schröder. Tübingen: H. Laupp, 1871.

Humbert of Romans. *Opera de vita regulari.* Ed. Joachim Joseph Berthier. 2 vols. Rome: A. Befani, 1888–89.

Jansen, Sabine. "Die Texte des Kirchberg-Corpus: Überlieferung und Textgeschichte vom 15. bis zum 19. Jahrhundert." Doctoral dissertation, Universität Köln, 2005.

König, J. "Die Chronik der Anna von Munzingen nach der ältesten Abschrift mit Einleitung und Beilagen." *Freiburger Diözesan-Archiv* 13 (1880): 129–236.

"Liber Constitutionum Ordinis Fratrum Praedicatorum (iuxta codicem prototypum B. Humberti in Archivo Generali Ordinis Romae asservatum)." *Analecta Sacri Ordinis Fratrum Praedicatorum* 3 (1897): 26–60, 98–122, 162–81.

"Liber Constitutionum Sororum Ordinis Praedicatorum (ex exemplari codicis Ruthenensis in Archivo Generali Ordinis Romae asservato)." *Analecta Sacri Ordinis Fratrum Praedicatorum* 3 (1897): 337–48.

Litterae encyclicae magistrorum generalium. Ed. Benedict Maria Reichert. Rome: In Domo Generalitia, 1900.

Löhr, Gabriel Maria. *Die Teutonia im 15. Jahrhundert: Studien und Texte vornehmlich zur Geschichte ihrer Reform.* Leipzig: Harrassowitz Verlag, 1924.

Mechthild of Hackeborn and the Nuns of Helfta. *The Book of Special Grace.* Trans. Barbara Newman. New York: Paulist Press, 2017.

Meister Eckhart. *Werke. Texte und Übersetzungen von Josef Quint.* Ed. Niklaus Largier. 2 vols. Frankfurt am Main: Deutscher Klassiker Verlag, 2008.

Meyer, Johannes. *Das Amptbuch.* Ed. Sarah Glenn DeMaris. Rome: Angelicum University Press, 2015.

Meyer, Ruth. *Das "St. Katharinentaler Schwesternbuch": Untersuchung, Edition, Kommentar.* Tübingen: Max Niemeyer, 1995.

Nider, Johannes. *Die vierundzwanzig goldenen Harfen: Edition und Kommentar.* Ed. Stefan Abel. Tübingen: Mohr Siebeck, 2011.

Ordinarium Juxta Ritum Sacri Ordinis Fratrum Praedicatorum. Ed. Franciscus-Maria Guerrini. Rome: Angelicum University Press, 1921.

Roth, F. W. E. "Aufzeichnungen über das mystische Leben der Nonnen von Kirchberg bei Sulz Predigerordens waehrend des XIV. und XV. Jahrhunderts." *Alemannia* 21 (1893): 103–48.

Seuse, Heinrich. *The Exemplar, with Two German Sermons.* Trans. Frank J. Tobin. New York: Paulist, 1989.

———. *Horologium Sapientiae: Erste kritische Ausgabe.* Ed. Pius Künzle. Freiburg: Universitätsverlag Freiburg Schweiz, 1977.

Simon, André. "Statuts des soeurs de Sainte Marie-Madeleine." In *L'ordre des pénitentes de Sainte Marie-Madeleine en Allemagne au XIIIme siècle,* 154–69. Fribourg: Oeuvre de Saint-Paul, 1918.

Tanner, Norman P., ed. *Decrees of the Ecumenical Councils.* London: Sheed and Ward, 1990.

Verheijen, Luc. *La règle de Saint Augustin.* Paris: Études Augustiniennes, 1967.

Vetter, Ferdinand, ed. *Das Leben der Schwestern zu Töß beschrieben von Elsbeth Stagel samt der Vorrede von Johannes Meier und dem Leben der Prinzessin Elisabet von Ungarn.* Berlin: Weidmann, 1906.

Zeller-Werdmüller, Heinrich, and Jakob Bächtold. *Die Stiftung des Klosters Oetenbach und das Leben der seligen Schwestern daselbst, aus der Nürnberger Handschrift.* Zürich, 1889.

SECONDARY SOURCES

Abel, Stefan. *Die vierundzwanzig goldenen Harfen. Edition und Kommentar.* Tübingen: Mohr Siebeck, 2011.

Acklin Zimmermann, Béatrice W. "Die Nonnenviten als Modell einer narrativen Theologie." In *Deutsche Mystik im abendländischen Zusammenhang: neu erschlossene Texte,*

neue methodische Ansätze, neue theoretische Konzepte; Kolloquium, Kloster Fischingen
1998, ed. Walter Haug, 563–80. Tübingen: Max Niemeyer, 2000.

———. Gott im Denken berühren: Die theologischen Implikationen der Nonnenviten. Freiburg: Universitätsverlag Freiburg Schweiz, 1993.

Anderson, Wendy Love. The Discernment of Spirits: Assessing Visions and Visionaries in the
Late Middle Ages. Tübingen: Mohr Siebeck, 2011.

Angenendt, Arnold. "Die Liturgie bei Heinrich Seuse." In Vita religiosa im Mittelalter:
Festschrift für Kaspar Elm zum 70. Geburtstag, ed. Franz J. Felten and Nikolas Jaspert,
877–97. Berlin: Duncker und Humblot, 1999.

Armgart, Martin. " 'Hat daß closter zugenommen nach der reformation in güttern, zinsen
und gulten': Klosterreform und Wirtschaft bei den Speyerer Dominikanerinnen." In
Lesen, Schreiben, Sticken und Erinnern, ed. Gabriela Signori, 11–26. Bielefeld: Verlag
für Regionalgeschichte, 2000.

Ayanna, Amiri. "Bodies of Crystal, Houses of Glass: Observing Reform and Improving
Piety in the St. Katharinental Sister Book." Journal of Medieval Religious Cultures 43,
no. 1 (2017): 24–57.

Bailey, Michael D. Battling Demons: Witchcraft, Heresy, and Reform in the Late Middle
Ages. University Park: Pennsylvania State University Press, 2003.

Barth, Médard. "Die Rolle des Dominikanerinnenklosters St. Marx zu Strassburg in der
Frühgeschichte des Ordens 1225–1242." Archiv für Elsässische Kirchengeschichte 7
(1932): 101–12.

Barthelmé, Annette. La réforme dominicaine au XVe siècle en Alsace et dans l'ensemble de la
province de Teutonie. Strasbourg: Imprimerie Heitz, 1931.

Bäuml, Franz H. "Varieties and Consequences of Medieval Literacy and Illiteracy." Speculum 55, no. 2 (1980): 237–65.

Beach, Alison I., ed. Manuscripts and Monastic Culture: Reform and Renewal in Twelfth-
Century Germany. Turnhout: Brepols, 2007.

———. Women as Scribes: Book Production and Monastic Reform in Twelfth-Century
Bavaria. Cambridge: Cambridge University Press, 2004.

Bell, David N. What Nuns Read: Books and Libraries in Medieval English Nunneries. Kalamazoo, Mich.: Cistercian Publications, 1995.

Benedict, Kimberley M. Empowering Collaborations: Writing Partnerships Between Religious Women and Scribes in the Middle Ages. London: Routledge, 2004.

Berger, Karol. "The Guidonian Hand." In The Medieval Craft of Memory: An Anthology of
Texts and Pictures, ed. Mary Carruthers and Jan M. Ziolkowski, 71–82. Philadelphia:
University of Pennsylvania Press, 2002.

Bernhardt, Susanne. "Die implizite Pragmatik der Gelassenheit in der Vita Heinrich
Seuses." In Semantik der Gelassenheit: Generierung, Etablierung, Transformation, ed.
Burkhard Hasebrink, Susanne Bernhardt, and Imke Früh, 115–42. Göttingen: Vande-
nhoeck & Ruprecht, 2012.

Bilinkoff, Jodi. Related Lives: Confessors and Their Female Penitents, 1450–1750. Ithaca,
N.Y.: Cornell University Press, 2005.

Blank, Walter. "Heinrich Seuses 'Vita.' Literarische Gestaltung und pastorale Funktion seines Schrifttums." *Zeitschrift für deutsches Altertum und deutsche Literatur* 122, no. 3 (1993): 285–311.

Blanton, Virgina, Veronica O'Mara, and Patricia Stoop, eds. *Nuns' Literacies in Medieval Europe: The Hull Dialogue.* Turnhout: Brepols, 2013.

———. *Nuns' Literacies in Medieval Europe: The Kansas City Dialogue.* Turnhout: Brepols, 2015.

Blumrich, Rüdiger. "Die Überlieferung der deutschen Schriften Seuses: Ein Forschungsbericht." In *Heinrich Seuses Philosophia spiritualis: Quellen, Konzept, Formen und Rezeption. Tagung Eichstätt 2.–4. Oktober 1991,* ed. Rüdiger Blumrich and Philipp Kaiser, 189–201. Wiesbaden: Reichert Verlag, 1994.

Bock, Friedrich. "Das Nürnberger Predigerkloster. Beiträge zu seiner Geschichte." *Mitteilungen des Vereins für Geschichte der Stadt Nürnberg* 25 (1924): 145–214.

Bonniwell, William R. *A History of the Dominican Liturgy.* New York: Joseph F. Wagner, 1944.

Borries, Ekkehard. *Schwesternspiegel im 15. Jahrhundert. Gattungskonstitution, Editionen, Untersuchungen.* Berlin: Walter de Gruyter, 2008.

Boyle, Leonard. "A Material Consideration of Santa Sabina ms. XIV L 1." In *Aux origines de la liturgie dominicaine: le manuscrit Santa Sabina XIV L 1,* ed. Leonard Boyle and Pierre-Marie Gy, 19–42. Rome/Paris: École Française de Rome/CNRS, 2004.

Boyle, Leonard, and Pierre-Marie Gy, eds. *Aux origines de la liturgie dominicaine: le manuscrit Santa Sabina XIV L 1.* Rome/Paris: École Française de Rome/CNRS, 2004.

Boynton, Susan. "The Bible and the Liturgy." In *The Practice of the Bible in the Middle Ages: Production, Reception, and Performance in Western Christianity,* ed. Susan Boynton and Diane J. Reilly, 10–33. New York: Columbia University Press, 2011.

Brand, Margit. *Studien zu Johannes Niders Deutschen Schriften.* Rome: Istituto Storico Domenicano, 1998.

Brandis, Wolfgang, ed. *Weltbild und Lebenswirklichkeit in den Lüneburger Klöstern: IX. Ebstorfer Kolloquium vom 23. bis 26. März 2011.* Berlin: Lukas, 2015.

Breitenbach, Almut. "'In der Schule des ewigen Königs': Wissen und Bildung in Klarissenklöstern zwischen Norm und Praxis." In *Gelobte Armut: Armutskonzepte der franziskanischen Ordensfamilie zwischen Ideal und Wirklichkeit vom Mittelalter bis in die Gegenwart,* ed. Hans-Dieter Heimann, Angelica Hilsebein, Bernd Schmies, and Christoph Stiegemann, 183–215. Paderborn: Schöningh, 2012.

Brett, Edward Tracy. *Humbert of Romans: His Life and Views of Thirteenth-Century Society.* Toronto: Pontifical Institute of Mediaeval Studies, 1984.

Briggs, Charles F. "Literacy, Reading, and Writing in the Medieval West." *Journal of Medieval History* 26, no. 4 (2000): 397–420.

Brückner, Undine. *Dorothea von Hof: 'Das buoch der götlichen liebe und summe der tugent'; Studien zu einer Konstanzer Kompilation geistlicher Texte des 14. und 15. Jahrhunderts.* Sigmaringen: Thorbecke, 2015.

Bürkle, Susanne. *Literatur im Kloster: Historische Funktion und rhetorische Legitimation frauenmystischer Texte des 14. Jahrhunderts.* Tübingen: Francke Verlag, 1999.

Bynum, Caroline Walker. "'Crowned with Many Crowns': Nuns and Their Statues in Late-Medieval Wienhausen." *Catholic Historical Review* 101, no. 1 (2015): 18–40.

———. *Fragmentation and Redemption: Essays on Gender and the Human Body in Medieval Religion.* New York: Zone Books, 1991.

Cabaniss, Allen. "Wisdom 18:14f.: An Early Christmas Text." *Vigiliae Christianae* 10, no. 2 (April 1956): 97–102.

Caciola, Nancy. *Discerning Spirits: Divine and Demonic Possession in the Middle Ages.* Ithaca, N.Y.: Cornell University Press, 2003.

Carroll, Jane. "Subversive Obedience: Images of Spiritual Reform by and for Fifteenth-Century Nuns." In *Reassessing the Roles of Women as "Makers" of Medieval Art and Architecture,* ed. Therese Martin, 2: 705–37. Leiden: Brill, 2012.

Clark, Anne L. "Elisabeth of Schönau." In *Medieval Holy Women in the Christian Tradition, c. 1100–c. 1500,* ed. A. J. Minnis and Rosalynn Voaden, 371–92. Turnhout: Brepols, 2010.

Classen, Albrecht. "From *Nonnenbuch* to Epistolarity: Elsbeth Stagel as a Late Medieval Woman Writer." In *Medieval German Literature: Proceedings from the 23rd International Congress on Medieval Studies, Kalamazoo, Michigan, May 5–6, 1988,* ed. Albrecht Classen, 147–70. Göppingen: Kümmerle Verlag, 1989.

Coakley, John Wayland. *Women, Men, and Spiritual Power: Female Saints and Their Male Collaborators.* New York: Columbia University Press, 2006.

Constable, Giles. "The Concern for Sincerity and Understanding in Liturgical Prayer, Especially in the Twelfth Century." In *Classica et Mediaevalia: Studies in Honor of Joseph Szövérffy,* ed. Irene Vaslef and Helmut Buschhausen, 17–30. Washington, D.C.: Classical Folia, 1986.

Creytens, Raymond. "L'ordinaire des frères prêcheurs au moyen âge." *Archivum Fratrum Praedicatorum* 24 (1954): 108–88.

Crusius, Martin. *Schwäbische Chronik.* Trans. Johann Jakob Moser. 2 vols. Frankfurt: Wohler, 1738.

Cyrus, Cynthia J. *The Scribes for Women's Convents in Late Medieval Germany.* Toronto: University of Toronto Press, 2009.

Dahmus, John. "Fifth-Century Monastic Wine in a Fifteenth-Century Bottle." In *Medieval Sermons and Society: Cloister, City, University,* ed. Jacqueline Hamesse, 243–59. Louvain-la-Neuve: Fédération Internationale des Instituts d'Études Médiévales, 1998.

———. "Preaching to the Laity in Fifteenth-Century Germany: Johannes Nider's 'Harps.'" *Journal of Ecclesiastical History* 34, no. 1 (1983): 55–68.

Decker, Otmar. *Die Stellung des Predigerordens zu den Dominikanerinnen (1207–1267).* Leipzig: Harrassowitz Verlag, 1935.

De Hamel, Christopher. *Gilding the Lilly: A Hundred Medieval and Illuminated Manuscripts in the Lilly Library.* Bloomington, Ind.: Lilly Library, 2010.

DeMaris, Sarah Glenn. "Introduction." In *Das Amptbuch*, ed. Sarah Glenn DeMaris, 1–145. Rome: Angelicum University Press, 2015.

Dinzelbacher, Peter. "Die Offenbarungen der heiligen Elisabeth von Schönau: Bildwelt, Erlebnisweise und Zeittypisches." *Studien und Mitteilungen zur Geschichte des Benediktiner-Ordens* 97 (1986): 462–82.

———. *Heilige oder Hexen? Schicksale auffälliger Frauen in Mittelalter und Frühneuzeit.* Zürich: Artemis & Winkler, 1995.

———. "Zur Interpretation erlebnismystischer Texte des Mittelalters." *Zeitschrift für deutsches Altertum und deutsche Literatur* 117, no. 1 (1988): 1–23.

Duval, Sylvie. *Comme des anges sur terre: les moniales dominicaines et les débuts de la réforme observante, 1385–1461.* Rome: École Française de Rome, 2015.

Ehrenschwendtner, Marie-Luise. "Creating the Sacred Space Within: Enclosure as a Defining Feature in the Convent Life of Medieval Dominican Sisters (13th–15th c.)." *Viator* 41, no. 2 (2010): 301–16.

———. "Das Bildungswesen in Frauenklöstern des Spätmittelalters. Beispiel: Dominikanerinnen." In *Handbuch der Geschichte des bayerischen Bildungswesens*, 1:332–48. Bad Heilbrunn/Obb: Verlag Julius Klinkhardt, 1991.

———. *Die Bildung der Dominikanerinnen in Süddeutschland vom 13. bis 15. Jahrhundert.* Stuttgart: Steiner, 2004.

———. "*Puellae Litteratae*: The Use of the Vernacular in the Dominican Convents of Southern Germany." In *Medieval Women in Their Communities*, ed. Diane Watt, 49–71. Toronto: University of Toronto Press, 1997.

———. "Virtual Pilgrimages? Enclosure and the Practice of Piety at St. Katherine's Convent, Augsburg." *Journal of Ecclesiastical History* 60, no. 1 (2009): 45–73.

Elliott, Dyan. *Proving Woman: Female Spirituality and Inquisitional Culture in the Later Middle Ages.* Princeton, N.J.: Princeton University Press, 2004.

———. *The Bride of Christ Goes to Hell: Metaphor and Embodiment in the Lives of Pious Women, 200–1500.* Philadelphia: University of Pennsylvania Press, 2012.

Elm, Kaspar, ed. *Reformbemühungen und Observanzbestrebungen im spätmittelalterlichen Ordenswesen.* Berlin: Duncker und Humblot, 1989.

Enders, Markus. "Selbsterfahrung als Gotteserfahrung: Zum Individualitätsbewusstsein bei Johannes Tauler." In *Individuum und Individualität im Mittelalter*, ed. Jan A. Aertsen and Andreas Speer, 642–64. Berlin: Walter de Gruyter, 1996.

Endres, Rudolf. "Das Schulwesen in Franken im ausgehenden Mittelalter." In *Studien zum städtischen Bildungswesen des späten Mittelalters und der frühen Neuzeit: Bericht über Kolloquien der Kommission zur Erforschung der Kultur des Spätmittelalters 1978–1981*, ed. Bernd Moeller, Hans Patze, and Karl Stackmann, 173–214. Göttingen: Vandenhoeck & Ruprecht, 1983.

Engler, Claudia. *Regelbuch und Observanz. Der Codex A 53 der Burgerbibliothek Bern als Reformprogramm des Johannes Meyer für die Berner Dominikanerinnen.* Berlin: Walter de Gruyter, 2017.

Fassler, Margot E. "Music and the Miraculous: Mary in the Mid-Thirteenth-Century Dominican Sequence Repertory." In *Aux origines de la liturgie dominicaine: le manuscrit Santa Sabina XIV L 1*, ed. Leonard Boyle and Pierre-Marie Gy, 229–78. Rome: École Française de Rome/CNRS, 2004.

Fassler, Margot E., and Jeffrey F. Hamburger. "The Desert in Paradise: A Newly-Discovered Office for John the Baptist from Paradies Bei Soest and Its Place in the Dominican Liturgy." In *Resounding Images: Medieval Intersections of Art, Music, and Sound*, ed. Susan Boynton and Diane J. Reilly, 251–79. Turnhout: Brepols, 2015.

Fechter, Werner. *Deutsche Handschriften des 15. und 16. Jahrhunderts aus der Bibliothek des ehemaligen Augustinerchorfrauenstifts Inzigkofen*. Sigmaringen: Thorbecke, 1997.

———. "Die Nürnberger Handschrift von Johannes Meyers 'Buch der Reformacio Predigerordens.'" *Zeitschrift für deutsches Altertum und deutsche Literatur* 110, no. 1 (1981): 57–69.

Fenten, Sandra. *Mystik und Körperlichkeit: Eine komplementär-vergleichende Lektüre von Heinrich Seuses geistlichen Schriften*. Würzburg: Königshausen & Neumann, 2007.

Frank, Karl Suso. *Das Klarissenkloster Söflingen: Ein Beitrag zur franziskanischen Ordensgeschichte Süddeutschlands und zur Ulmer Kirchengeschichte*. Ulm: Stadtarchiv, 1980.

Freckmann, Anja and Juliane Trede. *Katalog der lateinischen Handschriften der Bayerischen Staatsbibliothek München*. Vol. 4, *Die Handschriften aus den Klöstern Altenhohenau und Altomünster: Clm 2901–2966 sowie Streubestände gleicher Provenienz*. Wiesbaden: Harrassowitz Verlag, 2016.

Fries, Walter. "Kirche und Kloster zu St. Katharina in Nürnberg." *Mitteilungen des Vereins für Geschichte der Stadt Nürnberg* 25 (1924): 1–144.

Früh, Imke. "Im Zeichen und im Kontext von *gelossenheit*: Semantisierungsstrategien in den Predigten Johannes Taulers." In *Semantik der Gelassenheit: Generierung, Etablierung, Transformation*, ed. Burkhard Hasebrink, Susanne Bernhardt, and Imke Früh, 143–70. Göttingen: Vandenhoeck & Ruprecht, 2012.

Fuhrmann, Wolfgang. *Herz und Stimme: Innerlichkeit, Affekt und Gesang im Mittelalter*. Kassel: Bärenreiter Verlag, 2004.

Fulton, Rachel. "Praying with Anselm at Admont: A Meditation on Practice." *Speculum* 81, no. 3 (2006): 700–733.

———. "'Taste and See That the Lord Is Sweet' (Ps. 33:9): The Flavor of God in the Monastic West." *Journal of Religion* 86, no. 2 (2006): 169–204.

Galbraith, G. R. *The Constitution of the Dominican Order: 1216 to 1360*. Manchester: Manchester University Press, 1925.

Garber, Rebecca. *Feminine Figurae: Representations of Gender in Religious Texts by Medieval German Women Writers, 1100–1375*. New York: Routledge, 2003.

Gieraths, Gundolf. "Johannes Tauler und die Frömmigkeitshaltung des 15. Jahrhunderts." In *Johannes Tauler, ein deutscher Mystiker: Gedenkschrift zum 600. Todestag*, ed. Ephrem M. Filthaut, 422–34. Essen: Hans Driewer, 1961.

Gleeson, Philip. "The Pre-Humbertian Liturgical Sources Revisited." In *Aux origines de la liturgie dominicaine: le manuscrit Santa Sabina XIV L 1*, ed. Leonard Boyle and Pierre-Marie Gy, 99–114. Rome/Paris: École Française de Rome/CNRS, 2004.

Gnädinger, Louise. *Johannes Tauler: Lebenswelt und mystische Lehre*. München: C.H. Beck, 1993.

Gottschall, Dagmar. "Dô gedâhte ich ein glîchnisse. Gleichnisse des Sehens in den deutschen Predigten Meister Eckharts." In *Sprachbilder und Bildersprache bei Meister Eckhart und in seiner Zeit*, ed. Cora Dietl and Dietmar Mieth, 47–70. Stuttgart: Kohlhammer, 2015.

———. "Meister Eckhart-Rezeption in Nürnberg." *Zeitschrift für deutsches Altertum und deutsche Literatur* 138, no. 2 (2009): 199–213.

Griffiths, Fiona, and Julie Hotchin, eds. *Partners in Spirit: Women, Men, and Religious Life in Germany, 1100–1500*. Turnhout: Brepols, 2014.

Grubmüller, Klaus. "Die Viten der Schwestern von Töß und Elsbeth Stagel (Überlieferung und literarische Einheit)." *Zeitschrift für deutsches Altertum und deutsche Literatur* 98, no. 3 (1969): 171–204.

Grundmann, Herbert. "Jubel." In *Ausgewählte Aufsätze*, III: 130–62. Stuttgart: Hiersemann, 1978.

———. "Litteratus-illitteratus: der Wandel einer Bildungsnorm vom Alterum zum Mittelalter." *Archiv für Kulturgeschichte* 40, no. 1 (1958): 1–65.

———. *Religious Movements in the Middle Ages: The Historical Links Between Heresy, the Mendicant Orders, and the Women's Religious Movement in the Twelfth and Thirteenth Century with the Historical Foundations of German Mysticism*. Trans. Steven Rowan. Notre Dame, Ind.: University of Notre Dame Press, 1995.

Haas, Alois M. *Gottleiden, Gottlieben: Zur volkssprachlichen Mystik im Mittelalter*. Frankfurt am Main: Insel, 1989.

———. *Kunst rechter Gelassenheit: Themen und Schwerpunkte von Heinrich Seuses Mystik*. Bern: Peter Lang, 1995.

Halter, Annemarie. *Geschichte des Dominikanerinnen-Klosters Oetenbach in Zürich 1234–1525*. Winterthur: Verlag P.G. Keller, 1956.

Hamburger, Jeffrey F. "Another Perspective: The Book of Hours in Germany." In *Books of Hours Reconsidered*, ed. Sandra Hindman and James H. Marrow, 97–152. London: Harvey Miller, 2013.

———. "Visible, Yet Secret: Images as Signs of Friendship in Seuse." *Oxford German Studies* 36, no. 2 (2007): 141–62.

———. *The Visual and the Visionary: Art and Female Spirituality in Late Medieval Germany*. Cambridge, Mass.: MIT Press, 1998.

———. *Nuns as Artists: The Visual Culture of a Medieval Convent*. Berkeley: University of California Press, 1997.

———. *The Rothschild Canticles: Art and Mysticism in Flanders and the Rhineland Circa 1300*. New Haven, Conn.: Yale University Press, 1990.

Hamburger, Jeffrey F., and Eva Schlotheuber. "Books in Women's Hands: Liturgy, Learning, and the Libraries of Dominican Nuns in Westphalia." In *Entre stabilité et itinérance: livres et culture des ordres mendiants XIIIe–XVe siècle*, ed. Nicole Bériou, Martin Morard, and Donatella Nebbiai, 129–57. Turnhout: Brepols, 2014.

Hamburger, Jeffrey F., Eva Schlotheuber, Susan Marti, and Margot Fassler. *Liturgical Life and Latin Learning at Paradies Bei Soest, 1300–1425: Inscription and Illumination in the Choir Books of a North German Dominican Convent*. 2 vols. Münster: Aschendorff, 2017.

Harrison, Anna. "'I Am Wholly Your Own': Liturgical Piety and Community Among the Nuns of Helfta." *Church History* 78, no. 3 (September 2009): 549–83.

Hascher-Burger, Ulrike, Henrike Lähnemann, and Beate Braun-Niehr. *Liturgie und Reform im Kloster Medingen: Edition und Untersuchung des Propst-Handbuchs Oxford, Bodleian Library, MS. Lat. liturg. e. 18*. Tübingen: Mohr Siebeck, 2013.

Hasebrink, Burkhard. "Tischlesung und Bildungskultur im Nürnberger Katharinenkloster. Ein Beitrag zu ihrer Rekonstruktion." In *Schule und Schüler im Mittelalter: Beiträge zur europäischen Bildungsgeschichte des 9. bis 15. Jahrhunderts*, ed. Martin Kintzinger, Sönke Lorenz, and Michael Walter, 187–216. Cologne: Böhlau, 1996.

Heimann, Claudia. "Der Umfang der Dominikanerprovinz Teutonia im späteren Mittelalter." *Archivum Fratrum Praedicatorum* 75 (2005): 233–57.

Heinonen, Meri. "Between Friars and Nuns: The Relationships of Religious Men and Women in Johannes Meyer's *Buch der Reformacio Predigerordens*." *Oxford German Studies* 42, no. 3 (2013): 237–58.

Heinzer, Felix. "Claustrum non manufactum. Innenräume normativer Schriftlichkeit." In *Schriftkultur und religiöse Zentren im norddeutschen Raum*, ed. Patrizia Carmassi, 141–65. Wiesbaden: Harrassowitz Verlag, 2014.

———. "Imaginierte Passion: Vision im Spannungsfeld zwischen liturgischer Matrix und religiöser Erfahrung bei Elisabeth von Schönau." In *Nova de veteribus: mittel- und neulateinische Studien für Paul Gerhard Schimdt*, ed. Andreas Bihrer, 463–75. München: Saur, 2004.

Herzig, Tamar. "Female Mysticism, Heterodoxy, and Reform." In *A Companion to Observant Reform in the Late Middle Ages and Beyond*, ed. James D. Mixson and Bert Roest, 255–82. Leiden: Brill, 2015.

Hillenbrand, Eugen. "Die Observantenbewegung in der deutschen Ordensprovinz der Dominikaner." In *Reformbemühungen und Observanzbestrebungen im spätmittelalterlichen Ordenswesen*, ed. Kaspar Elm, 219–71. Berlin: Duncker und Humblot, 1989.

Hilpisch, Stephanus. "Chorgebet und Frömmigkeit im Spätmittelalter." In *Heilige Überlieferung: Ausschnitte aus der Geschichte des Mönchtums und des heiligen Kultes*, ed. Odo Casel, 263–84. Münster: Aschendorff, 1938.

Hindsley, Leonard P. *The Mystics of Engelthal: Writings from a Medieval Monastery*. New York: St. Martin's, 1998.

Hinnebusch, William A. *The Dominicans: A Short History*. New York: Alba House, 1975.

————. *The History of the Dominican Order*. 2 vols. New York: Alba House, 1966.

Hirbodian, Sigrid. "Dominikanerinnenreform und Familienpolitik: Die Einführung der Observanz im Kontext städtischer Sozialgeschichte." In *Schreiben und Lesen in der Stadt: Literaturbetrieb im spätmittelalterlichen Straßburg*, ed. Stephen Mossman, Nigel F. Palmer, and Felix Heinzer, 1–16. Berlin: Walter de Gruyter, 2012.

Hirbodian, Sigrid and Petra Kurz, eds. *Die Chronik der Magdalena Kremerin im interdisziplinären Dialog*. Ostfildern: Jan Thorbecke Verlag, 2016.

Hlaváček, Ivan, and Alexander Patschovsky, eds. *Reform von Kirche und Reich: Zur Zeit der Konzilien von Konstanz (1414–1418) und Basel (1431–1449)*. Konstanz: Universitätsverlag Konstanz, 1996.

Hohmann, Thomas, trans. *Heinrichs von Langenstein "Unterscheidung der Geister": lateinisch und deutsch*. Zürich: Artemis, 1977.

Hollywood, Amy. "Inside Out: Beatrice of Nazareth and Her Hagiographer." In *Gendered Voices: Medieval Saints and Their Interpreters*, ed. Catherine M. Mooney, 78–98. Philadelphia: University of Pennsylvania Press, 1999.

————. *The Soul as Virgin Wife: Mechthild of Magdeburg, Marguerite Porete, and Meister Eckhart*. Notre Dame, Ind.: University of Notre Dame Press, 1995.

Holsinger, Bruce W. *Music, Body, and Desire in Medieval Culture: Hildegard of Bingen to Chaucer*. Stanford, Calif.: Stanford University Press, 2001.

Huijbers, Anne. "'Observance' as Paradigm in Mendicant and Monastic Order Chronicles." In *A Companion to Observant Reform in the Late Middle Ages and Beyond*, ed. James D. Mixson and Bert Roest, 111–43. Leiden: Brill, 2015.

————. "Zealots for Souls: Dominican Narratives between Observant Reform and Humanism, c. 1388–1517." Doctoral dissertation, Radboud Universiteit Nijmegen, 2016.

Jäggi, Carola. *Frauenklöster im Spätmittelalter: Die Kirchen der Klarissen und Dominikanerinnen im 13. und 14. Jahrhundert*. Petersberg: Michael Imhof Verlag, 2006.

Jones, Claire Taylor. "Rekindling the Light of Faith: Hymn Translation and Spiritual Renewal in the Fifteenth-Century Observant Reform." *Journal of Medieval and Early Modern Studies* 42, no. 3 (2012): 567–96.

————. "Writing History to Make History: Johannes Meyer's Chronicles of Reform." In *Medieval Cantors and Their Craft: Music, Liturgy and the Shaping of History*, ed. Katie Ann-Marie Bugyis, A. B. Kraebel, and Margot E. Fassler, 340–56. York: York Medieval Press, 2017.

Justice, Steven. "Did the Middle Ages Believe in Their Miracles?" *Representations* 103, no. 1 (2008): 1–29.

Kaeppeli, Thomas. *Scriptores Ordinis Praedicatorum Medii Aevi*. Vol. 2. Rome: Ad S. Sabinae, 1975.

Kaminsky, Howard. "From Lateness to Waning to Crisis: The Burden of the Later Middle Ages." *Journal of Early Modern History* 4, no. 1 (2000): 85–125.

Kammeier-Nebel, Andrea. "Frauenbildung im Kaufmannsmilieu spätmittelalterlicher Städte." In *Geschichte der Mädchen- und Frauenbildung*, ed. Elke Kleinau and Claudia Opitz, 1:78–90. Frankfurt am Main: Campus Verlag, 1996.

Kieckhefer, Richard. "The Holy and the Unholy: Sainthood, Witchcraft and Magic in Late Medieval Europe." In *Christendom and Its Discontents: Exclusion, Persecution, and Rebellion, 1000–1500*, ed. Scott L. Waugh and Peter D. Diehl, 310–37. Cambridge: Cambridge University Press, 1996.

———. "The Notion of Passivity in the Sermons of John Tauler." *Recherches de Théologie Ancienne et Médiévale* 48 (1981): 198–211.

———. *Unquiet Souls: Fourteenth-Century Saints and Their Religious Milieu.* Chicago: University of Chicago Press, 1984.

Kist, Johannes. "Das Klarissenkloster in Nürnberg bis zum Beginn des 16. Jahrhunderts." Doctoral dissertation, Julius-Maximilians-Universität Würzburg, 1929.

Klaniczay, Gábor. "The Process of Trance: Heavenly and Diabolic Apparitions in Johannes Nider's Formicarius." In *Procession, Performance, Liturgy, and Ritual: Essays in Honor of Bryan R. Gillingham*, ed. Nancy van Deusen, 203–58. Ottawa: Institute of Medieval Music, 2007.

Köbele, Susanne. "*Emphasis, überswanc, underscheit*: Zur literarischen Produktivität spätmittelalterlicher Irrtumslisten (Eckhart und Seuse)." In *Literarische und religiöse Kommunikationen in Mittelalter und Früher Neuzeit: DFG-Symposion 2006*, ed. Peter Strohschneider, 969–1002. Berlin: Walter de Gruyter, 2009.

Koldau, Linda Maria, ed. *Passion und Ostern in den Lüneburger Klöstern.* Ebstorf: Kloster Ebstorf, 2010.

Kramp, Igna Marion. *Mittelalterliche und frühneuzeitliche deutsche Übersetzungen des pseudo-hugonischen Kommentars zur Augustinusregel.* Münster: Aschendorff, 2008.

———. *Renovamini spiritu / Ernüwent den geist üwers gemütes: deutsche Übersetzungen als Modernisierung im späten Mittelalter.* Münster: Aschendorff, 2008.

———. "Die Rezeption von Augustinusregelkommentaren bei den Dominikanerinnen." In *Regula Sancti Augustini: Normative Grundlage differenter Verbände im Mittelalter*, ed. Gert Melville and Anne Müller, 455–75. Paring: Augustiner-Chorherren-Verlag, 2002.

Kretzmann, Norman. "Philosophy of Mind." In *The Cambridge Companion to Aquinas*, ed. Norman Kretzmann and Eleonore Stump, 128–59. Cambridge: Cambridge University Press, 1993.

Kruppa, Nathalie, and Jürgen Wilke, eds. *Kloster und Bildung im Mittelalter.* Göttingen: Vandenhoeck & Ruprecht, 2006.

Kruse, Britta-Juliane, ed. *Rosenkränze und Seelengärten. Bildung und Frömmigkeit in niedersächsischen Frauenklöstern.* Wiesbaden: Harrassowitz Verlag, 2013.

Lähnemann, Henrike. "*Per organa*: Musikalische Unterweisung in Handschriften der Lüneburger Klöster." In *Dichtung und Didaxe: Lehrhaftes Sprechen in der deutschen Literatur des Mittelalters*, ed. Henrike Lähnemann and Sandra Linden, 397–412. Berlin: Walter de Gruyter, 2009.

Langer, Otto. *Mystische Erfahrung und spirituelle Theologie: Zu Meister Eckharts Auseinandersetzung mit der Frauenfrömmigkeit seiner Zeit.* München: Artemis, 1987.

Lappin, Anthony John. "From Osma to Bologna, from Canons to Friars, from the Preaching to the Preachers: The Dominican Path Towards Mendicancy." In *The Origin,*

Development, and Refinement of Medieval Religious Mendicancies, ed. Donald S. Prudlo, 31–58. Leiden: Brill, 2011.

Lentes, Thomas. "Bild, Reform und *cura monialium*. Bildverständnis und Bildgebrauch im *Buch der Reformacio Predigerordens* des Johannes Meyer (d. 1485)." In *Dominicains et dominicaines en Alsace: XIIIe–XXe S.*, ed. Jean-Luc Eichenlaub, 177–95. Colmar: Conseil Général du Haut-Rhin, 1996.

———. "Gebetbuch und Gebärde. Religiöses Ausdrucksverhalten in Gebetbüchern aus dem Dominikanerinnen-Kloster St. Nikolaus in undis zu Straßburg (1350–1550)." Doctoral dissertation, Westfälische Wilhelms-Universität Münster, 1996.

Lewis, Gertrud Jaron. *By Women, For Women, About Women: The Sister-Books of Fourteenth-Century Germany*. Toronto: Pontifical Institute of Medieval Studies, 1996.

Lindgren, Erika Lauren. *Sensual Encounters: Monastic Women and Spirituality in Medieval Germany*. New York: Columbia University Press, 2009.

Marti, Susan. "Schwester Elisabeth schreibt für ihre Brüder in Dortmund: das Graduale für das Dortmunder Dominikanerkloster." In *Die Dortmunder Dominikaner und die Propsteikirche als Erinnerungsort*, ed. Thomas Schilp and Barbara Welzel, 277–94. Bielefeld: Verlag für Regionalgeschichte, 2006.

———. "Sisters in the Margins? Scribes and Illuminators in the Scriptorium of Paradies near Soest." In *Leaves from Paradise: The Cult of John the Evangelist at the Dominican Convent of Paradies Bei Soest*, ed. Jeffrey F. Hamburger, 5–54. Cambridge, Mass.: Houghton Library of Harvard College Library, 2008.

Mayer, Johannes Gottfried. *Die "Vulgata"-Fassung der Predigten Johannes Taulers. Von der handschriftlichen Überlieferung des 14. Jahrhunderts bis zu den ersten Drucken*. Würzburg: Königshausen & Neumann, 1999.

McGinn, Bernard. *The Harvest of Mysticism in Medieval Germany*. New York: Crossroad, 2005.

———. "Theologians as Trinitarian Iconographers." In *The Mind's Eye: Art and Theological Argument in the Medieval West*, ed. Jeffrey F. Hamburger and Anne-Marie Bouché, 186–207. Princeton, N.J.: Princeton University Press, 2005.

Mecham, June L. *Sacred Communities, Shared Devotion: Gender, Material Culture, and Monasticism in Late Medieval Germany*. Ed. Alison I. Beach, Constance H. Berman, and Lisa M. Bitel. Turnhout: Brepols, 2014.

Melville, Gert. "Gehorsam und Ungehorsam als Verhaltensformen: Zu pragmatischen Beobachtungen und Deutungen Humberts de Romanis O.P." In *Oboedientia: Zu Formen und Grenzen von Macht und Unterordnung im mittelalterlichen Religiosentum*, ed. Sebastien Barret and Gert Melville, 181–204. Münster: Lit Verlag, 2005.

———. "Regeln, Consuetudines-Texte, Statuten. Positionen für eine Typologie des normativen Schrifttums religiöser Gemeinschaften im Mittelalter." In *Regulae, consuetudines, statuta: studi sulle fonti normative degli ordini religiosi nei secoli centrali del Medioevo*, ed. Cristina Andenna and Gert Melville, 5–38. Münster: Lit Verlag, 2005.

Mengis, Simone. *Schreibende Frauen um 1500: Scriptorium und Bibliothek des Dominikanerinnenklosters St. Katharina St. Gallen*. Berlin: Walter de Gruyter, 2013.

Miller, Max. "Der Streit um die Reform des Barfüßerklosters in Ulm und des Klarissenklosters in Söflingen und seine Beilegung (1484–1487)." In *Aus Archiv und Bibliothek: Festschrift für Max Huber*, ed. Alice Rössler, 175–93. Weißenhorn: Konrad, 1969.

Mixson, James D. "Observant Reform's Conceptual Frameworks Between Principle and Practice." In *A Companion to Observant Reform in the Late Middle Ages and Beyond*, ed. James D. Mixson and Bert Roest, 60–84. Leiden: Brill, 2015.

———. *Poverty's Proprietors: Ownership and Mortal Sin at the Origins of the Observant Movement*. Leiden: Brill, 2009.

Mixson, James D., and Bert Roest, eds. *A Companion to Observant Reform in the Late Middle Ages and Beyond*. Leiden: Brill, 2015.

Morgan, Ben. "The Spiritual Autobiographies of Visionary Nuns and Their Dominican Confessors in Fourteenth-Century Germany." In *Autobiography by Women in German*, ed. Mererid Puw Davies, Beth V. Linklater, and Gisela Shaw, 35–51. Oxford: Peter Lang, 2000.

Mulchahey, M. Michèle. *"First the Bow Is Bent in Study . . .": Dominican Education Before 1350*. Toronto: Pontifical Institute of Mediaeval Studies, 1998.

Muschiol, Gisela. "Geistliche Migrantinnen? Liturgietransfer und Reform im Spätmittelalter." In *Weltbild und Lebenswirklichkeit in den Lüneburger Klöstern, IX: Ebstorfer Kolloquium vom 23. bis 26. März 2011*, ed. Wolfgang Brandis, 129–43. Berlin: Lukas Verlag, 2015.

———. "Migrating Nuns—Migrating Liturgy: The Context of Reform in Female Convents of the Late Middle Ages." In *Liturgy in Migration: From the Upper Room to Cyberspace*, ed. Teresa Berger, 83–100. Collegeville, Minn.: Liturgical Press, 2012.

Naughton, Joan. "Books for a Dominican Nuns' Choir: Illustrated Liturgical Manuscripts at Saint-Louis de Poissy, c. 1330–1350." In *The Art of the Book: Its Place in Medieval Worship*, ed. Margaret M. Manion and Bernard J. Muir, 67–110. Exeter: University of Exeter Press, 1998.

———. "Friars and Their Books at Saint-Louis de Poissy, a Dominican Foundation for Nuns." *Scriptorium* 52 (1998): 83–102.

———. "Manuscripts from the Dominican Monastery of Saint-Louis de Poissy." Doctoral dissertation, University of Melbourne, 1995.

Neddermeyer, Uwe. *Von der Handschrift zum gedruckten Buch: Schriftlichkeit und Leseinteresse im Mittelalter und in der frühen Neuzeit: Quantitative und qualitative Aspekte*. Wiesbaden: Harrassowitz Verlag, 1998.

Neidiger, Bernhard. "Der Armutsbegriff der Dominikanerobservanten. Zur Diskussion in den Konventen der Provinz Teutonia (1389–1513)." *Zeitschrift für die Geschichte des Oberrheins* 145 (1997): 117–58.

———. "Selbstverständnis und Erfolgschancen der Dominikanerobservanten: Beobachtungen in der Provinz Teutonia und im Basler Konvent." *Rottenburger Jahrbuch für Kirchengeschichte* 17 (1998): 67–122.

———. "Standesgemäßes Leben oder frommes Gebet? die Haltung der weltlichen Gewalt zur Reform von Frauenklöstern im 15. Jahrhundert." *Rottenburger Jahrbuch für Kirchengeschichte* 22 (2003): 201–20.

Nemes, Balázs J. "Re-Skript und Re-Text—Wertlos und Entstellt? Oder: über die guten Seiten einer 'schlechten' Eckhart-Handschrift (ein Fundbericht)." *Zeitschrift für deutsche Philologie* 131 (2012): 73–102.

Newman, Barbara. "Annihilation and Authorship: Three Women Mystics of the 1290s." *Speculum* 91, no. 3 (2016): 591–630.

———. *God and the Goddesses: Vision, Poetry, and Belief in the Middle Ages*. Philadelphia: University of Pennsylvania Press, 2003.

———. "Henry Suso and the Medieval Devotion to Christ the Goddess." *Spiritus* 2, no. 1 (2002): 1–14.

———. "Love's Arrows: Christ as Cupid in Late Medieval Art and Devotion." In *The Mind's Eye: Art and Theological Argument in the Middle Ages*, ed. Jeffrey Hamburger and Anne-Marie Bouché, 263–86. Princeton, N.J.: Princeton University Press, 2006.

———. "Possessed by the Spirit: Devout Women, Demoniacs, and the Apostolic Life in the Thirteenth Century." *Speculum* 73, no. 3 (1998): 733–70.

———. "What Did It Mean to Say 'I Saw'? The Clash Between Theory and Practice in Medieval Visionary Culture." *Speculum* 80, no. 1 (2005): 1–43.

Nimmo, Duncan B. "The Franciscan Regular Observance: The Culmination of Medieval Franciscan Reform." In *Reformbemühungen und Observanzbestrebungen im spätmittelalterlichen Ordenswesen*, ed. Kaspar Elm, 189–205. Berlin: Duncker und Humblot, 1989.

Ochsenbein, Peter. "Latein und Deutsch im Alltag oberrheinischer Dominikanerinnenklöster des Spätmittelalters." In *Latein und Volkssprache im deutschen Mittelalter, 1100–1500*, ed. Nikolaus Henkel and Nigel F. Palmer, 42–51. Tübingen: Max Niemeyer, 1992.

Opitz, Claudia. "Erziehung und Bildung in Frauenklöstern des hohen und späten Mittelalters." In *Geschichte der Mädchen- und Frauenbildung*, ed. Elke Kleinau and Claudia Opitz, 1:63–77. Frankfurt am Main: Campus Verlag, 1996.

Peters, Ursula. *Religiöse Erfahrung als literarisches Faktum: Zur Vorgeschichte und Genese frauenmystischer Texte des 13. und 14. Jahrhunderts*. Tübingen: Max Niemeyer, 1988.

Pfaff, Carl. "Bild und Exempel: Die observante Dominikanerin in der Sicht des Johannes Meyer O.P." In *Personen der Geschichte. Geschichte der Personen: Studien zur Kreuzzugs-, Sozial- und Bildungsgeschichte*, ed. Christian Hesse, Beat Immenhauser, Oliver Landolt, and Barbara Studer, 221–35. Basel: Schwabe, 2003.

Poor, Sara S. "Transmission and Impact: Mechthild of Magdeburg's *Das fliessende Licht der Gottheit*." In *A Companion to Mysticism and Devotion in Northern Germany in the Late Middle Ages*, ed. Elizabeth Andersen, Henrike Lähnemann, and Anne Simon, 73–101. Leiden: Brill, 2014.

Radler, Charlotte C. "Meister Eckhart, Johannes Tauler, and Henry Suso." In *The Wiley-Blackwell Companion to Christian Mysticism*, ed. Julia A. Lamm, 340–56. Malden, Mass.: Wiley-Blackwell, 2013.

Ringler, Siegfried. *Viten- und Offenbarungsliteratur in Frauenklöstern des Mittelalters*. München: Artemis, 1980.

Ritzinger, E., and Heribert Christian Scheeben. "Beiträge zur Geschichte der Teutonia in der zweiten Hälfte des 13. Jahrhunderts." *Archiv der deutschen dominikaner* 3 (1941): 11–95.

Roest, Bert. *A History of Franciscan Education (c. 1210–1517)*. Leiden: Brill, 2000.

———. "Education and Religious Formation in the Medieval Order of the Poor Clares: Some Preliminary Observations." *Collectanea Franciscana* 73 (2003): 47–73.

———. *Franciscan Learning, Preaching and Mission c. 1220–1650*. Leiden: Brill, 2015.

———. "Observant Reform in Religious Orders." In *The Cambridge History of Christianity*, 4:446–57. Cambridge: Cambridge University Press, 2009.

———. *Order and Disorder: the Poor Clares between Foundation and Reform*. Leiden: Brill, 2013.

Rollo-Koster, Joelle, and Thomas M. Izbicki, eds. *A Companion to the Great Western Schism (1378–1417)*. Leiden: Brill, 2009.

Rozenski, Steven, Jr. "The Visual, the Textual, and the Auditory in Henry Suso's 'Vita' or 'Life of the Servant.'" *Mystics Quarterly* 34, no. 1 (January 2008): 35–72.

———. "*Von Aller Bilden Bildelosekeit*: The Trouble with Images of Heaven in the Works of Henry Suso." In *Envisaging Heaven in the Middle Ages*, ed. Carolyn Muessig and Ad Putter, 108–19. New York: Routledge, 2007.

Rüther, Andreas. "Schreibbetrieb, Bücheraustausch und Briefwechsel: Der Konvent St. Katharina in St. Gallen während der Reform." In *Vita religiosa im Mittelalter: Festschrift für Kaspar Elm zum 70. Geburtstag*, ed. Franz J. Felten and Nikolas Jaspert, 653–77. Berlin: Duncker und Humblot, 1999.

Rüther, Andreas, and Hans-Jochen Schiewer. "Die Predigthandschriften des Straßburger Dominikanerinnenklosters St. Nikolaus in undis: Historischer Bestand, Geschichte, Vergleich." In *Die deutsche Predigt im Mittelalter: Internationales Symposium am Fachbereich Germanistik der Freien Universität Berlin vom 3.–6. Oktober 1989*, ed. Volker Mertens and Hans-Jochen Schiewer, 169–93. Tübingen: Max Niemeyer, 1992.

Sack, Vera. "Bruchstücke von Regel und Konstitutionen südwestdeutscher Dominikanerinnen aus der Mitte des 13. Jahrhunderts (um 1241/42)." *Zeitschrift für die Geschichte des Oberrheins* 123 (1975): 115–67.

Sauer, Christine. "Zwischen Kloster und Welt: Illuminierte Handschriften aus dem Dominikanerinnenkonvent St. Katharina in Nürnberg." In *Frauen-Kloster-Kunst: Neue Forschungen zur Kulturgeschichte des Mittelalters: Beiträge zum internationalen Kolloquium vom 13. bis 16. Mai 2005 anlässlich der Ausstellung "Krone und Schleier"*, ed. Jeffrey F. Hamburger, Carola Jäggi, Susan Marti, and Hedwig Röcklein, 113–29. Turnhout: Brepols, 2007.

Schieler, Kaspar Erich. *Magister Johannes Nider aus dem Orden der Prediger-Brüder: ein Beitrag zur Kirchengeschichte des fünfzehnten Jahrhunderts*. Mainz: Franz Kirchheim, 1885.

Schiewer, Regina D. "Sermons for Nuns of the Dominican Observance Movement." In
     Medieval Monastic Preaching, ed. Carolyn Muessig, 75–92. Leiden: Brill, 1998.

Schlotheuber, Eva. "Bücher und Bildung in den Frauengemeinschaften der Bettelorden."
     In *Nonnen, Kanonissen und Mystikerinnen: Religiöse Frauengemeinschaften in Süddeutschland*, ed. Eva Schlotheuber, Helmut Flachenecker, and Ingrid Gardill, 241–62.
     Göttingen: Vandenhoeck & Ruprecht, 2008.

———. *Klostereintritt und Bildung: Die Lebenswelt der Nonnen im späten Mittelalter, mit
     einer Edition des "Konventstagebuchs" einer Zisterzienserin von Heilig-Kreuz bei Braunschweig (1484–1507)*. Tübingen: Mohr-Siebeck, 2004.

———. "Sprachkompetenz und Lateinvermittlung: Die intellektuelle Ausbildung der
     Nonnen im Spätmittelalter." In *Kloster und Bildung im Mittelalter*, ed. Nathalie
     Kruppa and Jürgen Wilke, 61–83. Göttingen: Vandenhoeck & Ruprecht, 2006.

Schmitt, Jean-Claude. *The Conversion of Herman the Jew: Autobiography, History, and
     Fiction in the Twelfth Century*. Trans. Alex J. Novikoff. Philadelphia: University of
     Pennsylvania Press, 2003.

Schneider, Karin. "Beziehungen zwischen den Dominikanerinnenklöstern Nürnberg und
     Altenhohenau im ausgehenden Mittelalter." In *Würzburger Prosastudien II: Untersuchungen zur Literatur und Sprache des Mittelalters*, ed. Peter Kesting, 211–18. München: Wilhelm Fink, 1975.

———. "Die Bibliothek des Katharinenklosters in Nürnberg und die städtische Gesellschaft." In *Studien zum städtischen Bildungswesen des späten Mittelalters und der frühen
     Neuzeit: Bericht über Kolloquien der Kommission zur Erforschung der Kultur des Spätmittelalters, 1978 bis 1981*, ed. Bernd Moeller, Hans Patze, Karl Stackmann, and
     Ludger Grenzmann, 70–83. Göttingen: Vandenhoeck & Ruprecht, 1983.

———. *Die Handschriften der Stadtbibliothek Nürnberg*. Vol. 1, *Die deutschen mittelalterlichen Handschriften*. Wiesbaden: Harrassowitz Verlag, 1965.

Schneider-Lastin, Wolfram. "Leben und Offenbarungen der Elsbeth von Oye: Textkritische Edition der Vita aus dem Ötenbacher Schwesternbuch." In *Kulturtopographie
     des deutschsprachigen Südwestens im späteren Mittelalter: Studien und Texte*, ed. Barbara Fleith and René Wetzel, 395–467. Berlin: Walter de Gruyter, 2009.

———. "Von der Begine zur Chorschwester: Die Vita der Adelheit von Freiburg aus dem
     'Ötenbacher Schwesternbuch': Textkritische Edition mit Kommentar." In *Deutsche
     Mystik im abendländischen Zusammenhang: Neu erschlossene Texte, neue methodische
     Ansätze, neue theoretische Konzepte: Kolloquium Kloster Fischingen 1998*, ed. Walter
     Haug and Wolfram Schneider-Lastin, 515–61. Tübingen: Max Niemeyer, 2000.

Schreiner, Klaus. "*Communio*: Semantik, Spiritualität und Wirkungsgeschichte einer in
     der Augustinusregel verankerten Lebensform." In *Gemeinsam leben: Spiritualität,
     Lebens- und Verfassungsformen klösterlicher Gemeinschaften in Kirche und Gesellschaft
     des Mittelalters*, ed. Mirko Breitenstein and Gert Melville, 205–41. Berlin: Lit Verlag,
     2013.

———. "Ein Herz und eine Seele: eine urchristliche Lebensform und ihre Institutionalisierung im augustinisch geprägten Mönchtum des hohen und späten Mittelalters."

In *Regula sancti Augustini: normative Grundlage differenter Verbände im Mittelalter*, ed. Gert Melville and Anne Müller, 1–47. Paring: Augustiner-Chorherren-Verlag, 2002.

———. "Gebildete Analphabeten? Spätmittelalterliche Laienbrüder als Leser und Schreiber wissensvermittelnder und frömmigkeitsbildender Literatur." In *Wissensliteratur im Mittelalter und in der Frühen Neuzeit*, ed. Horst Brunner and Norbert Richard Wolf, 296–327. Wiesbaden: Reichert Verlag, 1993.

———. "Laienbildung als Herausforderung für Kirche und Gesellschaft. Religiöse Vorbehalte und soziale Widerstände gegen die Verbreitung von Wissen im späten Mittelalter und in der Reformation." *Zeitschrift für historische Forschung*, 11 (1984): 257–354.

———. "Laienfrömmigkeit-Frömmigkeit von Eliten oder Frömmigkeit des Volkes? Zur sozialen Verfaßtheit laikaler Frömmigkeitspraxis im späten Mittelalter." In *Laienfrömmigkeit im späten Mittelalter*, ed. Klaus Schreiner, 1–78. München: R. Oldenbourg, 1992.

———. "Verschriftlichung als Faktor monastischer Reform. Funktionen von Schriftlichkeit im Ordenswesen des hohen und späten Mittelalters." In *Pragmatische Schriftlichkeit im Mittelalter. Erscheinungsformen und Entwicklungsstufen*, ed. Hagen Keller, Klaus Grubmüller, and Nikolaus Staubach, 37–75. München: Wilhelm Fink, 1992.

Schromm, Arnold. *Die Bibliothek des ehemaligen Zisterzienserinnenklosters Kirchheim am Ries: Buchpflege und geistiges Leben in einem schwäbischen Frauenstift*. Tübingen: Max Niemeyer, 1998.

Seebald, Christian. "Schreiben für die Reform: Reflexionen von Autorschaft in den Schriften des Dominikaners Johannes Meyer." In *Schriftstellerische Inszenierungspraktiken: Typologie und Geschichte*, ed. Christoph Jürgensen and Gerhard Kaiser, 33–53. Heidelberg: Universitätsverlag Winter, 2011.

———. "Zu den Handschriftenverhältnissen von Johannes Meyers 'Buch der Ämter' und 'Buch der Ersetzung.'" *Zeitschrift für deutsche Philologie* 134, no. 3 (2015): 394–430.

Signori, Gabriela, ed. *Lesen, Schreiben, Sticken und Erinnern*. Bielefeld: Verlag für Regionalgeschichte, 2000.

Simon, Anne. *The Cult of St. Katherine of Alexandria in Late-Medieval Nuremberg: Saint and the City*. Burlington, Vt.: Ashgate, 2012.

Sluhovsky, Moshe. *Believe Not Every Spirit: Possession, Mysticism, and Discernment in Early Modern Catholicism*. Chicago: University of Chicago Press, 2007.

Smith, Julie Ann. "An Apostolic Vocation: The Formation of the Religious Life for the Dominican Sisters in the Thirteenth Century." *Medieval Feminist Forum* 47, no. 2 (2011): 4–33.

———. "Prouille, Madrid, Rome: The Evolution of the Earliest Dominican Instituta for Nuns." *Journal of Medieval History* 35, no. 4 (2009): 340–52.

———. "'The Hours That They Ought to Direct to the Study of Letters': Literate Practices in the Constitutions and Rule for the Dominican Sisters." *Parergon* 31, no. 1 (2014): 73–94.

Steinke, Barbara. *Paradiesgarten oder Gefängnis? das Nürnberger Katharinenkloster zwischen Klosterreform und Reformation*. Tübingen: Mohr-Siebeck, 2006.

Steinmetz, Karl-Heinz. "Schule der heiligen Katharina. Triangulärer Wissenstransfer in der Katharinenpredigt und der Vierzehnten Harfe des Johannes Nider O.P." In *Kirchenbild und Spiritualität: dominikanische Beiträge zur Ekklesiologie und zum kirchlichen Leben im Mittelalter. Festschrift für Ulrich Horst OP zum 75. Geburtstag*, ed. Thomas Prügl and Marianne Schlosser, 339–55. Paderborn: Schöningh, 2007.

Störmer-Caysa, Uta. "Das Gespräch mit dem Wilden bei Seuse. Votum für eine folgenschwere Konjektur." In *Literarisches Leben: Rollenentwürfe in der Literatur des Hoch- und Spätmittelalters. Festschrift für Volker Mertens zum 65. Geburtstag*, ed. Matthias Meyer and Hans-Jochen Schiewer, 755–80. Tübingen: Max Niemeyer, 2002.

Stoudt, Debra L. "The Influence of Preaching on Dominican Women in Fourteenth-Century Teutonia." *Medieval Sermon Studies* 44 (2000): 53–67.

Studer, Monika. *Exempla im Kontext. Studien zu deutschen Prosaexempla des Spätmittelalters und zu einer Handschrift der Strassburger Reuerinnen*. Berlin: Walter de Gruyter, 2013.

Sturlese, Loris. "Einleitung." In *Das Buch der Wahrheit = Daz büchli der warheit*, ed. Loris Sturlese, IX-LXIII. Hamburg: F. Meiner, 1993.

Tanneberger, Tobias. ". . . usz latin in tutsch gebracht . . .": Normative Basistexte religiöser Gemeinschaften in volkssprachlichen Übertragungen. Katalog-Untersuchung-Fallstudie. Berlin: Lit Verlag, 2014.

Thali, Johanna. *Beten, Schreiben, Lesen: Literarisches Leben und Marienspiritualität im Kloster Engelthal*. Tübingen: A. Francke, 2003.

———. "Gehorsam, Armut und Nachfolge im Leiden: Zu den Leitthemen des 'Oetenbacher Schwesternbuchs.'" In *Bettelorden, Bruderschaften und Beginen in Zürich: Stadtkultur und Seelenheil im Mittelalter*, ed. Barbara Helbling, Magdalen Bless-Grabher, and Ines Buhofer, 198–213. Zürich: Verlag Neue Zürcher Zeitung, 2002.

Theisen, Joachim. *Predigt und Gottesdienst: Liturgische Strukturen in den Predigten Meister Eckharts*. Frankfurt am Main: Peter Lang, 1990.

———. "Tauler und die Liturgie." In *Deutsche Mystik im abendländischen Zusammenhang: Neu erschlossene Texte, neue methodische Ansätze, neue theoretische Konzepte: Kolloquium Kloster Fischingen 1998*, ed. Walter Haug and Wolfram Schneider-Lastin, 409–23. Tübingen: Max Niemeyer, 2000.

Thomas, Antoninus Hendrik. *De oudste constituties van de Dominicanen: Voorgeschiedenis, tekst, bronnen, ontstaan en ontwikkeling (1215–1237)*. Leuven: Bureel van de R.H.E. Universiteitsbibliotheek, 1965.

Tinsley, David. "Gender, Paleography, and the Question of Authorship in Late Medieval Dominican Spirituality." *Medieval Feminist Forum* 26 (1998): 23–31.

———. *The Scourge and the Cross: Ascetic Mentalities of the Later Middle Ages*. Paris: Peeters, 2010.

Tobin, Frank. "Henry Suso and Elsbeth Stagel: Was the *Vita* a Cooperative Effort?" In *Gendered Voices: Medieval Saints and Their Interpreters*, ed. Catherine M. Mooney, 118–35. Philadelphia: University of Pennsylvania Press, 1999.

Tschacher, Werner. *Der Formicarius des Johannes Nider von 1437: Studien zu den Anfängen der europäischen Hexenverfolgungen im Spätmittelalter*. Aachen: Shaker Verlag, 2000.

Tugwell, Simon. "The Evolution of Dominican Structures of Government, II: The First Dominican Provinces." *Archivum Fratrum Praedicatorum* 70 (2000): 5–109.

———. "The Evolution of Dominican Structures of Government, III: The Early Development of the Second Distinction of the Constitutions." *Archivum Fratrum Praedicatorum* 71 (2001): 5–183.

———. "Were the Magdalen Nuns Really Turned Into Dominicans in 1287?" *Archivum Fratrum Praedicatorum* 76 (2006): 39–77.

Uffmann, Heike. "Inside and Outside the Convent Walls: The Norm and Practice of Enclosure in the Reformed Nunneries of Late Medieval Germany." *Medieval History Journal* 4, no. 1 (2001): 83–108.

———. *Wie in einem Rosengarten: Monastische Reformen des späten Mittelalters in den Vorstellungen von Klosterfrauen.* Bielefeld: Verlag für Regionalgeschichte, 2008.

Ulrich, Peter. "Zur Bedeutung des Leidens in der Konzeption der *philosophia spiritualis* Heinrich Seuses." In *Heinrich Seuses* philosophia spiritualis*: Quellen, Konzept, Formen und Rezeption: Tagung Eichstätt 2.–4. Oktober 1991*, ed. Rüdiger Blumrich and Philipp Kaiser, 124–38. Wiesbaden: Reichert, 1994.

van Aelst, José. "Visualizing the Spiritual: Images in the Life and Teachings of Henry Suso (c. 1295–1366)." In *Speaking to the Eye: Sight and Insight Through Text and Image (1150–1650)*, ed. Thérèse de Hemptine, Veerle Fraeters, and María Eugenia Góngora, 129–51. Turnhout: Brepols, 2013.

Van Engen, John. "Communal Life: The Sister-Books." In *Medieval Holy Women in the Christian Tradition, c. 1100–1500*, ed. Alastair Minnis and Rosalynn Voaden, 105–31. Turnhout: Brepols, 2010.

———. "Friar Johannes Nyder on Laypeople Living as Religious in the World." In *Vita religiosa im Mittelalter: Festschrift für Kaspar Elm zum 70. Geburtstag*, ed. Franz J. Felten and Nikolas Jaspert, 583–615. Berlin: Duncker und Humblot, 1999.

———. "From Canons to Preachers: A Revolution in Medieval Governance." In *Domenico Di Caleruega e la Nascita dell'ordine Dei Frati Predicatori: Atti del XLI Convegno Storico Internazionale: Todi, 10–12 Ottobre 2004*, 261–95. Spoleto: Fondazione Centro italiano di studi sull'alto Medioevo, 2005.

Vargas, Michael A. *Taming a Brood of Vipers: Conflict and Change in Fourteenth-Century Dominican Convents.* Leiden: Brill, 2011.

———. "Weak Obedience, Undisciplined Friars, and Failed Reforms in the Medieval Order of Preachers." *Viator* 42, no. 1 (2011): 283–308.

Voaden, Rosalynn. *God's Words, Women's Voices: The Discernment of Spirits in the Writing of Late-Medieval Women Visionaries.* Suffolk: York Medieval Press, 1999.

———. "Mechthild of Hackeborn." In *Medieval Holy Women in the Christian Tradition, c. 1100–c. 1500*, ed. A. J. Minnis and Rosalynn Voaden, 431–51. Turnhout: Brepols, 2010.

von Heusinger, Sabine. *Johannes Mulberg OP (d. 1414). Ein Leben im Spannungsfeld von Dominikanerobservanz und Beginenstreit.* Berlin: Akademie Verlag, 2000.

von Kern, Theodor. "Die Reformation des Katharinenklosters zu Nürnberg im Jahre 1428." *Jahresbericht des historischen Vereins für Mittelfranken* 31 (1863): 1–20.

von Loe, Paulus. *Statistisches über die Ordensprovinz Saxonia.* Leipzig: Harrassowitz Verlag, 1910.

———. *Statistisches über die Ordensprovinz Teutonia.* Leipzig: Harrassowitz Verlag, 1907.

Wallach-Faller, Marianne. *Ein alemannischer Psalter aus dem 14. Jahrhundert. Hs. A. IV. 44 der Universitätsbibliothek Basel, Bl. 61–178.* Freiburg: Universitätsverlag Freiburg Schweiz, 1981.

Wegener, Lydia. *Der "Frankfurter" / "Theologia Deutsch": Spielräume und Grenzen des Sagbaren.* Berlin: Walter de Gruyter, 2016.

———. "Eckhart and the World of Women's Spirituality in the Context of the 'Free Spirit' and Marguerite Porete." In *A Companion to Meister Eckhart,* ed. Jeremiah Hackett, 415–43. Leiden: Brill, 2012.

Wehrli-Johns, Martina. "Das 'Exemplar': eine Reformschrift der Dominikanerobservanz? Untersuchungen zum Johannesmotiv im 'Horologium' und in der 'Vita.'" In *Predigt im Kontext. Internationales Symposium am Fachbereich Germanistik der Freien Universität Berlin vom 5.–8. Dezember 1996,* ed. Volker Mertens, Hans-Jochen Schiewer, Regina D. Schiewer, and Wolfram Schneider-Lastin, 347–76. Tübingen: Max Niemeyer, 2013.

Wiethaus, Ulrike. "Thieves and Carnivals: Gender in German Dominican Literature of the Fourteenth Century." In *The Vernacular Spirit: Essays on Medieval and Religious Literature,* ed. Renate Blumenfeld-Kosinski, Duncan Robertson, and Nancy Bradley Warren, 209–38. New York: Palgrave, 2002.

Williams, Ulla. *Die alemannischen Vitaspatrum: Untersuchungen und Edition.* Tübingen: Max Niemeyer, 1996.

———. "Schul der weisheit: Spirituelle *artes*-Auslegung bei Johannes Nider. Mit Edition der '14. Harfe.'" In *Überlieferungsgeschichtliche Editionen und Studien zur deutschen Literatur des Mittelalters: Kurt Ruh zum 75. Geburtstag,* ed. Konrad Kunze, Johannes G. Mayer, and Bernhard Schnell, 391–424. Tübingen: Max Niemeyer, 1989.

Williams, Ulla, and Werner Williams-Krapp, eds. *Die "Offenbarungen" der Katharina Tucher.* Tübingen: Max Niemeyer, 1998.

Williams-Krapp, Werner. "Die Bedeutung der reformierten Klöster des Predigerordens für das literarische Leben in Nürnberg im 15. Jahrhundert." In *Studien und Texte zur literarischen und materiellen Kultur der Frauenklöster im späten Mittelalter,* ed. Falk Eisermann, Eva Schlotheuber, and Volker Honemann, 311–29. Leiden: Brill, 2004.

———. "Dise ding sint dennoch nit ware zeichen der heiligkeit: Zur Bewertung mystischer Erfahrungen im 15. Jahrhundert." *Zeitschrift für Literaturwissenschaft und Linguistik* 80 (1990): 61–71.

———. "Frauenmystik und Ordensreform im 15. Jahrhundert." In *Literarische Interessenbildung im Mittelalter. DFG-Symposion 1991,* ed. Joachim Heinzle, 301–13. Stuttgart: Metzler, 1993.

———. "Henry Suso's 'Vita' Between Mystagogy and Hagiography." In *Seeing and Knowing: Women and Learning in Medieval Europe, 1200–1550,* ed. Anneke B. Mulder-Bakker, 35–47. Turnhout: Brepols, 2004.

————. "Nucleus totius perfectionis. Die Altväterspiritualität in der Vita Heinrich Seuses." In *Festschrift Walter Haug und Burghart Wachinger*, ed. Johannes Janota, 407–21. Tübingen: Max Niemeyer, 1992.

————. "Observanzbewegungen, monastische Spiritualität und geistliche Literatur im 15. Jahrhundert." *Internationales Archiv für Sozialgeschichte der deutschen Literatur* 20 (1995): 1–15.

————. "Ordensreform und Literatur im 15. Jahrhundert." *Jahrbuch der Oswald von Wolkenstein Gesellschaft* 4 (July 1986): 41–51.

————. " 'Praxis pietatis': Heilsverkündigung und Frömmigkeit der 'illiterati' im 15. Jahrhundert." In *Die Literatur im Übergang vom Mittelalter zur Neuzeit*, ed. Werner Röcke and Marina Münkler, 139–65. Hansers Sozialgeschichte der deutschen Literatur vom 16. Jahrhundert bis zur Gegenwart, I. München: Carl Hanser, 2004.

Williams-Krapp, Werner, and Ulla Williams. "Die Dominikaner im Kampf gegen weibliche Irrtümer: Eberhard Mardachs 'Sendbrief von wahrer Andacht': Mit einer Textedition." In *Deutsch-böhmische Literaturbeziehungen-Germano-Bohemica: Festschrift für Václav Bok zum 65. Geburtstag*, ed. Hans-Joachim Behr, 427–46. Hamburg: Kovac, 2004.

————. "Eine Warnung an alle, dy sych etwaz duncken. Der 'Sendbrief vom Betrug teuflischer Erscheinungen' (mit einer Edition)." In *Forschungen zur deutschen Literatur des späten Mittelalters: Festschrift für Johannes Janota*, ed. Horst Brunner and Werner Williams-Krapp, 167–89. Tübingen: Max Niemeyer, 2003.

Willing, Antje, ed. *Das "Konventsbuch" und das "Schwesternbuch" aus St. Katharina in St. Gallen. Kritische Edition und Kommentar.* Berlin: Erich Schmidt, 2016.

————. *Die Bibliothek des Klosters St. Katharina zu Nürnberg: Synoptische Darstellung der Bücherverzeichnisse.* Berlin: Akademie Verlag, 2012.

————. *Literatur und Ordensreform im 15. Jahrhundert: Deutsche Abendmahlsschriften im Nürnberger Katharinenkloster.* Münster: Waxmann, 2004.

————. *Nürnberger Eucharistiepredigten des Gerhard Comitis.* Erlangen: Palm & Enke, 2003.

Wilms, Hieronymus. *Das Beten der Mystikerinnen dargestellt nach den Chroniken der Dominikanerinnen-klöster zu Adelhausen, Diessenhofen, Engeltal, Kirchberg, Oetenbach, Töß und Unterlinden.* Leipzig: Harrassowitz Verlag, 1916.

Winston-Allen, Anne. *Convent Chronicles: Women Writing About Women and Reform in the Late Middle Ages.* University Park: Pennsylvania State University Press, 2004.

————. " 'Es [ist] nit wol zu gelobind, daz ain frowen bild so wol kan arbaiten': Artistic Production and Exchange in Women's Convents of the Observant Reform." In *Frauen-Kloster-Kunst: Neue Forschungen zur Kulturgeschichte des Mittelalters: Beiträge zum internationalen Kolloquium vom 13. bis 16. Mai 2005 anlässlich der Ausstellung "Krone und Schleier"*, ed. Jeffrey Hamburger, 187–95. Turnhout: Brepols, 2007.

————. "Making Manuscripts as Political Engagement by Women in the Fifteenth-Century Observant Reform Movement." *Journal of Medieval Religious Cultures* 42, no. 2 (2016): 224–47.

————. "Networking in Medieval Strasbourg: Cross-Order Collaboration in Book Illustration Among Women's Reformed Convents." In *Schreiben und Lesen in der Stadt: Literaturbetrieb im spätmittelalterlichen Straßburg*, ed. Stephen Mossman, Nigel F. Palmer, and Felix Heinzer, 197–212. Berlin: Walter de Gruyter, 2012.

————. "Rewriting Women's History: Medieval Nuns' *Vitae* by Johannes Meyer." In *Medieval German Voices in the 21st Century: The Paradigmatic Function of Medieval German Studies for German Studies*, ed. Albrecht Classen, 145–54. Amsterdam: Rodopi, 2000.

Wiora, W. "Jubilare sine verbis." In *In memoriam Jacques Handschin*, ed. H. Anglès, 39–65. Strasbourg: P.H. Heitz, 1962.

Wittmer, Charles. "Berceau de la réforme dominicaine 1389." *Annuaire de Colmar/Colmarer Jahrbuch* 4 (1938): 52–61.

Wolf, Klaus. *Hof-Universität-Laien: Literatur- und sprachgeschichtliche Untersuchungen zum deutschen Schrifttum der Wiener Schule des Spätmittelalters*. Wiesbaden: Reichert, 2006.

Woodford, Charlotte. *Nuns as Historians in Early Modern Germany*. Oxford: Oxford University Press, 2002.

Wrigge, Anke, and Falk Eisermann. "Der Nürnberger Pfarrer und Prediger Albrecht Fleischmann." In *Predigt im Kontext. Internationales Symposium am Fachbereich Germanistik der Freien Universität Berlin vom 5.–8. Dezember 1996*, ed. Volker Mertens, Hans-Jochen Schiewer, Regina D. Schiewer, and Wolfram Schneider-Lastin, 193–232. Berlin: Walter de Gruyter, 2013.

Wyser, Paul. "Taulers Terminologie vom Seelengrund." In *Altdeutsche und altniederländische Mystik*, ed. Kurt Ruh, 324–52. Darmstadt: Wissenschaftliche Buchgesellschaft, 1964.

Yardley, Anne Bagnall. "The Musical Education of Young Girls in Medieval English Nunneries." In *Young Choristers: 650–1700*, ed. Susan Boynton and Eric Rice, 49–67. Woodbridge: Boydell & Brewer, 2008.

Zarri, Gabriella. "Ecclesiastial Institutions and Religious Life in the Observant Century." In *A Companion to Observant Reform in the Late Middle Ages and Beyond*, ed. James D. Mixson and Bert Roest, 23–59. Leiden: Brill, 2015.

Zekorn, Stefan. *Gelassenheit und Einkehr: Zu Grundlage und Gestalt geistlichen Lebens bei Johannes Tauler*. Würzburg: Echter Verlag, 1993.

Zieman, Katherine. "Reading, Singing, and Understanding: Constructions of the Literacy of Women Religious in Late Medieval England." In *Learning and Literacy in Medieval England and Abroad*, ed. Sarah Rees Jones, 97–120. Turnhout: Brepols, 2003.

INDEX

ACKNOWLEDGMENTS

This book was both a very short and a very long time in the making. I wrote most of what you read in these pages feverishly between May and September 2016. That work was made possible, however, by years of learning, researching, thinking and conversing with extraordinary scholars and wonderful friends, whom I will never be able to thank adequately.

Several institutions have supported my archival research, beginning with the Deutscher Akademischer Austauschdienst (DAAD), which funded a research year at the Stadtarchiv in Freiburg im Breisgau in 2009–2010. I must also thank the Hill Monastic Manuscript Library (HMML) for digitized images of a number of important manuscripts, as well as the Alice Paul Center for Research on Women, Gender and Sexuality at the University of Pennsylvania which provided the funds for these images with a Phyllis Rackin Fellowship for Feminist Scholarship in the Humanities. Numerous units at the University of Notre Dame have also been exceedingly generous in supporting my research; I owe thanks to the Office of Research for a Francis M. Kobayashi Research Travel Grant, to the Institute for Scholarship in the Liberal Arts (ISLA) in the College of Arts and Letters for two Small Research Grants and an Indexing Support Grant, and to the Nanovic Institute for European Studies. A sabbatical year supported by the Andrew W. Mellon Foundation allowed me to take advantage of the marvelous resources at the Pontifical Institute of Mediaeval Studies in Toronto, where I wrote Chapter 5.

There are many more people to thank than there are institutions and these brief words seem a paltry gesture with which to repay the mentoring and friendships that have shaped me into the scholar I am today. Numerous mentors have pointed me in certain directions and exposed me to certain lines of inquiry that remain fruitful for me, among whom I count David Wallace, E. Ann Matter, Amy Hollywood, Kevin Brownlee, Rita Copeland,

Donald F. Duclow, Bethany Wiggin, and Jean-Michel Rabaté. Catriona
MacLeod and Sara S. Poor have far exceeded any bonds of obligation and I
am deeply grateful for their continued support. At Notre Dame, John Van
Engen, Margot Fassler, D'Arcy Jonathan Dacre Boulton, Maureen Boulton,
and my colleagues in the German department have taken me under their
wings and provided much support and advice. I am also grateful for the
generosity of PIMS and the Toronto community, especially my three fellow
"Mel(l)ons" Stephen Metzger, Annalia Marchisio, and Shami Ghosh, as well
as Jonathan Black, Fred Unwalla, Brian Stock, Markus Stock, Ann Hutchi-
son, and Rachel Koopmans, who encouraged me to get my hands dirty. I
must also acknowledge the support of Barbara North at PIMS and especially
of JoAnne Dubil at the University of Pennsylvania, without whom none of
us would make it. Finally, I would like to thank my editor Jerome Singerman,
as well as Barbara Newman and the anonymous second reader, for providing
excellent advice and giving me the chance to act on it.

Many of my friends and colleagues have helped me work through ideas
either in conversation or by reading my writing in various stages of comple-
tion and coherence. I would like specially to acknowledge Leif Weatherby,
Ian Cornelius, Lucas Wood, Elizaveta Strakhov, Emily Zazulia, Kathryn Mal-
czyk, Katherine Aid, Mary Marshall Campbell, Moritz Wedell, Kathrin
Gollwitzer-Oh, Alison Beringer, Allison Edgren, Amy Nelson, and Steven
Rozenski. Anne Bornschein and Lydia Yaitsky Kertz cheered me through the
finish line and I cannot give high enough praise to Tara Mendola for helping
me articulate this final book. I owe my deepest gratitude to Courtney Rydel,
who has been "a second self," and to Christopher Liebtag Miller, who kept
me alive while I was writing this book and still feeds me intellectually every
day.